STUDIES IN HISTORY, ECONOMICS AND PUBLIC LAW

Edited by the

FACULTY OF POLITICAL SCIENCE
OF COLUMBIA UNIVERSITY

NUMBER 379

THE ECONOMIC RESULTS OF PROHIBITION

BY

CLARK WARBURTON

THE ECONOMIC RESULTS OF PROHIBITION

BY

CLARK WARBURTON, PH.D.

NEW YORK
COLUMBIA UNIVERSITY PRESS
LONDON: P. S. KING & SON, LTD.
1932

PRINTED IN THE UNITED STATES OF AMERICA

PREFACE

This study of the economic results of prohibition was initiated early in 1929 at the request of the Association Against the Prohibition Amendment, and I am indebted to the Association for financial support during the first few months of the investigation. The major part of the work has been done during the past two years, since the termination of my connection with that organization.

The paper read by Mr. John C. Gebhart before the American Statistical Association at Washington, D. C., in December, 1929, and published for the Committee on Social Statistics of that Association in *Statistics in Social Studies,* and the pamphlet published by the Association Against the Prohibition Amendment entitled "Does Prohibition Pay?" were based in part upon a preliminary report which I presented to that Association.* Since the publication of this paper and pamphlet all of my estimates and analyses have been revised; and all figures, tables and statements taken from my report are replaced, so far as my responsibility for them is concerned, by revised computations and conclusions given in this book.

I wish to thank Mr. John C. Gebhart for suggestions as to sources of information, Mr. John Parker for the collection of much material from library sources, and the many trade associations, business firms, and newspaper

* The parts of these studies which are based on this preliminary report are as follows:

Statistics in Social Studies, pp. 133-148; and

Does Prohibition Pay? the section on liquor consumption, pp. 6-15, and that on increase in savings, pp. 21-24 and p. 37.

editors and reporters who have responded to my inquiries and without whose co-operation it would have been impossible to assemble much of the information in the study. Professors Wesley C. Mitchell, Harold Hotelling and Joseph Dorfman have contributed helpful advice. I am especially indebted to Professor Arthur R. Burns for his painstaking care in reading the entire manuscript and proof and for his many valuable suggestions and criticisms.

It is not likely that the tables and figures presented in this book are entirely free from error, especially as I have had no assistance in checking the accuracy of transcripts or the hundreds of thousands of computations involved in the statistical analysis; but I feel sure that no such errors are sufficiently great to affect the conclusions drawn from the data and the analysis.

It has been my aim throughout the study to be strictly impartial as to the merits of prohibition and to analyze without bias the statistical evidence regarding its effects.

CLARK WARBURTON

WASHINGTON, D. C.,
SEPTEMBER, 1932.

CONTENTS

PAGE

INTRODUCTION: Economic Aspects of Prohibition 17

PART ONE

THE CONSUMPTION OF ALCOHOL

CHAPTER I

PRE-PROHIBITION CONSUMPTION OF ALCOHOLIC BEVERAGES. . 23

CHAPTER II

CONSUMPTION OF ALCOHOLIC BEVERAGES UNDER PROHIBITION: ESTIMATE FROM SOURCES OF PRODUCTION

Consumption of Beer 27
Consumption of Wine. 34
Consumption of Spirits 40
Industrial alcohol. 40
Corn sugar 49
Corn syrup and corn starch 54
Corn meal 54
Corn, rye and other grains 56
Cane and beet sugar. 57
Molasses 63
Malt syrup 65
Fruits and vegetables 65
Total production of beverage spirits 66
Smuggled spirits 67
Medicinal alcohol 68
Consumption of alcoholic spirits 69

CHAPTER III

CONSUMPTION OF ALCOHOLIC BEVERAGES UNDER PROHIBITION: ESTIMATE FROM DEATH RATES 73

Alcohol consumption and death rates in the United Kingdom . . 74
Alcohol consumption and death rates in Denmark 81
Alcohol consumption and death rates in the United States 84

PAGE

CHAPTER IV

Consumption of Alcoholic Beverages Under Prohibition: Estimate from Arrests for Drunkenness 99

CHAPTER V

Consumption of Alcoholic Beverages Under Prohibition: Comparison of Estimates. 104

PART TWO

The Effect of Prohibition Upon Expenditures

CHAPTER VI

Pre-Prohibition Expenditures for Alcoholic Beverages

The National Liquor Bill 111
Pre-prohibition prices of alcoholic beverages. 111
Annual liquor bill prior to prohibition 113
Business fluctuations and the liquor bill 115
Influence of price changes. 118
Family and Group Expenditures for Liquor 119
Average per capita and per family expenditure 119
Regional expenditures. 120
Influence of urban life. 121
Influence of age, sex and marital status 121
Influence of nationality 122
Influence of occupation 125
Influence of permanent poverty and economic status 125
Influence of family incomes 127
Liquor Expenditures by Economic Classes. 130
Distribution of population among the principal economic classes 130
Class consumption of alcoholic beverages. 132
Class expenditures upon alcoholic beverages 134
Allocation of the liquor bill in 1910 among the principal economic classes 137

CHAPTER VII

Expenditures for Alcoholic Beverages Under Prohibition

Probable Liquor Bill in the Absence of Prohibition. 139
Liquor bill for 1921-1930 as predicted from conditions of 1911-1914 140

PAGE
Liquor bill for 1921-1930 as predicted from the trend in the proportion of the national income spent on liquor. 150
Actual Liquor Bill Under Prohibition 151
Prices of alcoholic beverages. 152
Liquor bill under prohibition 165
Effect of Prohibition upon Expenditures for Liquor 168

CHAPTER VIII

PROHIBITION AND THE SHIFTING PATTERN OF CONSUMPTION. 172
Consumption of and expenditure upon selected articles 173
Relation of prohibition to savings 180
Substitutes for beer 184

PART THREE

OTHER ECONOMIC PHASES OF PROHIBITION

CHAPTER IX

PROHIBITION AND INDUSTRIAL EFFICIENCY

Effect of drinking upon efficiency 195
Statistical evidence regarding the effect of prohibition upon productivity 196
Effect of prohibition upon industrial accidents 199
Effect of prohibition upon absenteeism. 203
Efficient use of productive resources 206

CHAPTER X

PROHIBITION AND PUBLIC HEALTH AND SAFETY

Effect of prohibition upon deaths directly associated with the use of alcohol. 212
Effect of prohibition upon the general death rate and the death rate from tuberculosis 217
Effect of prohibition upon automobile accidents. 221
Effect of prohibition upon crime. 223

CHAPTER XI

PROHIBITION AND ECONOMIC GROUPS

Farming class. 228
Wage-earning class 233
Business, professional and salaried class 237
Producers of alcoholic beverages. 242

PAGE

CHAPTER XII

Prohibition and Public Finance

Cost of enforcing prohibition 245
Loss of government revenues 248
Incidence of liquor taxation 254

PART FOUR

Summary and Conclusions

CHAPTER XIII

Economic Results of Prohibition

Effect of prohibition upon the consumption of alcoholic beverages. 259
Effect of prohibition upon national expenditures 260
Effect of prohibition upon industrial efficiency 261
Effect of prohibition upon economic groups 261
Effect of prohibition upon public health and safety and upon public finance 262

Bibliography. 264

Index 271

LIST OF TABLES

TABLE PAGE

1. Per capita consumption of alcoholic beverages in the United States, 1840 to 1922 24
2. Average annual per capita consumption of alcoholic liquors in various countries, 1910–1914. 26
3. Use of hops in the United States. 28
4. Estimated production of beer in the United States, 1921 to 1931 31
5. Estimated consumption of beer in the United States, 1921 to 1931 32
6. Estimated consumption of illegal beer, 1921 to 1930. 33
7. Production and use of grapes in the United States, 1899, 1909 and 1917 35
8. Estimated production of wine in the United States, 1921 to 1931 (first method) 37
9. Estimated production of wine in the United States, 1921 to 1931 (second method) 38
10. Estimated consumption of wine, 1921 to 1931. 40
11. Use of industrial alcohol in the United States, 1907 to 1931. 43
12. Estimate of alcohol used for automobile anti-freeze 44
13. Estimated diversion of industrial alcohol, 1921 to 1931. . . . 46
14. Industrial alcohol withdrawn, 1921 to 1931—important formulas not included in Table 13. 48
15. Estimate of beverage spirits produced from diverted industrial alcohol. 49
16. Use of corn sugar in the United States, 1909 to 1930 52
17. Production of corn syrup and of starch, 1919 to 1930 55
18. Production and use of corn meal in the United States. . . . 56
19. Factors influencing the consumption of sugar in the United States, 1890–1916 58
20. Factors influencing the consumption of sugar in the United States, 1917–1930 60
21. Estimate of beverage spirits produced from cane and beet sugar. 62
22. Production and importation of molasses 63
23. Use of molasses in the United States. 64
24. Estimate of beverage-spirit production in the United States, 1921 to 1930. 66

TABLE PAGE

25. Relative importance of materials used in producing beverage spirits 67
26. Estimate of spirits smuggled into the United States 68
27. Medicinal alcohol used in the United States 69
28. Estimate of alcoholic spirits consumed in the United States, 1921 to 1930. 70
29. Consumption of alcoholic beverages in the United States, 1921 to 1930: estimates obtained from sources of production. 71
30. Consumption of pure alcohol in the United States, 1921 to 1930; estimates obtained from sources of production . . . 72
31. Alcoholic deaths as related to alcohol consumption in the United Kingdom of Great Britain and Ireland 75
32. Consumption of alcohol and the alcoholic death rate in Great Britain and Ireland 78
33. Coefficients of relationship in respect to the death rate from alcoholism and cirrhosis of the liver 80
34. Consumption of alcohol and the alcoholic death rate in Denmark. 82
35. Alcoholic deaths as related to alcoholic consumption in the United States, 1910 to 1919 85
36. Consumption of alcohol and the alcoholic death rate in the United States, 1910 to 1919 86
37. Consumption of alcohol in the United States, 1920–1931, estimated from the death rate 89
38. Death rates in the United States, 1910 to 1929 90
39. Measures of relationship between alcoholism, cirrhosis of the liver, the general death rate and the consumption of alcoholic beverages, 1910–1919. 91
40. Estimates of the consumption of spirits and of beer, 1910–1919, derived from death rates 97
41. Estimates of consumption of spirits and of beer, 1920–1929, derived from death rates. 98
42. Consumption of spirits and convictions for drunkenness, England and Wales, 1891–1914 and 1919–1928. 99
43. Arrests for drunkenness and the consumption of alcoholic beverages, United States, 1910–1919 101
44. Consumption of spirits and of pure alcohol, 1920 to 1929: estimates from arrests for drunkenness. 102
45. Estimates of the consumption of pure alcohol in the United States, 1920 to 1930 104
46. Estimates of the consumption of alcoholic beverages in the United States, 1920 to 1930 106

TABLE PAGE
47. Consumption of alcoholic beverages in the United States before and after the adoption of prohibition. 107
48. Wholesale prices of alcoholic beverages in the United States, 1890 to 1918. 112
49. Estimated retail prices of alcoholic beverages in the United States prior to 1915 113
50. Estimated expenditures on alcoholic beverages in the United States, 1890-1916 114
51. Estimated percentage of the national income spent for alcoholic beverages in the United States. 115
52. Business fluctuations and the consumption of alcoholic beverages. 116
53. Estimated expenditures per capita for alcoholic beverages, 1890–1916. 119
54. Estimated expenditure per family for alcoholic beverages in the United States, 1890–1916. 120
55. Reported expenditure for liquor by workingmen's families in geographical regions 121
56. Urban and rural death rates from alcoholism and cirrhosis of the liver 122
57. Expenditures for liquor by all families, by "normal families," and by single men, in Bombay 123
58. Reported expenditures for liquor by nationalities: workingmen's families, 1890. 124
59. Reported expenditures for liquor by income classes: European and American workingmen's families, 1890. 124
60. Reported expenditures for liquor by workingmen's families in various industries, 1890 125
61. Workingmen's family incomes and expenditures for liquor in the United States. 128
62. Workingmen's family incomes and expenditures for liquor in foreign countries 129
63. An estimate of the number of unmarried males and of families in the principal economic classes in the United States, 1910 131
64. Estimated division of the liquor bill among economic classes in 1910 138
65. The 1921–1930 liquor bill as predicted from conditions of 1911–1914 141
66. Prices of principal materials used in producing alcoholic beverages. 144
67. Estimated commercial costs of producing alcoholic beverages, 1914 and 1929, taxes excluded 145

TABLE PAGE

68. Estimated probable post-war prices of alcoholic beverages had prohibition not been adopted 148
69. The 1921–1930 liquor bill as predicted from 1911–1914 consumption, 1921–1929 price level, and 1917–1919 rates of taxation 149
70. Estimated probable national expenditure for alcoholic beverages, 1920 to 1930, without national prohibition 151
71. Prices of alcoholic beverages in fourteen cities in December, 1929 152
72. Prices of alcoholic beverages at various places and dates . . 153
73. Prices of alcoholic beverages in July, 1930, in the United States 155
74. Prices of beer in American cities in July, 1930 156
75. Prices of wine in American cities in July, 1930 157
76. Prices of beverage spirits in American cities in July, 1930. . 158
77. Average prices of alcoholic beverages in the United States, 1929–1930. 160
78. Index of price of gin in Washington and adjusted prices of alcoholic beverages in the United States 161
79. Estimated average cost to users of alcoholic beverages, 1929–1930 164
80. Estimated expenditures per capita upon alcoholic beverages, 1921–1930 166
81. Estimated total expenditures on alcoholic beverages in the United States, 1921–1930 167
82. Effect of prohibition upon the liquor bill 168
83. Effect of prohibition upon the amount spent for spirits, for wine and for beer 170
84. Apparent consumption per capita of selected articles 174
85. Apparent average annual percentage change in per capita consumption of selected articles 176
86. Estimated total consumer expenditure for selected articles. . 177
87. Total savings deposits in the United States, 1910 to 1930 . . 179
88. Savings deposits before and since prohibition. 180
89. Life insurance issued and in force, 1910 to 1930. 181
90. Assets of building and loan associations 182
91. Life insurance issued and in force, and assets of building and loan associations, before and since prohibition 183
92. Per capita consumption of non-alcoholic beverages, 1890 to 1930 186
93. Per capita consumption of ice cream, confectionery and tobacco, and attendance at motion pictures, 1899 to 1929 . . 191
94. Indexes of productivity and of alcohol consumption, 1899 to 1927 198

TABLE PAGE
95. Indexes of accident frequency rates and of alcohol consumption, 1913 to 1930 200
96. Industrial accident death rates and the consumption of alcohol, 1912–1924. 203
97. Absenteeism in a Delaware powder plant. 205
98. Average annual percentage decline in absenteeism in a Delaware powder plant 205
99. Resources devoted to the production of alcoholic beverages, 1899 to 1914. 209
100. Resources seized by Federal prohibition agents, 1921 to 1930. 210
101. Death rates from diseases associated with the use of alcohol, 1900 to 1930. 213
102. Average annual death rates from diseases associated with the use of alcohol before and since the adoption of prohibition. 214
103. Hospitalization of alcoholic cases, 1912 to 1930 215
104. Average annual rates of hospitalization of alcohol cases before and since the adoption of prohibition 216
105. Death rates from all causes and from tuberculosis, 1900 to 1930 218
106. Death rates, hours of labor, and the consumption of alcohol. 220
107. Indexes of motor-vehicle fatalities and of alcohol consumption, 1913 to 1929 222
108. Alcohol consumption and criminal activity, 1900 to 1929 . . 224
109. Alcohol consumption and criminal activity: average annual rates for various periods. 226
110. Estimated annual losses of farmers on account of reduced production of beer. 231
111. Changes in death rates from diseases associated with the use of alcohol. 234
112. Urban and rural death rates from alcoholism and cirrhosis of the liver, 1911–14 and 1926–28 239
113. Federal expenditures upon the enforcement of prohibition, 1920 to 1930. 246
114. Internal revenue tax rates on alcoholic beverages since 1862. 248
115. Government revenue from alcoholic beverages, 1890 to 1919. 249
116. Estimates of loss of Federal government revenue as a result of prohibition, 1920 to 1931 250

INTRODUCTION

The Economic Aspects of Prohibition

Among the arguments offered for and against national prohibition of the manufacture and sale of alcoholic beverages are several which are primarily economic in character.

In favor of prohibition it is argued:

(1) That for some years after the adoption of prohibition there was a notable decline in the national expenditure for alcoholic beverages and that the money thus saved promoted prosperity by being spent for other things.

(2) That prohibition has resulted in great additions to deposits in savings accounts, in increased holdings of life insurance, in employee purchases of corporate stocks, and has thus increased the productive resources of the nation.

(3) That workingmen are more sober since the adoption of prohibition, and that this sobriety has been an important element in the increased efficiency of American industry in recent years.

(4) That reduction in industrial and motor accidents and improvement in public health, traceable to prohibition, have aided productivity.

(5) That resources formerly devoted to the production of alcoholic beverages are now used in other industries which yield greater returns to their owners and to the communities in which they are located.

(6) That the economic arguments presented in opposition to prohibition are fallacious or relatively insignificant.[1]

[1] The literature on prohibition is voluminous, and it is not possible to refer to more than a small part of the books, pamphlets and journals

In opposition to prohibition it is argued:

(1) That the foregoing arguments in favor of prohi-

in which these arguments appear. Among the more important, however, are the following:

Thomas Nixon Carver, "The Effects of Prohibition on Our Economic Structure," *The New York Times*, February 1, 1931, IX, p. 5.

Ernest H. Cherrington, "Education and Prohibition," *Congressional Record*, October 8, 1929.

Ernest H. Cherrington, "A Study of the Social Effect of National Prohibition," *Congressional Record*, November 19, 1929.

Ernest H. Cherrington, "Working and Results of Prohibition in the United States," *Congressional Record*, April 3, 1930.

Samuel Crowther, *Prohibition and Prosperity* (New York, 1930).

Herman Feldman, *Prohibition: Its Economic and Industrial Aspects* (New York, 1927).

Irving Fisher, *Prohibition at Its Worst* (New York, 1927).

Irving Fisher, *Prohibition Still at Its Worst* (New York, 1928).

Irving Fisher, *The Noble Experiment* (New York, 1930).

Paul H. Nystrom, *Economic Principles of Consumption* (New York, 1929).

Board of Temperance, Prohibition and Public Morals of the Methodist Episcopal Church, Pamphlet No. 126, *What Has Prohibition Done?*

Board of Temperance, Prohibition and Public Morals of the Methodist Episcopal Church, Pamphlet No. 160, *Prohibition Prosperity.*

Board of Temperance, Prohibition and Public Morals of the Methodist Episcopal Church, Pamphlet No. 161, *Why I Am for Prohibition.*

Board of Temperance, Prohibition and Public Morals of the Methodist Episcopal Church, pamphlet entitled *The Facts About Prohibition—Illustrated—Trust Your Eye* (Washington, 1927).

Bureau of Prohibition, United States Department of Justice, *The Value of Law Observance* (Washington, 1930).

U. S. Congress, Senate, Subcommittee of the Committee on the Judiciary, *The National Prohibition Law* (Washington, 1926).

U. S. Congress, House, Committee on the Judiciary, *The Prohibition Amendment* (Washington, 1930).

National Commission on Law Observance and Enforcement, *Report on the Enforcement of the Prohibition Laws of the United States* (Washington, 1930).

The Monitor Bureau, "From Vacuum Cleaners to Bathtubs People Have Bought More in Dry Era," *The Christian Science Monitor*, June 10, 1930.

bition are either fallacious or their importance is much exaggerated.

(2) That prohibition has fostered crime, and consequently increased the cost of government and law enforcement.

(3) That prohibition has resulted in a serious loss of public revenue.

(4) That certain groups of producers, especially the farmers, have been seriously affected by the loss of markets for their products.

(5) That alcoholic beverages, if used wisely, contribute to national efficiency by promoting the relaxation necessary at the close of a day's work.

(6) That reduced alcohol consumption, and whatever economic benefits may be derived therefrom, can be achieved more economically by some other method than national prohibition.[2]

"The Debate on Prohibition: A Summing Up," *The New York Times*, March 30, 1930, IX, p. 3.

Department of Research and Education, Federal Council of the Churches of Christ in America, Research Bulletin No. 5, *The Prohibition Situation.*

[2] Many of these arguments are discussed in the references mentioned as containing arguments in favor of prohibition. Other sources are the following:

Rheta Childe Dorr, *Drink: Coercion or Control?* (New York, 1929).

Fabian Franklin, *The A B C of Prohibition* (New York, 1927).

John C. Gebhart, "Prohibition: Statistical Studies of Enforcement and Social Effect," *Statistics in Social Studies* (Philadelphia, 1930).

Reginald E. Hose, *Prohibition or Control?* (New York, 1928).

Ernest H. Starling, *The Action of Alcohol on Man* (New York, 1923).

Millard E. Tydings, *Before and After Prohibition* (New York, 1930).

The Hearst Temperance Contest Committee, *Temperance—or Prohibition?* (New York, 1929).

Association Against the Prohibition Amendment, *Government Liquor Control in Canada* (Washington, 1929).

The following chapters are an analysis, largely statistical, of the available facts relevant to the foregoing arguments, both for and against prohibition. This study is by no means a complete survey of the economic aspects of prohibition. It is especially deficient in its lack of a field survey, for field studies, if made by competent investigators, would have been invaluable in showing the regional distribution and variability of many phenomena which can be handled statistically only on a national basis. It is hoped, however, that, even without the support of a field survey, the analysis throws some light upon the much-discussed relation of prohibition to public welfare.

Association Against the Prohibition Amendment, *Cost of Prohibition and Your Income Tax* (Washington, 1929).

Association Against the Prohibition Amendment, *Scandals of Prohibition Enforcement* (Washington, 1929).

Association Against the Prohibition Amendment, *Does Prohibition Pay?* (Washington, 1930).

PART ONE

The Consumption of Alcohol

CHAPTER I

Pre-Prohibition Consumption of Alcoholic Beverages

The validity of most of the economic arguments both for and against prohibition depends upon the extent to which prohibition has modified the consumption of alcoholic beverages. For this reason it is necessary, before examining these arguments, to compare the quantities of such beverages used before and since the adoption of prohibition.

In Table 1 the per capita consumption of spirits, wine and beer in the United States, as reported by the Commissioner of Internal Revenue, is given, for ten-year intervals from 1840 to 1900, and by years from 1900 to 1922. To this is added a computation of the total alcohol consumed per capita, based on an average alcoholic content of 4.25 per cent by volume for beer and 14 per cent for wine. The consumption of spirits is given in proof gallons, containing 50 per cent alcohol by volume, or 42.47 per cent by weight.

The above figures for spirits and for beer are based upon the withdrawals for sale on which internal revenue taxes were paid. For wine they are computed from the estimated annual production and foreign trade. None of these figures is precisely accurate. There has always been some manufacture of alcoholic spirits, especially in the southern Appalachian region, by persons evading the Federal tax, as well as some production of cider and fruit wines in homes and rural areas, which also paid no Federal tax. It is probable, also, that the consumption of wine varied less from year to year than did its production,

TABLE 1

PER CAPITA CONSUMPTION OF ALCOHOLIC BEVERAGES IN THE UNITED STATES, 1840 TO 1922

Year ending June 30	Spirits (proof gallons)	Wine (gallons)	Beer (gallons)	Total pure alcohol (gallons)
1840	2.52	.29	1.36	1.36
1850	2.23	.27	1.58	1.22
1860	2.86	.34	3.22	1.62
1870	2.07	.32	5.31	1.31
1880	1.27	.56	8.26	1.06
1890	1.39	.46	13.57	1.34
1900	1.28	.39	16.06	1.38
1901	1.31	.36	15.95	1.38
1902	1.34	.62	17.15	1.49
1903	1.43	.47	17.64	1.53
1904	1.44	.52	17.88	1.55
1905	1.41	.41	17.99	1.53
1906	1.47	.53	19.51	1.64
1907	1.58	.65	20.53	1.75
1908	1.39	.58	20.23	1.64
1909	1.32	.67	19.04	1.56
1910	1.42	.65	19.77	1.64
1911	1.46	.67	20.69	1.70
1912	1.45	.58	20.02	1.66
1913	1.51	.56	20.72	1.71
1914	1.44	.53	20.69	1.67
1915	1.26	.33	18.40	1.46
1916	1.37	.47	17.78	1.51
1917	1.62	.41	18.17	1.64
1918	.85	.49	14.87	1.13
1919	.77	.51	8.00	.80
1920	.26	.12	2.45	.25
1921	.32	.19	....	.19
1922	.17	.09	....	.10

SOURCES OF DATA:

Spirits, wine and beer: *Statistical Abstract of the United States*, 1922, pp. 692-697.

Total alcohol: computed from the preceding columns, assuming the average alcoholic content of beer to be 4.25 per cent, and of wine to be 14 per cent.

and, consequently, less than is indicated in the table. However, it is generally recognized that these errors, for the years prior to 1919, are not large, and the per capita consumption recorded in this table, up to 1919, may be considered approximately correct.[1] The figures for 1920 to 1922, inclusive, represent withdrawals from bonded warehouses for medicinal, sacramental and scientific purposes.

It may be noted that during the years from 1911 to 1914 the consumption of alcoholic liquors was relatively steady. The slightly lower figures for 1915 and 1916 are probably due partly to the extension of state-wide prohibition laws and partly to changed habits associated with the European war.[2] The unusually great per capita consumption of spirits in the year ending June 30, 1917, may have been due to a reaction against the comparative abstemiousness of the two preceding years, but more probably to the withdrawal of spirits in anticipation of increased taxation or of war-time restrictions.[3]

During the year ending June 30, 1918, the production of alcoholic beverages was limited by the Food Control Act. In view of these facts, it is best to take the fiscal

[1] In 1915, which appears to be a typical year, Federal officials seized 3,764 illicit stills, and 34,381 gallons of distilled spirits (U. S. Treasury Dept., Bureau of Industrial Alcohol, *Statistics Concerning Intoxicating Liquors*, December, 1930, p. 72). If this were one per cent of the amount of distilled spirits which escaped the tax, the consumption of spirits per capita given in the above table would be .03 gallons, or 2 per cent, too low.

[2] During 1914 and 1915 ten states, Colorado, Virginia, Arizona, Oregon, Washington, Arkansas, Idaho, Iowa, Alabama and South Carolina, adopted prohibitory laws or constitutional amendments. These states in 1910 contained 14 per cent of the population of the United States.

[3] From the middle of April, 1917, to the end of the fiscal year Congressional Committees were considering increases in the liquor taxes. An attempt was also made to introduce a prohibition clause in a bill dealing with German spies. Cf. Charles Merz, *The Dry Decade* (Garden City, N. Y., 1930), p. 26.

years 1911 to 1914 as the period of normal consumption of alcoholic beverages prior to prohibition, with which consumption in recent years may be compared.

In Table 2, the average consumption of alcoholic beverages during the fiscal years 1911 to 1914 is compared with the consumption in other countries during approximately the same period.

TABLE 2

AVERAGE ANNUAL PER CAPITA CONSUMPTION OF ALCOHOLIC LIQUORS IN VARIOUS COUNTRIES, 1910-1914

Country	Spirits (U. S. proof gallons)	Wine (gallons)	Beer (gallons)	Total pure alcohol (gallons)
United States	1.47	.59	20.53	1.69
United Kingdom	.92	.31	32.43	1.96
Belgium	1.49	1.11	59.66	3.29
Holland	1.41	.34	7.52	1.05
France	2.04	37.49	8.87	5.12
Italy	.35	33.79	.57	3.58
Switzerland	1.05	15.05	21.12	2.88
Germany	1.52	1.24	27.46	2.03
Denmark	2.84	.37	22.76	2.38
Sweden	1.78	.15	13.00	1.41
Norway	.89	.40	5.62	.73
Canada	1.48	.16	8.22	1.11

SOURCES OF DATA:

United States: Table 1, *supra*, p. 24, average for 1911-1914.

United Kingdom: *The Alliance Year Book for 1931*, p. 321. Figures converted from Imperial gallons to United States gallons and from British proof to United States proof. It is assumed that wine averages 14 per cent alcohol, and beer 4.5 per cent.

Other European countries: *Annuaire Statistique de la France, 1928*, pp. 375, 376, 379. For beer and wine figures are for the years 1911-1913. All figures converted from liters to United States gallons. It is assumed that beer averages 4 per cent alcohol; wine 10 per cent in France, Italy and Switzerland, and 14 per cent elsewhere.

Canada: "Liquor Traffic in Canada," Canadian Department of Trade and Commerce, and *Canada Year Book*, 1914, p. 558. Figures are for the years 1911-1914, and converted from Imperial gallons to United States gallons, and from British proof to United States proof. It is assumed that wine averages 14 per cent alcohol, and beer 4.25 per cent.

CHAPTER II

The Consumption of Alcoholic Beverages Under Prohibition: Estimate by Sources of Production

Since the adoption of prohibition estimates of the quantity of alcoholic beverages consumed in the United States can be made only indirectly. There are three feasible methods: from the materials used in producing alcoholic beverages; from sickness and death rates associated with the use of alcohol; and from police and court cases resulting from the use of liquor.[1] These three methods are completely independent of each other, and this chapter is devoted to the first of them.

THE CONSUMPTION OF BEER

With the exception of hops, the materials used in malt liquors are also used for other purposes to such an extent that it is not possible to estimate the quantity used in the production of beer. But hops are used only to a slight extent for purposes other than the manufacture of beverages, and, consequently, it is reasonable to assume that practically all the hops unaccounted for by the legitimate manufacture of cereal beverages and by exportation are used in the production of beer in American homes and in illegal breweries.

The available statistics in regard to the use of hops in the United States since 1916 are given in Table 3.

[1] Were a field study to be made, it might also be possible to obtain estimates of the sale of alcoholic beverages in specific cities and regions from persons engaged in their production and sale, and to estimate the national consumption from these samples.

TABLE 3

USE OF HOPS IN THE UNITED STATES

(thousands of pounds)

Year ending June 30	Production	Net exports	Used by brewers	Balance	Consumption unaccounted for (smoothed)	Farm price Dec. 1, cents per lb.
1916	52,986	21,869	37,452	—6,335		11.7
1917	50,595	4,664	41,949	3,982		12.0
1918	29,388	3,411	33,481	—7,504		33.3
1919	21,481	7,472	13,925	7,556		19.3
			Used by beverage and spirit manufacturers			
1920	24,970	28,187	6,441	—9,658		77.6
1921	34,280	18,226	5,989	10,065	3,000	35.7
1922	29,340	19,116	4,453	5,771	4,000	24.1
1923	27,744	12,401	4,556	10,787	5,500	8.6
1924	19,751	19,832	3,815	—3,896	7,000	18.8
1925	27,670	15,737	3,314	8,619	9,000	10.3
1926	28,573	14,592	3,498	10,483	11,000	21.8
1927	31,522	12,936	3,150	15,436	13,500	23.0
1928	30,658	11,087	3,078	16,493	16,000	22.9
1929	32,944	8,172	2,735	22,037	20,000	19.3
1930	33,220	5,867	2,627	24,726	23,000	11.4
1931	23,447	4,570	2,197	16,680	19,500	14.8

SOURCES OF DATA:

Production, net exports, and farm price: 1916-1929, *Yearbook of Agriculture, 1930,* p. 812; 1930-1931, *Crops and Markets,* Dec. 1930, p. 481, and *Monthly Summary of Foreign Commerce of the United States.*

Used by brewers, and used by beverage and spirit manufacturers: *Statistics Concerning Intoxicating Liquors,* December, 1931, pp. 59, 78 and 79.

Balance: production minus net exports and quantities used by brewers and manufacturers.

Consumption unaccounted for: obtained from the column headed "balance" by allowing for carryover, for miscellaneous uses, smoothing, and expressing the results in round numbers.

In the above table, the column headed "Balance" gives the surplus each year, after allowing for net exports and for the quantities used by manufacturers of cereal beverages and distilled spirits. These figures cannot be used directly as an estimate of the quantity of hops used in the manufacture of beer, on account of the fluctuations in carryover from year to year.

Unfortunately, estimates of carryover are available only for recent years, and even these refer to various dates in the year. However, it may be noted that in two of the last four pre-prohibition years the quantity of hops exported and used by brewers was greater than the production, and that this deficiency of supply was greater than the excess during the other two years. During the year 1919-1920, the first full year of prohibition, there was also a deficiency and the price of hops in the fall of 1919 reached the exceedingly high figure of 77.6 cents per pound. These facts indicate a definite shortage of supply, and it may, therefore, reasonably be assumed that the carryover at the end of the crop year 1919-1920 was negligible.

The exceedingly low price of 8.6 cents per pound in the fall of 1922, together with the fact that the quantity exported and used by legitimate beverage manufacturers during 1923-1924 exceeded production, indicates that the carryover from the 1922-1923 season was exceptionally large. Again, the fairly high price prevailing from 1926 to 1928, gives ground for belief that the carryover in the fall of 1927 was small, and this is corroborated by references in trade journals.[2] On March 1, 1928, stocks in the hands of growers and merchants on the Pacific Coast were estimated at four million pounds, and a year later at seven million pounds. On August 1, 1930, the Pacific Coast carryover was approximately six million pounds, and on July 1, 1931, four million pounds.[3]

[2] See *The Malt Age*, May, 1928, p. 32.

[3] Federal-State Marketing Service, Sacramento, Cal., "Market Infor-

When all of these facts are taken into consideration, and allowance made for the use of a small quantity of hops in medicine, it is possible to make, in round numbers, a smoothed estimate of the consumption of hops unaccounted for, year by year, since 1920.[4] This is a reasonable estimate of the quantity of hops used in the production of beer.

Between 1911 and 1918 the breweries in the United States used from .64 to .71 pounds of hops per barrel of beer.[5] When the entire process of making beer is carried on at home, the use of hops is doubtless much greater than this, and it is probable that such was the case during the early years of prohibition. However, in recent years "home-brew" is made principally from hop-flavored malt extract or from "wort," which is "embryo beer before the yeast is added." It is not likely that the manufacturers of malt extract and of "wort" use a greater ratio of hops to beer than the pre-war manufacturers of beer. It is, therefore, reasonable to assume that there is now used about three-fourths of a pound of hops per barrel of beer produced; that is, that forty-one gallons of beer are manufactured for each pound of hops used. In

mation on Hops," March 20, 1929, p. 9 (dealer estimates averaged and converted from bales into pounds); and Grain, Hay and Feed Market News Service, San Francisco, Cal., the "Hop Market Review," July 3, 1931, and August 5, 1931.

[4] Professor Irving Fisher agrees with Mr. Hugh F. Fox in estimating the quantity of hops used annually for other than brewing purposes at 250,000 pounds (Fisher, *The Noble Experiment*, p. 261). Both of these men assume that hops are used in the manufacture of yeast, but an official of the company believed to be the largest manufacturer of yeast in the United States says that his company does not do so (letter to the author).

[5] Computed from statistics of hops used and of beer produced, as given in the annual reports of the Commissioner of Internal Revenue of the United States.

order to make allowance for wastage, however, this is reduced to forty gallons of beer per pound of hops in the following estimate of the production of beer in the United States.[6]

TABLE 4

ESTIMATED PRODUCTION OF BEER IN THE UNITED STATES, 1921 TO 1931

Year ending June 30	Estimate of hops used (millions of pounds)	Estimate of beer produced (millions of gallons)	Beer produced per capita (gallons)
1921	3	120	1.11
1922	4	160	1.47
1923	5½	220	1.97
1924	7	280	2.46
1925	9	360	3.13
1926	11	440	3.76
1927	13½	540	4.64
1928	16	640	5.33
1929	20	800	6.58
1930	23	920	7.57
1931	19½	780	6.33

SOURCES OF DATA:
Hops used: Table 3, *supra*, p. 28.
Beer produced: computed at 40 gallons of beer per pound of hops used.

In order to obtain an estimate of the total consumption of beer in the United States, there must be added to the domestic production the beer smuggled into the nation and deducted that seized by prohibition agents. The only figures available regarding smuggled liquor are those of liquor cleared for export from Canada to the United States.[7] It is sometimes asserted that the quantity of

[6] The Bureau of Prohibition reduces this to 28 gallons of beer per pound of hops, on the testimony of retail dealers regarding the use of hops in home brew (*Possible Production of Illegal Liquor in the United States for the fiscal year ending June 30, 1930*). It is doubtful, however, whether much of the beer consumed in American cities is brewed at home by methods involving the direct use of hops.

[7] Since prohibition in the United States involved no change in

TABLE 5

ESTIMATED CONSUMPTION OF BEER IN THE UNITED STATES, 1921 TO 1931

Year ending June 30	Beer produced in the United States (millions of gallons)	Smuggled Beer (millions of gallons) From Canada	Smuggled Beer (millions of gallons) From all countries (rough estimate)	Malt liquor seized by Federal officials (millions of gallons)	Beer consumed (millions of gallons)
1921	120	0	0	5	115
1922	160	.4	1	4	157
1923	220	1.6	3	5	218
1924	280	3.4	7	5	282
1925	360	3.6	7	7	360
1926	440	4.5	9	14	435
1927	540	5.1	10	6	544
1928	640	4.6	9	4	645
1929	800	4.9	10	3	807
1930	920	1.7	4	4	920
1931	780		4	5	779

SOURCES OF DATA:

Beer produced in the United States: Table 4, *supra*, p. 31.

Beer smuggled from Canada: Dominion Bureau of Statistics. Figures are for fiscal years ending March 31, and have been converted from Imperial gallons to United States gallons.

Beer smuggled from all countries: estimated at twice the quantity exported from Canada to the United States (see footnote 6, *supra*, p. 31).

Malt liquors seized by Federal officials: *Statistics Concerning Intoxicating Liquors*, December, 1930, p. 73.

Beer consumed: beer produced plus smuggled beer minus malt liquors seized.

liquor actually sent from Canada to the United States is much greater than that cleared for export; and, on the other hand, that part of the liquor cleared for export to the United States is bootlegged back into Canada to escape

Canadian law, Canadian officials continued to issue clearance papers for cargoes of alcoholic beverages exported from Canada to the United States, and these cargoes were presumably smuggled into the United States. There is no indication in the Canadian export statistics that liquor designed for smuggling into the United States was cleared for export to other countries.

taxation. There is no valid evidence regarding either of these assertions. With no other data available, we may use twice the quantity exported from Canada to the United States as a rough estimate of the quantity smuggled into the United States from all countries.[8]

In Table 5 this estimate of smuggled beer is added, and the seizures of malt liquor by Federal officials subtracted, from the estimates of beer produced in the United States. Both the quantity smuggled into the country and the quantity seized are relatively insignificant, and the resulting estimate of the consumption of beer in the United States does not differ appreciably from the estimate of domestic production.

In Table 6 the estimated consumption of illegal beer is given for calendar years.

TABLE 6

ESTIMATED CONSUMPTION OF ILLEGAL BEER, 1921 TO 1930

Calendar years	Millions of gallons	Gallons per capita
1921	136	1.26
1922	188	1.71
1923	250	2.24
1924	321	2.84
1925	398	3.46
1926	490	4.21
1927	595	5.03
1928	726	6.05
1929	864	7.11
1930	850	6.90

SOURCE OF DATA: Table 5, *supra*, p. 32.

[8] The Bureau of Prohibition estimated the total quantity of all alcoholic beverages smuggled into the United States during the fiscal year ending June 30, 1930, at 4,858,200 gallons, which may be compared with 2,620,190 gallons exported from Canada to the United States (*Possible Production of Illegal Liquor in the United States for the fiscal year ending June 30, 1930*, pp. 48 and 46). This estimate of smuggled liquor appears reasonable, in the light of all available statistics regarding exports of alcoholic beverages to the United States, and to nearby countries from which smuggling into the United States is convenient.

THE CONSUMPTION OF WINE

Two methods may be used in estimating the probable quantity of wine produced in the United States in recent years: one by deducting grapes exported (in the form of raisins) and those probably used for table purposes from the total annual production, and the other by assuming that all wine grapes and fresh raisin grapes, and a small percentage of table grapes and raisins, are used in wine-making.

To use the first method we must first estimate the quantity of grapes used for other than wine purposes in the United States. In Table 7 such an estimate is made for three pre-prohibition years, 1899, 1909 and 1917, the only years for which sufficient data are available to make even approximate estimates.

It will be seen from this computation that the per capita use of grapes for other purposes than exports and the production of liquors increased from 1899 to 1909 at the rate of .4 of a pound per year, and from 1909 to 1917 at the rate of .5 of a pound per year. It may be suggested that there has been an unusually rapid increase in the use of grapes for table purposes and of raisins in food in recent years as a result of advertising. This argument, however, must be offset against others: the fact that grapes have now to compete for table use with a greater variety of fruits than in former years, and the fact that the greatest increase in the consumption of raisins, which have been more widely advertised than any other form of grapes, occurred before 1917.[9] It appears

[9] From 1910 to 1914 the per capita consumption of raisins was approximately 1½ pounds per year. By 1917 it had increased to 2¾ pounds, remaining approximately at that level until 1924, when it increased to about 3½ pounds per capita. (Shear, *Economic Status of the Grape Industry*, p. 124). Extensive advertising of raisins began in 1914.

TABLE 7

PRODUCTION AND USE OF GRAPES IN THE UNITED STATES, 1899, 1909 AND 1917

	1899	1909	1917
Production of grapes in California, tons	392,000	858,000	1,254,000
Production of grapes outside California, tons	290,000	296,000	192,000
Production of vinous liquors in California, gallons	5,492,000	16,006,000	
Production of vinous liquors outside California, gallons	2,754,000	2,630,000	
Ratio of production of vinous liquors outside California to that in California	50.1%	16.4%	
Grapes used for wine and brandy in California, tons	236,000	490,000	441,000
Grapes used for wine and brandy outside California, estimated	118,000	80,000	64,000
Grapes and raisins exported, tons of fresh grapes	8,000	18,000	96,000
Total grapes used for liquors and exported	362,000	588,000	601,000
Grapes available for other purposes, tons	320,000	566,000	845,000
Grapes available for other purposes, pounds per capita	8.6	12.5	16.5

SOURCES OF DATA:

Production of grapes in California: S. W. Shear, *Economic Status of the Grape Industry,* Bulletin 429, University of California, College of Agriculture Agricultural Experiment Station, June, 1927.

Production of grapes outside California: 1899, *United States Census of Agriculture,* 1910, p. 716; 1909 and 1917, Shear, *op. cit.*, p. 24.

Production of vinous liquors: *U. S. Census,* 1910, v. 5, p. 717.

Grapes used for wine and brandy in California: Shear, *op. cit.*, p. 111.

Grapes used for wine and brandy outside California: 1899 and 1909, computed by applying the ratio of production of vinous liquors outside California to that in California; 1917, computed by assuming that one-third of the crop outside California was used for wine, *Standard Encyclopedia of the Alcohol Problem,* (Westerville, Ohio, 1925) v. 3, p. 1135.

Grapes and raisins exported: 1899, *Statistical Abstract of the United States*, 1906, p. 339; 1909 and 1917, Shear *op. cit.*, p. 124. Raisins converted to fresh fruit on the basis of 3½ pounds of fresh fruit per pound of raisins (letter from the Sun-Maid Raisin Growers of California).

Total grapes used for liquors and exported: total of the preceding three items.

Grapes available for other purposes: total production minus grapes used for liquors and exported.

reasonable, therefore, to estimate the maximum increase in per capita consumption for other purposes at one-half pound per year since 1917.

Making this allowance, and allowing for grapes exported and for grapes used in the officially reported production of wine and spirits, the production of illicit and home-made wine in the United States may be estimated. This method necessitates the assumption that when the grape crop is short, as in 1921 and in 1924, there is no reduction in the use of grapes for table purposes, but that the entire shortage is met by a reduction in grapes used for wine purposes; and the assumption that when the grape crop is large, as in 1923, the surplus all goes into the increased use of wine. These assumptions are not strictly accurate and the estimates in the following table of illicit and home-made wine are, therefore, probably too high in some years and too low in others. It is quite possible, also, that the line of trend in the use of grapes for table purposes has tended to flatten out, instead of increasing uniformly at the rate of one-half pound per year. If so, the estimate of wine produced given in Table 8 is too low for the more recent years.

The Bureau of Prohibition states that investigators in various departments of the United States Government agree that all of the wine grapes and fresh raisin grapes are used in making wine; and estimates that about 10 per cent of the table grapes and raisins produced are also used

TABLE 8

ESTIMATED PRODUCTION OF WINE IN THE UNITED STATES, 1921 TO 1931
(First method)

Year ending June 30	Production of grapes (1000 tons)	Exports and used for legal wine and spirits	Used for other purposes Pounds per capita	(1000 tons)	Balance available for home-made wine (1000 tons)	Illicit and home-made wine produced (million gallons)
1921	1,523	190	18	958	375	56
1922	1,212	139	18½	997	76	11
1923	1,981	290	19	1,037	654	98
1924	2,227	226	19½	1,089	912	137
1925	1,778	264	20	1,137	377	57
1926	2,064	286	20½	1,183	595	89
1927	2,423	324	21	1,230	869	130
1928	2,463	419	21½	1,275	769	115
1929	2,518	484	22	1,320	714	107
1930	2,022	269	22½	1,383	370	56
1931	2,245	250	23	1,426	569	85

SOURCES OF DATA:

Production of grapes: Shear, *op. cit.*, p. 24, *Yearbook of Agriculture,* 1930, p. 731, and *Crops and Markets,* December, 1930, p. 481. Grapes produced in California but not harvested have been deducted.

Exports and used for legal wine and spirits: computed by totalling (a) domestic exports of grapes *(Yearbook of Agriculture,* 1930, p. 731, and issues of the *Monthly Summary of Foreign Commerce of the United States),* (b) domestic exports of raisins (Shear, *op. cit.*, p. 124, and issues of the *Monthly Summary of Foreign Commerce of the United States)* multiplied by 3½ to convert to fresh fruit, (c) grapes used for legitimate wine production, at 150 gallons of wine per ton *(Statistics Concerning Intoxicating Liquors,* December, 1930, p. 57, and December, 1931, p. 61), and (d) grapes used in the legitimate production of spirits (*Statistics Concerning Intoxicating Liquors*, December, 1930, p. 63).

Used for other purposes, pounds per capita: increase of one-half pound per year after 1917.

Balance available: production minus exports and used for wine and spirits and minus used for other purposes.

Illicit and home-made wine produced: computed at the rate of 150 gallons of wine per ton of grapes. See Shear, *op. cit.*, p. 111, and Irving Fisher, *The Noble Experiment*, p. 273. Fisher gives the yield as from 1¾ to 2 gallons of wine per box of 25 or 26 pounds of grapes, which is the equivalent of from 140 to 160 gallons per ton.

for this purpose. These assumptions are used as the basis of the estimates in Table 9.

TABLE 9

ESTIMATED PRODUCTION OF WINE IN THE UNITED STATES, 1921 TO 1931

(Second method)

Year ending June 30	Fresh raisin and wine grapes produced in California (1000 tons)	Raisins and table grapes produced in California (1000 tons)	Grapes produced in other states (1000 tons)	Grapes used for making wine (1000 tons)	Total wine produced (millions of gallons)	Produced by licensed wineries (millions of gallons)	Illegal and home-m wine (millio of gallon
1921	375	874	250	487	73	21	52
1922	310	743	112	396	59	6	53
1923	450	1,161	275	594	89	15	74
1924	558	1,472	197	725	109	9	100
1925	530	1,005	243	655	98	4	94
1926	773	1,139	152	922	138	6	132
1927	643	1,471	309	821	123	4	119
1928	776	1,488	199	945	142	5	137
1929	844	1,369	305	1,011	152	11	141
1930	654	1,097	271	791	119	3	116
1931	981	986	278	1,108	166	7	159

SOURCES OF DATA:

Production of grapes, all three classes: *Yearbook of Agriculture*, 1927, p. 848; 1930, pp. 731-732, and *Crops and Markets*, December, 1930, p. 481. Raisins converted to fresh grape basis.

Grapes used for making wine: 100 per cent of the wine and fresh raisin grapes produced in California, plus 10 per cent of the table grapes and raisins on fresh grape basis produced in California, plus ten per cent of the total production in other states.

Total wine produced: computed from grapes available for wine at the rate of 150 gallons per ton of grapes. The estimates in this column differ slightly from the estimates of the Bureau of Prohibition *(Possible Production of Illegal Liquor in the United States for the fiscal year ending June 30, 1930)*, inasmuch as the Bureau failed to deduct in some years the quantities of grapes produced but not harvested in California, while in this table no allowance has been made for the small quantities of grapes exported and imported.

Produced by licensed wineries: *Statistics Concerning Intoxicating Liquors*, December, 1930, p. 57 and December, 1931, p. 61.

Illegal and homemade wine produced: total wine produced less that produced by licensed wineries.

It will be noted that the estimated production of illegal and home-made wine as computed by this method is greater in most years than as computed by the first method. Since this method is at least as reasonable as the first, an average of the two estimates may be considered a conservative estimate of the production of illegal and home-made wine during the years since the adoption of prohibition.

To obtain an estimate of wine consumption, there should be added to the estimate of production the wine smuggled into the country, that withdrawn for medicinal and sacramental use, and that made from other fruits than grapes. There should be deducted the wine seized by prohibition agents. Smuggled wine is insignificant. The largest quantity cleared for export from Canada to the United States in any year since 1920 is about one-fourth of a million gallons, and if we assume an equal quantity to be smuggled in from other countries, the total is not more than half a million gallons.[10] It is impossible to make any estimate of the quantity of wine made from any other fruits. The Bureau of Prohibition does not report the quantity of wine seized separately, but combines it with cider, mash and pomace. No estimate can, therefore, be made of the quantity of wine seized by prohibition agents. So the following estimate of consumption differs from the estimate of production of grape wine only by the addition of wine legally withdrawn from bonded wineries.

In view of the convenience of computing the estimates of consumption of spirits by calendar instead of fiscal years, this estimate of the consumption of wine, like that of beer, is converted to calendar years. This has the added advantage of reducing the overestimate of production in years of a large crop and the underestimate in years of a small crop.

[10] *Cf.* footnote 6, *supra*, p. 31. Figures of Canadian exports to the United States furnished by the Dominion Bureau of Statistics.

TABLE 10

ESTIMATED CONSUMPTION OF WINE, 1921 TO 1931

Year ending June 30	Illegal and home-made wine (millions of gallons)	Removed from bonded wineries, tax-paid (millions of gallons)	Calendar year	Wine Consumed Millions of gallons	Wine Consumed Gallons per capita
1921	54	6	1921	48	.44
1922	32	3	1922	63	.57
1923	86	4	1923	106	.95
1924	118	4	1924	102	.90
1925	76	5	1925	99	.86
1926	111	5	1926	122	1.05
1927	125	2	1927	128	1.08
1928	126	2	1928	128	1.07
1929	124	3	1929	108	.89
1930	86	3	1930	107	.87
1931	122	2			

SOURCES OF DATA:

Illegal and home-made wine: average of estimates in Table 8, *supra*, p. 37, and Table 9, *supra*, p. 38.

Removed from bonded wineries, tax paid: *Statistics Concerning Intoxicating Liquors*, December, 1931, p. 75.

Wine consumed, calendar years: averages of figures for successive fiscal years. For example, the illegal and home-made wine produced in the United States plus that removed from bonded wineries was 60 million gallons for the fiscal year ending June 30, 1921, and 35 million gallons for the fiscal year ending June 30, 1922. The average for these two fiscal years is 48 million gallons, and this is used as the estimate of consumption during the calendar year 1921.

THE CONSUMPTION OF SPIRITS

It is more difficult to make an estimate from sources of production of the consumption of spirits than of beer or of wine. There is no one material which can be selected because of its especial use in the manufacture of distilled liquors. Account must be taken of several possible sources of distilled spirits for beverage purposes, and of the probable quantity obtained from each of these sources.

Industrial Alcohol. It is popularly supposed that there

is a vast quantity of industrial alcohol diverted to the beverage industry, but the estimates which have been made, even by government officials, vary widely.[11]

There are three forms of industrial alcohol which must be considered: pure alcohol released on payment of tax, completely denatured alcohol and specially denatured alcohol.[12] Up to 1915 the volume of pure alcohol released on payment of tax was far greater than the production of denatured alcohol, though there had been a steady growth in the use of denatured alcohol after 1907. In 1916 the production of specially denatured alcohol increased immensely, due to the war demand. After the increase in the tax rate on spirits in 1917, the withdrawals of pure alcohol decreased sharply; but on account of the war demand for denatured alcohol, it is impossible to tell whether this is due to the substitution of denatured alcohol, or simply to a decrease in the demand for the products for which the pure alcohol had been used. During the first few years of prohibition the withdrawals of pure alcohol decreased still further, due, presumably, though not certainly, to the substitution of denatured alcohol.

In pre-war days large quantities of pure alcohol were used in patent medicines, many of which contained large

[11] See, for example, the statements of Emory R. Buckner, United States Attorney for the Southern District of New York, and of J. M. Doran, at that time chemist in the Bureau of Internal Revenue, U. S. Congress, Senate, Subcommittee of the Committee on the Judiciary, *The National Prohibition Law,* pp. 1309 and 1656. Mr. Buckner estimated a diversion of 60 million gallons, and Mr. Doran of between 13 and 14 million gallons, both in 1925. The latter estimate is much the more reliable.

[12] The Bureau of Industrial Alcohol classifies the various formulas used for denaturing alcohol into two groups: completely denatured alcohol and specially denatured alcohol. (*Statistics Concerning Intoxicating Liquors,* December, 1931, pp. 26-32.)

percentages of alcohol, and doubtless considerable quantities were also used in fortifying beverages. It is thus absolutely impossible to estimate the quantity of alcohol, pure or denatured, formerly used for those purposes which are today considered industrial.

In the following table it is assumed that the decline in the use of pure alcohol for proprietary medicines and for fortifying beverages is approximately offset by the increased use of specially denatured alcohol for various purposes in industry, which is known to have been very great in recent years. That is, the per-capita use of all three classes of industrial alcohol for all purposes, except as anti-freeze in automobiles and in the lacquer industry, for which it is possible to make separate estimates, is assumed to have remained at .4 of a gallon, the average from 1907 to 1915.

When allowance is made for annual fluctuations from the estimated normal it is apparent that legitimate demands for alcohol account for nearly all the withdrawals of industrial alcohol, and there is no evidence from this analysis of substantial diversion to beverage use. The years when diversion was most likely were 1924-1925 and 1925-1926, when the large "balance" indicates that it may have been from ten to fifteen million gallons annually. On the other hand, the character of the assumptions involved in the estimate of normal industrial demand precludes the definite conclusion that there has been no significant quantity diverted.

Another, and probably more reliable, method of estimating the quantity of industrial alcohol diverted to beverage use is that of considering each formula for industrial alcohol and the probable diversion therefrom. Mr. Doran, now Commissioner of Industrial Alcohol, estimates by this method that between thirteen and four-

TABLE 11

THE USE OF INDUSTRIAL ALCOHOL IN THE UNITED STATES, 1907 TO 1931

(Millions of wine gallons, 190 proof)

Year ending June 30	Alcohol withdrawn: Pure	Alcohol withdrawn: Completely denatured	Alcohol withdrawn: Specially denatured	Alcohol withdrawn: Total	Estimated normal legitimate use: For miscellaneous purposes	Estimated normal legitimate use: For auto anti-freeze	Estimated normal legitimate use: In lacquer industry (calendar years)	Estimated normal legitimate use: Total	Balance
1907	37.6	1.4	.4	39.4	34.3			34.3	5.1
1908	31.7	1.8	1.5	35.0	35.0			35.0	0.0
1909	25.8	2.4	2.2	30.4	35.6			35.6	—5.2
1910	29.2	3.1	3.0	35.3	36.3			36.3	—1.0
1911	29.2	3.4	3.5	36.1	36.9			36.9	—0.8
1912	29.8	4.2	3.9	37.9	37.5			37.5	0.4
1913	31.2	5.2	4.6	41.0	38.0			38.0	3.0
1914	30.9	5.2	5.2	41.3	38.6			38.6	2.7
1915	28.3	5.4	8.6	42.3	39.2			39.2	3.1
1916	30.9	7.9	38.8	77.6	39.7			39.7	37.9
1917	37.4	10.5	45.2	93.1	40.3	.7		41.0	52.1
1918	15.4	10.3	39.8	65.5	40.9	2.0		42.9	22.6
1919	9.5	10.0	28.3	47.8	41.4	4.9		46.3	1.5
1920	11.9	13.5	15.3	40.7	42.0	6.3	1.4	49.7	—9.0
1921	13.4	12.4	10.0	35.8	42.6	9.0	1.3	52.9	—17.1
1922	8.6	16.2	17.2	42.0	43.1	11.9	1.3	56.3	—14.3
1923	5.7	27.1	30.4	63.2	43.7	18.2	2.3	64.2	—1.0
1924	4.9	34.6	33.1	72.6	44.7	24.6	2.5	71.8	0.8
1925	4.5	47.0	34.8	86.3	45.5	28.9	4.0	78.4	7.9
1926	4.6	65.9	39.5	110.0	46.2	44.1	6.8	97.1	12.9
1927	4.3	56.1	39.4	99.8	46.9	43.8	9.5	100.2	0.4
1928	4.6	47.0	45.5	97.1	47.5	44.4	14.0	105.9	—8.8
1929	4.7	52.4	54.6	111.6	48.0	48.5	15.7	112.2	—0.6
1930	4.3	58.1	47.6	110.0	48.6	51.2	11.0	110.8	—0.8
1931	3.9	49.1	37.2	90.2	49.3	53.0	8.0	110.3	—20.1

SOURCES OF DATA:

Alcohol withdrawn: *Statistics Concerning Intoxicating Liquors,* December, 1930, pp. 4 and 27, and December, 1931, pp. 18-19. Figures for pure alcohol converted from tax or proof gallons to gallons of 190 proof, by dividing by 1.9.

Estimated normal use for miscellaneous purposes: computed at .4 of a gallon per capita, the average from 1907 to 1915.

Estimated use for auto anti-freeze: see footnote 13.[13]

Estimated use in lacquer industry: furnished by the E. I. du Pont de Nemours & Company for the years from 1920 to 1930; figure for 1931 estimated from automobile production.

Balance: difference between total alcohol withdrawn and total estimated normal legitimate use.

[13] Previous to 1917 few cars were used during the winter. Closed car production was in 1917 about 4 per cent of the total, but had risen to more than 50 per cent in 1925. In computing the estimate of alcohol used as anti-freeze, it is assumed that its use grew gradually from 1917 to 1925, reaching two gallons per car per winter of normal weather in 1925-26, and remaining at that figure since then.

It is assumed that little or no use in parts of the United States is offset by the use of more than two gallons per car in other parts. This rate of use is then modified by an index of weather severity obtained by averaging the number of months with a minimum temperature below 32 degrees Fahrenheit in 69 cities (data from Annual and Monthly Reports of the Weather Bureau), the ten-year average from 1919-20 to 1928-29 being taken as unity. The data and computations are shown in the following table.

TABLE 12

ESTIMATE OF ALCOHOL USED FOR ANTI-FREEZE

Year	Number of automobiles registered December 31 (thousands)	Estimate of alcohol used per car in a winter of average temperature (gallons)	Average number of freezing months in 69 cities	Index of weather severity	Total alcohol used (millions of gallons)
1916-17	3,513	0.2			7
1917-18	4,983	0.4			2.0
1918-19	6,147	0.6			4.9
1919-20	7,565	0.8	5.74	1.041	6.3
1920-21	9,232	1.0	5.32	.965	9.0
1921-22	10,465	1.2	5.25	.951	11.9
1922-23	12,240	1.4	5.87	1.064	18.2
1923-24	15,092	1.6	5.62	1.020	24.6
1924-25	17,595	1.8	5.03	.912	28.9
1925-26	19,954	2.0	6.09	1.104	44.1
1926-27	22,001	2.0	5.49	.996	43.8
1927-28	23,133	2.0	5.29	.959	44.4
1928-29	24,493	2.0	5.45	.988	48.5
1929-30	26,501	2.0	5.33	.966	51.2
1930-31	26,524	2.0	5.51	.999	53.0

This estimate may be compared with an estimate made by a more detailed method by the Prohibition Unit, Bureau of Internal Revenue, for the calendar year, 1925, of 36.5 million gallons (U. S. Congress, Senate, Subcommittee of the Committee on the Judiciary, *The National Prohibition Law*, p. 1315).

teen million gallons were diverted in 1925.[14] The Bureau of Prohibition, using the same method, estimates a diversion of five million gallons in 1929-1930, a total with which Mr. Doran is in substantial agreement, despite his dissent from the Bureau's estimate of diversion from certain kinds of denatured alcohol.[15] These estimates may be accepted, with one minor change in that of the Bureau of Prohibition, as the best that can be made for those years. Mr. Doran estimated that perhaps a million gallons of completely denatured alcohol No. 5, used principally for automobile anti-freeze preparations, was diverted to beverage use in 1925, but the Bureau of Prohibition omitted this formula from its calculations. Deaths from wood alcohol poisoning have been nearly as great in recent years as in 1925, and it is said, too, that many hardened drinkers are able to consume alcohol denatured with aldehol and 4 per cent wood alcohol, the denaturant in this formula, without poisoning.[16] Some allowance ought, therefore, to be made for diversion from this formula.

For other years since 1921 it is possible to interpolate from these two estimates, with due regard for the total production of each kind of denatured alcohol. This is the basis of Table 13.

[14] Statement of J. M. Doran, U. S. Congress, Senate, Subcommittee of the Committee on the Judiciary, *The National Prohibition Law*, pp. 1309-1315.

[15] Bureau of Prohibition, *Possible Production of Illegal Liquor in the United States for the fiscal year ending June 30, 1930*, p. 32. Mr. Doran disagreed with the Bureau of Prohibition regarding diversion of alcohol from the perfumery and toilet water trade, terming this figure excessive (*The Atlanta Journal*, October 12, 1930, p. 17). In July, 1930, however, he estimated that diversion had been reduced to less than 5 per cent of the total supply (*New York Times*, July 9, 1930, p. 1). Five per cent of the withdrawals of denatured alcohol would be 5¼ million gallons in 1929-30.

[16] *The New York Times*, April 29, 1931, p. 27.

TABLE 13

ESTIMATED DIVERSION OF INDUSTRIAL ALCOHOL, 1921 to 1931
(millions of gallons)

Year ending June 30	Pure alcohol		Completely denatured alcohol					
			No. 4		No. 5		No. 6	
	Withdrawn	Estimated diversion	Withdrawn	Estimated diversion	Withdrawn	Estimated diversion	Withdrawn	Estimated diversion
1921	13.4	5	.3	..	6.5	2	5.1	..
1922	8.6	4	..	..	9.8	1	5.8	1
1923	5.7	1	..	..	18.8	1	6.9	2
1924	4.9	½	..	..	25.8	1	7.2	3
1925	4.5	..	..	..	36.1	1	8.7	4
1926	4.6	..	..	..	47.9	1	12.4	8
1927	4.3	..	1.5	1½	47.0	1	.3	..
1928	4.6	..	..	..	40.4	1	..	..
1929	4.7	..	..	..	41.6	1	..	..
1930	4.6	..	..	..	47.2	1	..	..
1931	3.9	..	..	..	41.5	1	..	..

Year ending June 30	Specially denatured alcohol								Total diversion
	No. 2-B		No. 4		Nos. 36, 39-A 39-B, 39-C, 40		No. 44-A		
	Withdrawn	Estimated diversion	Withdrawn	Estimated diversion	Withdrawn	Estimated diversion	Withdrawn	Estimated diversion	
1921	2.0	..	.7	..	.1	..	..	..	7
1922	2.5	..	.9	..	3.2	1	..	..	7
1923	4.7	..	.7	..	10.4	6	..	..	10
1924	5.2	..	.8	..	12.1	7	..	..	11½
1925	6.7	..	1.0	..	12.8	8	..	..	13
1926	9.1	2	1.7	½	12.2	7½	..	..	19
1927	11.3	3	1.4	..	6.9	3	..	..	8½
1928	12.1	3	1.3	..	6.8	3	.2	..	7
1929	13.9	3½	1.3	..	6.8	3	3.2	3	10½
1930	13.3	2	1.3	..	5.5	2	1.1	1	6
1931	8.9	1	1.3	..	3.4	1	.1	..	3

SOURCES OF DATA:

Alcohol withdrawn: *Statistics Concerning Intoxicating Liquors,* December, 1931, pp. 18-25.

Estimated diversion, pure alcohol. Mr. Doran estimated the diversion in 1925 as negligible, but stated that in 1921 and 1922 difficulties were experienced in the ready conversion of pure alcohol to illegal liquor. Not all the difference between the 1921 production and that of later years is to be considered diverted, however, since the toilet goods, and perhaps other industries, used pure alcohol at that time.

Estimated diversion, completely denatured No. 4. This formula was produced only in small quantities previous to 1927, and discontinued thereafter. Most of the 1926-27 production was probably diverted.

Estimated diversion, completely denatured No. 5. Mr. Doran estimated a million gallons a year diversion as a maximum in 1925. The number of deaths from wood alcohol poisoning has remained fairly constant during the whole period, except for 1921, and diversion in other years than 1925 has been estimated accordingly. This is the formula used principally for automobile anti-freeze preparations.

Estimated diversion, completely denatured No. 6. Mr. Doran estimated no substantial diversion in 1921, and 4 million gallons in 1925. The formula was discontinued early in 1926.

Estimated diversion, specially denatured No. 2-B. This is the formula chiefly used in making ethyl acetate, and it is estimated that about a third of the alcohol produced under this formula is used in its production. The Bureau of Prohibition estimates that in 1929-30 about half the acetate produced was "cracked" and the alcohol (about 2 million gallons) recovered. Mr. Doran thought none was diverted in 1925.

Estimated diversion, specially denatured No. 4. This formula is used chiefly in tobacco manufacture and production in recent years has not been excessive. However, Mr. Doran estimated that about a half million gallons were diverted in 1925.

Estimated diversion, specially denatured Nos. 36, 39-A, 39-B, 39-C and 40. These formulas cover the fields of perfumes, hair tonics and other toilet preparations. Mr. Doran estimated a diversion of 8 million gallons in 1925 and the Bureau of Prohibition of 2 million gallons in 1929-30.

Estimated diversion, specially denatured No. 44-A. This formula was authorized for lacquer thinners and solvents, but the Bureau of Prohibition estimates that in 1929-30 most of the production was diverted.

It may be well to examine, also, formulas not included in the above estimates. Accordingly, there are given in Table 14 the quantities withdrawn of all other formulas in which the withdrawals have in any year since 1921 amounted to as much as a million gallons.

TABLE 14

INDUSTRIAL ALCOHOL WITHDRAWN, 1921 TO 1931

Important Formulas not Included in Table 13

(millions of gallons)

Year ending June 30	Completely denatured No. 1	Specially denatured No. 1	No. 3-A	No. 13-A	No. 18	No. 23-A	No. 32
1921	...	4.0	.2	1.0	.7	.1	...
1922	.2	5.0	.5	1.8	1.0	.5	...
1923	.4	7.2	.7	2.3	.8	.5	...
1924	.5	7.1	.8	1.9	1.7	.5	.3
1925	1.1	7.2	.7	1.3	1.3	.5	.8
1926	4.5	7.5	1.1	1.4	1.7	1.1	1.1
1927	5.3	7.6	.9	1.6	3.6	1.5	1.2
1928	7.5	7.8	.7	1.4	7.3	2.3	1.2
1929	9.7	9.0	.8	1.6	8.3	4.1	1.1
1930	9.9	7.4	.7	1.4	8.1	3.4	1.1
1931	7.6	7.6	.6	1.2	6.1	3.2	.4

SOURCE OF DATA:
Statistics Concerning Intoxicating Liquors, December, 1931, p. 22-25.

Examination of these formulas and their uses does not reveal any likelihood of substantial diversion. Completely denatured No. 1 is used for a wide variety of purposes, and contains more wood alcohol than any other formula. Specially denatured No. 1 and No. 23-A are used in the manufacture of many chemicals, and especially in lacquers, which accounts for the marked increase in withdrawals in recent years. No. 3-A is also used for a wide variety of purposes. Nos. 13-A and 32 are used in various medical and food preparations. No. 18 is used in the production of vinegar and acetone, the latter being used in the production of rayon and accounting for large withdrawals in recent years.

To estimate the beverage spirits, proof strength, produced from diverted industrial alcohol, the estimates of total diversion may be multiplied by 1.9 and converted to calendar years. This is done in Table 15.

TABLE 15

ESTIMATE OF BEVERAGE SPIRITS PRODUCED FROM DIVERTED INDUSTRIAL ALCOHOL

Year ending June 30	Estimated diversion (millions of gallons 190 proof)	Calendar year	Beverage spirits produced (millions of proof gallons)
1921	7	1921	13
1922	7	1922	16
1923	10	1923	20
1924	11½	1924	23
1925	13	1925	30
1926	19	1926	26
1927	8½	1927	15
1928	7	1928	17
1929	10½	1929	16
1930	6	1930	9
1931	3	....	..

SOURCES OF DATA:

Estimated diversion: Table 13, *supra*, p. 46.

Beverage spirits produced: quantities diverted multiplied by 1.9, and fiscal years averaged to convert to calendar years.

Corn Sugar (Solid Glucose). The comparatively small use of industrial alcohol for beverage purposes is due to the fact that denatured alcohol must be de-denatured. The process of diversion and of de-denaturing is as difficult and more easily detected than the direct distillation of alcohol from sugar, glucose or molasses.

Among the various products which are capable of being used for the production of beverage alcohol, solid glucose, now called corn sugar in the reports of the Census of Manufactures, and formerly called grape sugar, is the most convenient and one of the most extensively used. The production of corn sugar has increased enormously since 1923, for which there seems to be no explanation except its use in the making of beverage alcohol.

It has been suggested that corn sugar is being used

extensively in a number of industries: in foods, such as bakery products, confectionery, condensed milk, vinegar, caramel, sugar coloring and stock foods; in dyes, chemicals and finishes, such as pigments, lacquers, waterproofing materials and medicines; in soap, cosmetics and laundries, and in the manufacture of leather, textiles and artificial silk.[17]

Some of these alleged uses, however, have not been substantiated by investigation, and the quantity necessary for other uses is slight. In respect to some uses corn sugar has been confused with cornstarch and corn syrup.[18] Thus "linit" has been claimed to be corn sugar, but its manufacturer says it is a special form of cornstarch; the director of research of the national association of laundry owners reports that he has no knowledge of the use of corn sugar as a laundry sizing, and a cotton manufacturer reports that it is liquid glucose, rather than solid, that is used for textile sizing.[19] In other cases, persons associated with the industries concerned report that only slight use, if any, is made of corn sugar. Candy manufacturers say that they have experimented with the

[17] Irving Fisher, *The Noble Experiment*, pp. 279-281; and *Possible Production of Illegal Liquor in the United States for the fiscal year ending June 30, 1930*, pp. 13-14.

[18] Perhaps the most striking example of this confusion is the following statement made by Mr. Robert E. Corradini, Research Secretary of the World League Against Alcoholism; "Do you happen to know that linit is corn sugar? Corn sugar exclusively, and nothing else but corn sugar? I suppose that every man in this audience carries an ounce and a half of corn sugar on his shirt and collar. There isn't a lady here that hasn't some corn sugar on her dress, or her gown, or whatever she is wearing today. Corn sugar is used by every manufacturer in the line of textiles, by every Chinese laundry, and all of us have some corn sugar on our clothes." (Stenographic report of debate at the Women's University Club, New York City, January 24, 1930.)

[19] Letters to the author.

use of corn sugar, but that its uses have proven very limited. A large soap manufacturer states that cane sugar is used almost exclusively in the manufacture of soap.[20] A survey of ice-cream manufacture in 1927 indicated that only 2.1 per cent of the sugar used in that industry was corn sugar.[21]

The most reliable list of uses of corn sugar is that published by the Associated Corn Products Manufacturers, as follows:[22]

REFINED WHITE CORN SUGAR	In fruit canning
For infant feeding	In the manufacture of candy
For diabetics	70 AND 80 CORN SUGAR
For sugar tolerance test	Caramel or sugar coloring
For surgical shock	Vinegar
In the manufacture of ice cream	In the manufacture of lactic acid
In bread making	In tanning
In condensed milk	In the manufacture of artificial silk

Unfortunately, estimates of the quantities of corn sugar used in these various industries are not available, except for artificial silk, and for the year 1929 only, the total use of refined white sugar and the amount used in tanning. There is probably a great deal of significance in the fact that the manufacturers of corn products submit to trade compilers and to the Department of Commerce the distribution of sales of liquid glucose (corn syrup), but do not give any information whatever concerning the distribution among trades of the sales of solid glucose (corn sugar).

20 Letters to the author.

21 International Association of Ice Cream Manufacturers, *Dairy Products and Kinds of Sugar Used in the Manufacture of Ice Cream*, based on the sixth production and distribution survey of the Bureau of Service and Statistics.

22 Associated Corn Products Manufacturers, *The Story of a Grain of Corn* (Chicago, 1930), p. 20.

TABLE 16

THE USE OF CORN SUGAR IN THE UNITED STATES, 1909 TO 1930

Year	Consumption: Millions of pounds	Consumption: Pounds per capita	Legitimate use (millions of pounds): Miscellaneous purposes	Legitimate use (millions of pounds): Rayon manufacture	Balance (millions of pounds)	Beverage spirits produced (millions of proof gallons)
1909	159	1.8	...	..	...	..
1914	174	1.8	...	..	...	..
1919	116	1.1	...	..	...	..
1920	85	0.8	...	..	...	..
1921	149	1.4	...	..	...	..
1922	270	2.5	197	18	55	6
1923	484	4.3	201	24	259	26
1924	557	4.9	205	26	326	33
1925	535	4.6	208	34	293	29
1926	697	6.0	211	40	446	45
1927	897	7.6	213	47	637	64
1928	969	8.3	216	60	693	69
1929	895	7.4	219	72	604	60
1930	849	6.9	221	59	569	57

SOURCES OF DATA:

Consumption: 1909 and 1914 from the *Census of Manufactures;* 1919 to 1930 supplied by the Associated Corn Products Manufacturers, figures referring to sales rather than to production.

Used for miscellaneous purposes: computed at 1.8 pounds per capita.

Used in rayon manufacture: estimated from the amount used in 1929 by companies making 85 per cent of the total production of rayon (letters to the author).

Balance: consumption minus legitimate use.

Beverage spirits produced: computed at the rate of 10 gallons of spirits, proof strength, per 100 pounds of corn sugar. This computation is based on the assumption that most of the corn sugar used for alcohol production is "70," which contains 70 per cent dextrose and about 10 per cent other carbohydrates, and that between 80 and 85 per cent of these are converted to alcohol. This output of spirits per 100 pounds of corn sugar is also used by the Bureau of Prohibition (cf. *Possible Production of Illegal Liquor in the United States for the fiscal year ending June 30, 1930,* p. 14).

The total use of corn sugar showed no increase during the decade prior to the adoption of prohibition, and, with the exception of rayon, there is no evidence that the use of corn sugar for legitimate purposes has increased appreciably during the decade since its adoption. It is true that sales of refined white corn sugar, first put on the market in 1924, have grown rapidly; but, for the most part, this form of corn sugar has replaced other forms, especially pressed corn sugar, which is no longer made in large quantities.

In Table 16, in which the production of beverage alcohol from corn sugar is estimated, it is assumed that the legitimate use of corn sugar, apart from the rayon industry, has since 1922 remained at 1.8 pounds per capita per year, the rate of consumption in 1909 and in 1914. This is a very liberal estimate in view of the fact that during the three years from 1919 to 1921 consumption declined to an average of 1.1 pounds per capita per year, and makes ample allowance for increased use of refined corn sugar in recent years.

As indicated above, more detailed figures are available of the use of corn sugar for legitimate purposes during the year 1929. In that year the total production of refined corn sugar amounted to 130 million pounds, leaving 765 million pounds as the production of grades 70 and 80. Of this amount approximately 72 million pounds were used in the rayon industry, 10 million pounds in tanning and 7 million pounds were exported.[23] It is hardly conceivable that more than 10 million pounds were used in the production of caramel, vinegar and lactic acid, especially in view of the fact that some manufacturers of these products report they do not use corn sugar. These include all of the uses for corn sugar claimed by the Associated

[23] Production of refined corn sugar and exports in 1929 are given in *Possible Production of Illegal Liquor in the United States for the fiscal year ending June 30, 1930*, p. 13; the estimate of the amount used in tanning was furnished by the American Leather Chemists' Association.

Corn Products Manufacturers, and, after deducting these amounts, the balance unaccounted for in 1929 is 666 million pounds. This is 62 million pounds, or nearly 10 per cent more than the estimate in Table 16 above, and indicates that that estimate is very conservative.

Corn Syrup (Liquid Glucose) and Corn Starch. Beverage alcohol can, of course, be produced from corn syrup (liquid glucose) and from starch, though the process is more complicated if the latter material is used. However, the production of these commodities has changed little since 1920, and is mostly accounted for by known industrial uses. Confectioners, bakers, manufacturers of mixed corn syrups, jams, jellies, preserves and tobacco and the textile and paper trades all use corn syrup; glucose in this form being more convenient than in the solid form. The quantities of corn syrup sold to these various industries are published annually, and the important changes since 1922 can be accounted for, thus indicating that there is no appreciable diversion to the production of alcohol. The bulk of corn starch is sold to grocers, to manufacturers of food products and confectionery, to textile mills and laundries, and to exporters. In Table 17 the sales of corn syrup, corn starch and the total production of starch are given since 1919.

Corn Meal. The mountaineers of the South have made "corn liquor" from corn meal since Colonial days, and it is to be presumed that many of the smaller stills in operation since the adoption of prohibition use corn meal as their principal material.

The per-capita consumption of corn meal, as indicated by production reported by the Census of Manufactures, declined steadily from 1899 to 1919 at the rate of 2.7 pounds per year. The decline was then halted for a few years, being resumed between 1923 and 1925, and again halted. To assume, as one might be at first inclined to

TABLE 17

PRODUCTION OF CORN SYRUP AND OF STARCH, 1919 TO 1930
(millions of pounds)

Year	Sales of corn syrup	Sales of corn starch	Production of starch
1919	1,406	773	784
1920	1,236	671	...
1921	1,025	839	894
1922	1,086	1,022	...
1923	1,012	788	858
1924	1,196	876	...
1925	1,060	799	874
1926	1,109	836	...
1927	1,065	906	1,033
1928	1,107	839	...
1929	1,111	880	731
1930	1,026	710	...

SOURCES OF DATA:

Sales of corn syrup, and sales of corn starch: Associated Corn Products Manufacturers.

Production of starch: *Census of Manufactures.*

assume, that this halt in the declining consumption of corn meal is due entirely or chiefly to its use in the production of beverage alcohol would not be reasonable, for continuation of the annual rate of decline of 2.7 pounds a year would have completely eliminated the normal consumption in 1927.

It is much more reasonable to assume that the curve of normal use has flattened out since 1919, but at what level is hardly more than a guess. Since it is common knowledge that some corn meal is used for beverage alcohol, but it may be presumed that there is still considerable use of corn meal for other purposes, it is assumed, in the computations given in the following table, that the normal use of corn meal per capita has not declined below 14 pounds per year, as compared with 20 pounds in 1919 and 32 pounds in 1914.

TABLE 18

PRODUCTION AND USE OF CORN MEAL IN THE UNITED STATES

Year	Production: Millions of gallons	Production: Pounds per capita	Estimated normal use (pounds per capita)	Balance (millions of pounds)	Beverage spirits produced (millions of proof gallons)
1899	27.8	73.3	..	...	..
1904	23.6	56.0	..	...	..
1909	21.6	46.7	..	...	..
1914	16.3	32.6	..	...	..
1919	10.7	20.0	..	...	..
1921	10.9	19.8	17	300	13
1923	12.2	21.4	15	715	31
1925	9.0	15.3	14	150	7
1927	9.5	15.7	14	200	9
1929	10.1	16.3	14	280	12

SOURCES OF DATA:

Production: *Census of Manufactures.*

Estimated normal use: based on the assumption that the precipitate and steady decline from 1899 to 1919 was halted, and that the curve of normal use has flattened out since 1919.

Balance: computed from production and estimated normal use per capita.

Beverage spirits produced: computed from the "balance" at the rate of 4.4 gallons of alcohol, proof strength, per 100 pounds of corn meal. For this yield, which is equivalent to 17½ pints of pure alcohol per 100 pounds of corn meal, see the *Scientific American Cyclopedia of Formulas,* (New York, 1911), p. 934.

Corn, Rye and Other Grains. In the foregoing paragraph regarding the use of corn meal in making beverage alcohol no allowance has been made for corn purchased at small mills not reporting to the Census of Manufactures, or ground by the distillers. To a certain extent, of course, the quantity produced in this way is offset by a similar unrecorded production in pre-prohibition days. It is quite impossible to estimate how much more of this rurally produced and unrecorded "corn liquor" is produced now than in pre-war times. It is also impossible to estimate how much rye and other grains are used in producing beverage spirits under prohibition. So-called " rye " whisky may be made from other materials than rye and artifically flavored.[24]

Cane and Beet Sugar. While ordinary sugar is not as convenient to use in the production of alcohol as corn sugar, the fact that cane and beet sugar can be obtained more readily than corn sugar or corn meal makes it probable that it is used rather extensively in the production of beverage alcohol. To obtain an estimate of the quantity so used, however, is difficult, because of the extensive use of sugar for other purposes.

The consumption of sugar has been growing steadily for many years, and also varies with the price of sugar and with the general price level. The best estimate of the normal consumption of sugar since 1920, aside from the effect of prohibition, is the following equation, derived by multiple correlation from data for the period from 1890 to 1916:

$$Y = 14.512\,X_1 - .198\,X_2 + 1.057\,X_3 - 13.092\,X_4 - 691.520$$

where Y is the annual consumption of sugar in 10,000 tons;

X_1 is the population of the United States in millions;

X_2 is the average annual wholesale price of sugar in cents per 100 pounds;

X_3 is the Bureau of Labor wholesale price index (1913 base); and

X_4 is the number of years since 1889.

The coefficient of multiple determination, showing what per cent of the factors influencing the consumption of sugar are accounted for in this equation, is .998 after correction for the number of observations and variables, and the standard error of estimate 9.4 ten thousand tons.

In order to enable readers not familiar with the significance of the coefficient of multiple determination and

[24] In pre-prohibition years about one-fourth as much rye as corn was used in producing alcoholic spirits. (*Statistics Concerning Intoxicating Liquors, 1930, p. 63*).

the standard error of estimate to note the degree of accuracy of this equation, there are given in the following table the data on which the equation is based, and a comparison of the estimate of consumption obtained from the equation with the original estimate furnished by trade sources.

TABLE 19

FACTORS INFLUENCING THE CONSUMPTION OF SUGAR IN THE UNITED STATES, 1890-1916

Year	Population in millions	Average wholesale price of sugar (cents per 100 pounds)	Index of wholesale prices	Number of years since 1889	Consumption of sugar (10,000 tons) Estimated from equation	Estimate from trade sources	Error of estimate from equation (10,000 tons)
	X_1	X_2	X_3	X_4		Y	
1890	62.9	617	81	1	172	165	7
1891	63.8	464	80	2	201	212	—11
1892	65.1	435	75	3	207	208	— 1
1893	66.3	484	77	4	204	214	—10
1894	67.6	412	69	5	215	225	—10
1895	68.9	415	70	6	222	218	4
1896	70.3	453	67	7	218	220	— 2
1897	71.6	450	67	8	225	232	— 7
1898	72.9	497	70	9	224	224	0
1899	74.3	492	75	10	238	233	5
1900	76.1	532	81	11	249	249	0
1901	77.7	505	79	12	263	266	— 3
1902	79.4	446	84	13	291	287	4
1903	81.0	464	86	14	300	286	14
1904	82.6	477	86	15	307	310	— 3
1905	84.2	526	86	16	308	295	13
1906	85.8	452	89	17	336	321	15
1907	87.4	465	94	18	348	335	13
1908	89.1	496	90	19	350	357	— 7
1909	90.7	477	97	20	371	365	6
1910	92.3	497	101	21	381	375	6
1911	93.7	535	93	22	373	375	— 2
1912	95.1	504	99	23	392	393	— 1
1913	96.5	428	100	24	416	419	— 3
1914	97.9	468	98	25	413	421	— 8
1915	99.3	556	100	26	405	426	—21
1916	100.8	686	123	27	412	410	2

SOURCES OF DATA:

Population of the United States, *Statistical Abstract of the United States*, 1931, p. 3.

Average wholesale price of sugar: United States Beet Sugar Association.

Index of wholesale prices: *Bulletin of the Bureau of Labor Statistics*, No. 440, p. 9.

Consumption of sugar, estimate from equation: computed by applying the equation $Y = 15.412\,X_1 - .198\,X_2 + 1.057\,X_3 - 13.092\,X_4 - 691.520$ to the preceeding columns.

Consumption of sugar, estimate from trade sources: furnished by the United States Beet Sugar Association.

In the next table, which carries the data and estimates of the preceding table from 1917 to 1930, the last column, "Error of estimate from equation," includes both the errors of estimate of the same sort as those in the preceding table and changes in consumption resulting from additional factors not operating during the period from 1890 to 1916. From 1917 to 1919 war-time restrictions were the additional factors. Since 1920 prohibition has undoubtedly been the chief new influence on the consumption of sugar.

The consumption of sugar since 1922 in excess of the quantity estimated from the equation of relationship established above may reasonably be considered the result of prohibition. It may, at first, be supposed that this excess is due to the increased use of sugar in the form of confectionery, ice cream and soft drinks, all stimulated by reduced consumption of alcoholic beverages. Statistical examination, however, indicates that this explanation is incorrect. The value of confectionery produced in the United States per capita, when adjusted for changes in the general price level, increased from 1899 to 1919 at the rate of five cents per year, dropped seven cents between 1919 and 1921, and has increased since 1921 at approxi-

TABLE 20

FACTORS INFLUENCING THE CONSUMPTION OF SUGAR IN THE UNITED STATES, 1917 – 1930

Year	Population in millions	Average wholesale price of sugar (cents per 100 pounds)	Index of wholesale prices	Number of years since 1889	Consumption of sugar (10,000 tons) Estimated from equation	Estimate from trade sources	Error of estimate from equation (10,000 tons)
	X_1	X_2	X_3	X_4		Y	
1917	102.2	766	168	28	451	413	38
1918	103.6	783	188	29	476	392	84
1919	105.0	900	199	30	471	456	15
1920	106.5	1139	221	31	458	457	1
1921	108.2	621	140	32	485	460	25
1922	109.9	590	139	33	501	570	—69
1923	111.5	844	144	34	467	535	—68
1924	113.2	747	141	35	494	544	—50
1925	114.8	548	148	36	551	617	—66
1926	116.5	547	143	37	558	635	—77
1927	118.1	583	137	38	554	593	—39
1928	119.8	554	140	39	575	621	—46
1929	121.5	503	138	40	594	651	—57
1930	123.1	441	124	41	602	626	—24

SOURCES OF DATA:

Same as Table 19, except index of wholesale prices, *Bulletin of the Bureau of Labor Statistics*, No. 493, p. 9, and issues of the *Monthly Labor Review*.

mately the pre-prohibition rate.[25] Between 1910 and 1916 the consumption of ice cream increased at the rate of .18 gallons per capita per year, while since 1919 the rate of increase has been only .08 gallons per capita per year.[26] Since 1919 the consumption of carbonated beverages has increased at a rate slightly greater than that

[25] *Cf.* Table 93, *infra*, p. 191. The value of confectionery, even when adjusted for changes in the general price level, is not an accurate measure of the quantity of confectionery consumed. It is, however, the best measure available, since no quantity figures are available except for very recent years.

[26] *Cf.* Table 93, *infra*, p. 191.

prior to prohibition. The sugar consumed in bottled carbonated beverages has increased in recent years at a rate of one-fourth of a pound per capita per year, whereas the consumption of sugar unaccounted for by forces operating in pre-prohibition days varied from 9 to 13 pounds per year per capita between 1922 and 1926, and between 4 and 9 pounds per capita per year between 1927 and 1930. The sugar consumed in other soft drinks cannot be estimated, but is doubtless less than that in carbonated beverages.[27]

Since confectionery, ice cream and soft drinks do not account in any appreciable degree for the abnormally large consumption of sugar since 1921, it is reasonable to assume that that consumption is due to the use of sugar in the production of alcoholic beverages, and that the figures given in the last column of Table 20 are the approximate quantities so used.

But before using these figures as an estimate of the sugar used in the production of alcoholic beverages, we should make what allowance we can for the ordinary errors of estimate. For this, we may assume that no such error is greater than three times the standard error, or 28 ten thousand tons.[28] If we adjust the maximum positive and the maximum negative deviations in the last column of Table 20 by this amount, and the other deviations in proportion to their difference from the mid-

[27] For the consumption of carbonated beverages see Table 92, *infra*, p. 186. The sugar content is estimated to be about .85 of an ounce per half-pint bottle (letter from the American Bottlers of Carbonated Beverages).

[28] "In most statistical work, three times the standard error is taken as the greatest extent to which a given result is likely to be wrong." (Mordecai Ezekiel, *Methods of Correlation Analysis*, New York, 1930, p. 23). In the present case, there is about one chance in 170 of an error greater than this.

point between the maximum positive and the maximum negative deviations, we will be reasonably certain of avoiding an overestimate of the excess of sugar consumption above normal, and at the same time will have "smoothed" the annual variations in the estimate of excess consumption of sugar on account of prohibition.

In the following table this adjusted estimate of the excess of sugar consumed above normal, which is the most reasonable estimate we can make of the quantity of cane and beet sugar used in the production of beverage alcohol, is given, and also the estimated quantity of beverage spirits produced therefrom.[29]

TABLE 21

ESTIMATE OF BEVERAGE SPIRITS PRODUCED FROM CANE AND BEET SUGAR

	Deviation of sugar consumption from the computed normal (10,000 tons)	Adjusted deviation of sugar consumption from the computed normal (10,000 tons)	Estimated production of beverage spirits (millions of proof gallons)
1921	—25	3	7
1922	69	45	108
1923	68	45	108
1924	50	37	89
1925	66	44	106
1926	77	49	118
1927	39	32	77
1928	46	35	84
1929	57	40	96
1930	24	25	60

[29] A part of the sugar estimated to have been used in the production of beverage spirits may have been used in the production of home-made beer, since sugar is often added to malt syrup when beer is made at home. In so far as this is the case, the estimate of beverage spirits produced given in Table 21 is too high. The estimate of pure alcohol consumed given in Table 30, *infra*, p. 72, is not, however, too high; for when sugar is added to malt syrup in making beer, the alcoholic content is likely to be higher than 4 per cent.

SOURCES OF DATA:

Deviation of sugar consumption from the computed normal: from last column, "Error of estimate from equation," Table 20, *supra*, p. 60.

Adjusted deviation of sugar consumption from the computed normal: the extreme cases, 1921 and 1926, modified by three times the standard error of estimate, or 28 ten thousand tons; other years modified in proportion to their difference from the mid-point, 26.

Estimated production of beverage spirits: computed from the adjusted deviation of sugar consumption at the rate of 12 gallons per 100 pounds, or 2.4 million gallons per 10,000 tons of sugar. This is on the basis of 80 per cent conversion of sugar into alcohol, the theoretical maximum being about 15 gallons, proof strength. The larger stills probably obtain 85 per cent conversion, but doubtless much of the cane and beet sugar is used in small stills which are less efficient.

Molasses. Molasses, especially black-strap, is the most important material used in the production of industrial alcohol. It is likely, therefore, that it is used by makers of beverage alcohol. In the following table there are presented the available figures regarding the production and importation of molasses.

TABLE 22

THE PRODUCTION AND IMPORTATION OF MOLASSES
(millions of gallons)

Year	Beet sugar industry (a)	Cane sugar industry other than blackstrap	Cane sugar industry blackstrap	Cane sugar refining (a)	Total production	Net imports	Available for consumption
1914	26.5	20.7	(b)	35.4	82.9	50.4	133.3
1919	18.8	20.1	(b)	44.1	83.0	113.5	196.5
1921	26.9	9.7	12.2	31.8	80.6	72.5	153.1
1923	18.0	6.1	9.6	41.1	74.8	181.0	255.8
1925	24.5(c)	5.5	9.7	45.9	85.5	253.8	339.3
1927	13.1(c)	3.3	2.3	36.6	55.2	238.8	294.0
1929	13.0(c)	7.5	9.6	36.5	66.6	303.6	370.2

(a) Includes refiner's syrup, blackstrap and non-edible syrup.

(b) Not reported separately from other molasses.

(c) Converted from tons to gallons at the rate of 171 gallons per ton, this being the ratio in 1921, for which figures are available in both tons and gallons.

SOURCES OF DATA:

Census of Manufactures; Statistical Abstract of the United States, 1930.

The greater part of this molasses is used in the production of industrial alcohol. Other uses are probably diminishing, or, at least, not increasing. In the following computation of the quantity available for the production of beverage alcohol, it is assumed that since 1921 the normal consumption of molasses for miscellaneous purposes has remained at .52 gallons per capita per year, the average for the three years 1914, 1919 and 1921. It is believed that, while there are doubtless fluctuations from year to year, this figure is approximately correct for most years.

TABLE 23

USE OF MOLASSES IN THE UNITED STATES

Year	Available for consumption (millions of gallons)	Used for industrial alcohol (millions of gallons)	Balance (millions of gallons)	Balance (gallons per capita)	Available for beverage alcohol (millions of gallons)	Estimate of alcohol produced (millions of gallons)
1914	133.3	94.0	39.3	.41	...	..
1919	196.5	118.3	78.2	.74	...	..
1921	153.1	108.1	45.0	.41	...	..
1923	255.8	151.9	103.9	.93	45.7	34
1925	339.3	235.3	104.0	.91	44.8	34
1927	294.0	212.6	81.4	.69	20.1	15
1929	370.2	251.9	118.3	.97	54.7	41

SOURCES OF DATA:

Available for consumption: Table 22, *supra*, p. 63.

Used for industrial alcohol: *Statistics Concerning Intoxicating Liquors*, December, 1930, p. 63. For 1914 and 1919 the molasses used for beverage alcohol is included. Figures converted from fiscal to calendar years by averaging successive fiscal years.

Available for beverage alcohol: computed from the preceding column by allowing .52 gallons per capita, the average for 1914, 1919 and 1921, for miscellaneous purposes.

Beverage alcohol produced: computed from the quantity of molasses available for beverage alcohol at the rate of .75 gallons alcohol, proof strength, per gallon of molasses. This is on the basis of an average of 6.24 pounds of fermentable sugar per gallon and 80 per cent conversion. This rate may also be computed by deducting from the legitimate production of alcohol, as reported in *Statistics Concerning Alcoholic Liquors*, the quantities probably produced from other materials, for any recent year, and computing the ratio between the balance and the quantity of molasses used.

Malt Syrup. It has been stated that in some parts of the country malt syrup is used with corn sugar in making whisky.[30] If this is generally true, the carbohydrates contained in that syrup may contribute a substantial quantity of alcohol to the nation's consumption. However, no figures on the extent of this practice are available, nor even on the quantity of malt syrup used for all purposes. The alcohol obtained from this source is, accordingly, omitted from our computations.

Fruits and Vegetables. Alcoholic spirits can also be produced from any starchy vegetable or sugary fruit. In northern Europe potato whisky is a well-known beverage. It is not likely, however, that potatoes and other vegetables are used to a great extent in the United States for the production of beverage alcohol. This cannot be said of fruits, for there are frequent reports that considerable quantities of apple cider are converted into "applejack."[31] But statistical evidence regarding "applejack" is entirely lacking, so that this source of beverage spirits is also omitted from our computations.

[30] Hugh F. Fox, "The Present Consumption of Alcohol in the United States," *The Periscope,* April, 1927.

[31] Only one such report will be quoted here. "Concealed in a labyrinth of tunnels running under a garage and a dog kennel, a huge applejack plant, with equipment and liquor valued at $200,000 was discovered yesterday in Norwood, Bergen County, by ten agents from Federal prohibition headquarters in Newark. . . . Three 5,000-gallon continuous process stills and 12,500 gallons of applejack in barrels and tanks were reported found" (*The New York Times*, Feb. 1, 1931, p. 22).

The Total Production of Beverage Spirits. If we bring together the estimates in the foregoing paragraphs, we have the following table showing the estimated total production of beverage spirits in the United States.

TABLE 24

ESTIMATE OF BEVERAGE SPIRIT PRODUCTION IN THE UNITED STATES

(millions of proof gallons)

Year	From industrial alcohol	From corn sugar	From corn meal	From cane and beet sugar	From molasses	Total
1921	13	..	13	7	..	33
1922	16	6	22 (a)	108	17 (a)	169
1923	20	26	31	108	34	219
1924	23	33	19 (a)	89	34 (a)	198
1925	30	29	7	106	34	206
1926	26	45	8 (a)	118	24 (a)	221
1927	15	64	9	77	15	180
1928	17	69	10 (a)	84	29 (a)	209
1929	16	60	12	96	41	225
1930	9	57	10 (a)	80	30 (a)	166

(a) Interpolated.

SOURCES OF DATA:

From industrial alcohol: Table 15, *supra*, p. 49.
From corn sugar: Table 16, *supra*, p. 53.
From corn meal: Table 18, *supra*, p. 56.
From cane and beet sugar: Table 21, *supra*, p. 62.
From molasses: Table 23, *supra*, p. 64.

The relative importance of the various materials used for beverage alcohol, as indicated in the above table, may be compared with the relative importance of the same materials, as indicated by the reports of the Bureau of Prohibition regarding materials seized by prohibition agents.[32] The seizures by Federal agents are an actual

[32] Unfortunately these reports are available for only the first four months of 1930. The Bureau of Prohibition states that they were not compiled prior to January 1930, and refuses to disclose them since April of that year.

sample of the materials used throughout the country. They are not a perfect sample, however, since more seizures are made in some sections of the country than in other sections, and the materials used are not the same in all sections of the country. Federal agents probably seize a larger part of the corn sugar used at distilleries than of corn meal or ordinary sugar, since the corn sugar is principally used in the larger urban stills, and corn meal and ordinary sugar in smaller stills.

TABLE 25

RELATIVE IMPORTANCE OF MATERIALS USED IN PRODUCING BEVERAGE SPIRITS

Material	Seizures by Federal agents four months of 1930 (1000 proof gallons)	Percentage seizures by Federal agents	Percentage computed from Table 24 for the years 1929 and 1930: 1929	1930
Corn sugar	1,057	51.7	26.7	34.3
Cane and beet sugar	703	34.5	42.7	36.2
Alcohol and alcoholic preparations	151	7.4	7.1	5.4
Molasses	99	4.9	18.2	18.1
Corn meal and grain	30	1.5	5.3	6.0
	2,040	100.0	100.0	100.0

SOURCES OF DATA:

Seizures by Federal agents: "Stills and Distilling Material Seized by Prohibition Administrators and Special Agents," January to April, 1930, furnished by the Bureau of Prohibition.

Percentage seizures by Federal agents: computed from the previous column.

Percentage computed from Table 24: computed from the last two lines in that table, *supra*, p. 66.

Smuggled Spirits. For the fiscal year ending June 30, 1930, the Bureau of Prohibition estimated the total quantity of spirits smuggled into the United States at 3.6 million gallons, which compares with 1.4 million gallons exported from Canada to the United States.[33] This estimate is the most accurate that has been made regarding smuggled spirits, and it will not be unreasonable to assume that the total quantity of spirits smuggled into the United States each year since prohibition is approximately two and a half times the quantity shipped from Canada. This is the assumption in Table 26.

TABLE 26

ESTIMATE OF SPIRITS SMUGGLED INTO THE UNITED STATES

Year	From Canada (millions of U. S. gallons)	From all countries (millions of gallons)
1921	Less than .1	1/4
1922	.1	1/4
1923	.3	3/4
1924	.4	1
1925	.8	2
1926	1.4	3½
1927	1.6	4
1928	1.7	4
1929	1.5	4
1930	1.4	3½

SOURCES OF DATA:

From Canada: External Trade Branch, Dominion Bureau of Statistics. Figures are for fiscal years ending March 31, and have been multiplied by 1.2 to convert from Imperial gallons to United States gallons. No correction has been made for the difference between British proof and United States proof, since this would make no appreciable difference in the total estimate of smuggled spirits.

From all countries: computed at 2½ times the quantity shipped from Canada.

Medicinal Alcohol. As a final source of spirits consumed in the United States, there is medicinal alcohol. In

[33] *Possible Production of Illegal Liquor in the United States for the fiscal year ending June 30, 1930*, p. 48. In this report the Canadian figure is given as 1.1 gallons. The figure of 1.4 gallons given above is for the Canadian fiscal year ending March 31, 1930, converted from Imperial to United States gallons.

the following table there are given the quantities of alcohol and alcoholic liquors (whisky, brandy, gin and rum) received by physicians and reported as sold on physicians' prescriptions. In estimating the total equivalent in proof spirits it is assumed that the alcohol is 190 proof, and the alcoholic liquors 40 per cent by volume.

TABLE 27

MEDICINAL ALCOHOL USED IN THE UNITED STATES

Year ending June 30	Received by physicians and hospitals (1000 gallons)		Sold on physicians' prescriptions (1000 gallons)		Total (millions of proof gallons)
	Alcohol	Alcoholic liquors	Alcohol	Alcoholic liquors	
1922	Not reported		6	999	1.0
1923	67	63	2	1,399	1.3
1924	106	78	3	1,595	1.5
1925	122	95	2	1,659	1.6
1926	144	97	2	1,588	1.6
1927	175	99	1	1,444	1.6
1928	190	95	1	1,421	1.6
1929	208	95	1	1,400	1.6
1930	223	98	1	1,306	1.7
1931	317	119	1	1,157	1.6

SOURCES OF DATA:

Received by physicians and hospitals, and sold on physicians' prescriptions: *Statistics Concerning Intoxicating Liquors,* December, 1931, pp. 9-13.

Total: computed from the preceding columns on the basis of 190 proof for alcohol and 40 per cent alcoholic content for the liquors.

The Consumption of Alcoholic Spirits. By adding together the estimates of beverage spirits produced in the United States, spirits smuggled into the country and those legally sold for medicinal purposes, and deducting the alcohol equivalent of spirits and materials seized by Federal prohibition agents, an estimate is obtained of the total consumption of alcoholic spirits in the United States each year since 1921. No allowance is made in this estimate for seizures by local and State officials, nor, on the other hand, for spirits made from vegetables, fruits or directly from grains.

TABLE 28

ESTIMATE OF ALCOHOLIC SPIRITS CONSUMED IN THE UNITED STATES, 1921 TO 1930

(millions of proof gallons)

Year	Beverage spirits produced in the United States	Spirits smuggled into the United States	Medicinal spirits	Total	Spirits seized by prohibition agents	Estimate of spirits consumed
1921	33	..	1	34	1	33
1922	169	..	1	170	1	169
1923	219	1	1	221	2	219
1924	198	1	2	201	3	198
1925	206	2	2	210	3	207
1926	221	3	2	226	3	223
1927	180	4	2	186	5	181
1928	209	4	2	215	5	210
1929	225	4	2	231	5	226
1930	166	3	2	171	7	164

SOURCES OF DATA:

Beverage spirits produced in the United States: Table 24, *supra*, p. 66.

Spirits smuggled into the United States: Table 26, *supra*, p. 68, averaged for calendar years, and fractional parts of a million gallons omitted.

Medicinal spirits: Table 27, *supra*, p. 69.

Spirits seized by prohibition agents: *Statistics Concerning Intoxicating Liquors*, December, 1930, pp. 72-73. Seizures of wine, cider, mash and pomace, which are doubtless mostly mash, have been converted to spirits at the rate of 1 gallon of proof spirits for each 6.3 gallons of mash. This ratio is obtained from statistics presented in "Stills and Distilling Material Seized by Prohibition Administrators and Special Agents," January to April, 1930.

This completes the estimates of alcoholic beverages consumed since the adoption of prohibition as estimated from the sources of production. In Table 29 these estimates are summarized for spirits, wine and beer. The estimates for spirits are in terms of gallons of 50 per cent alcohol, by volume. Since spirits are usually sold, or, at least, drunk, in weaker solutions than this, the consumption in ordinary gallons is considerably larger than the figures in the table.

TABLE 29

THE CONSUMPTION OF ALCOHOLIC BEVERAGES IN THE UNITED STATES, 1921 TO 1930

Estimates Obtained From Sources of Production

	Millions of gallons			Gallons per capita		
Year	Spirits	Wine	Beer	Spirits	Wine	Beer
1921	33	48	136	.30	.44	1.26
1922	169	63	188	1.54	.57	1.71
1923	219	106	250	1.96	.95	2.24
1924	198	102	321	1.75	.90	2.84
1925	207	99	398	1.80	.86	3.46
1926	223	122	490	1.91	1.05	4.21
1927	181	128	595	1.53	1.08	5.03
1928	210	128	726	1.75	1.07	6.05
1929	226	108	864	1.86	.89	7.11
1930	164	107	850	1.33	.87	6.90

SOURCES OF DATA:
Spirits: Table 28, *supra*, p. 70.
Wine: Table 10, *supra*, p. 40.
Beer: Table 6, *supra*, p. 33.

The estimated consumption of pure alcohol in these beverages is given in Table 30.

TABLE 30

THE CONSUMPTION OF PURE ALCOHOL IN THE UNITED STATES, 1921 to 1930

Estimates Obtained From Sources of Production

Year	In spirits (millions of gallons)	In wine (millions of gallons)	In beer (millions of gallons)	Total (millions of gallons)	Total (gallons per capita)
1921	17	5	5	27	.26
1922	85	6	8	99	.90
1923	110	11	10	131	1.17
1924	99	10	13	122	1.08
1925	104	10	16	130	1.13
1926	112	12	20	144	1.24
1927	91	13	24	128	1.08
1928	105	13	29	147	1.23
1929	113	11	35	159	1.31
1930	82	11	34	127	1.03

SOURCES OF DATA: computed from Table 29, *supra*, p. 71, assuming wine to have an average alcoholic content of 10 per cent and beer of 4 per cent. The estimate of pure alcohol contained in spirits may be too high, and that contained in beer too low, on account of the use of sugar in making home-brew. *Cf.* footnote 29, *supra*, p. 62.

CHAPTER III

THE CONSUMPTION OF ALCOHOLIC BEVERAGES UNDER PROHIBITION: ESTIMATE FROM DEATH RATES

THE second method of estimating the consumption of alcohol at the present time is from its effects upon the death rate. Deaths from alcoholism and from cirrhosis of the liver are only a small part of the total deaths each year, and the use of alcohol is only a contributing cause of cirrhosis of the liver.[1] There is, however, so much association between death rates from these two causes and the consumption of alcohol per capita that it is possible to use these death rates to estimate within reasonable limits the consumption of alcohol.

[1] "With regard to the question whether or not alcohol is the cause of cirrhosis, clinical and experimental evidence are opposed. In practice there are few points more certain than that the abuse of alcoholic drinks is a frequent precursor of hepatic cirrhosis, while from experiments on animals the bulk of the evidence is in a contrary direction . . . Since alcohol alone is not sufficient to account for cirrhosis either in man or animals, the undoubted association between alcoholism and cirrhosis must be explained in some other way . . . *Per se* alcohol has no specific action of the liver except fatty degeneration. It gives rise to cirrhosis in a secondary manner, either by leading to the production of sclerogenic poisons or by enabling such poisons to have full sway on the liver." (Sir Humphrey Rolleston and John Wm. McNee, *Diseases of the Liver, Gall-bladder and Bileducts,* third edition, pp. 209-14.)

"Dr. A. M. Snell, of the Mayo clinic, Rochester, Minn., told the physicians that the common belief that the use of alcohol was the cause of cirrhosis, or the hardening of the liver, was erroneous. 'For years,' said Dr. Snell, 'it has been assumed by doctors and laymen that cirrhosis, or hardening of the liver, is due to alcoholism. However, we know now that cirrhosis occurs in only 4 per cent of alcoholic individuals.'" *(The New York Times,* March 26, 1931, p. 1).

Few countries have sufficiently accurate records of the annual per capita consumption of alcohol and the annual death rates from alcoholism and cirrhosis of the liver to make possible statistical studies of the relationship between them. Not many have death rates reliably recorded. In wine-consuming countries estimates of the per capita consumption of wine are based on estimates of production, which vary widely from year to year in accord with fluctuations in grape production. Only in Denmark, Great Britain, and the United States are the records of both the consumption of alcohol and the mortality of diseases related to the use of alcohol sufficiently reliable for comparison over a considerable length of time.

ALCOHOL CONSUMPTION AND THE DEATH RATE IN THE UNITED KINGDOM

In the United Kingdom of Great Britain and Ireland, where all the wine used is imported and where tax records provide accurate reports on the use of beer and spirits, there are reliable records, both of the consumption of alcoholic beverages and of deaths from alcoholism and from cirrhosis of the liver, back to 1891. In 1910 a new classification of deaths was adopted, but statistics were compiled according to the old classification up to 1920. There are thus consistent and continuous series of figures for the thirty-year period from 1891 to 1920, and also for the period since 1910.

When statistical methods are applied to these series, the coefficients of correlation given in Table 31 are derived.

The general type of equation of relationship in all these cases is $\log y = ax + b$, where y is the death rate from alcoholism, cirrhosis of the liver, or both causes, and x is the consumption per capita of spirits, beer or alcohol.

TABLE 31

ALCOHOLIC DEATHS AS RELATED TO ALCOHOL CONSUMPTION IN THE UNITED KINGDOM OF GREAT BRITAIN AND IRELAND

Correlation between		Correlation coefficient	
Consumption of	Death rate from	1890-1920	1911-1927
Spirits	alcoholism, no lag		.974
"	" 1 year lag		.927
"	cirrhosis, no lag		.919
"	" 1 year lag		.931
"	both causes, no lag	.926	.938
"	" " 1 year lag	.925	.936
Beer	alcoholism, no lag		.850
"	" 1 year lag		.872
"	cirrhosis, no lag		.769
"	" 1 year lag		.912
"	both causes, no lag	.932	.792
"	" " 1 year lag	.984	.916
Alcohol	alcoholism, no lag		.911
"	" 1 year lag		.916
"	cirrhosis, no lag		.832
"	" 1 year lag		.849
"	both causes, no lag	.943	.845
"	" " 1 year lag	.983	.949

SOURCES OF DATA:

Statistics of consumption: *The Alliance Year Book,* 1931, pp. 320-321.

Statistics of deaths: George B. Wilson, "A Statistical Review of the Variations during the Last Twenty Years in the Consumption of Intoxicating Drinks in the United Kingdom, and in Convictions for Offenses Connected with Intoxication, with a Discussion of the Causes to which these Variations may be Ascribed," *Journal of the Royal Statistical Society,* January, 1912, pp. 183-247; and annual reports of the Registrars-General for England and Wales, Scotland and Ireland.

Correlation coefficients: computed by the usual method for linear correlation, using the logarithms of the death rates.

In Great Britain during these years there was a tendency for the consumption of beer and that of spirits to increase or decrease together, and on that account the most significant of the correlations is that between the total consumption of alcohol and the combined death rates from alcoholism and cirrhosis of the liver. The relationship between these variates is closer if the death rate is lagged a year than if they are taken for the same period, due, presumably, to the delayed effect of alcohol upon the death rate from cirrhosis of the liver. In this case the equations of relationship are

$$\log y = .27x + 1.34 \text{ (for 1890-1920), and}$$
$$\log y = .28x + 1.23 \text{ (for 1911-1927),}$$

where y is the death rate from alcoholism and cirrhosis of the liver per million population, and x is the per capita consumption of alcohol expressed in gallons of proof spirits per capita.

These coefficients of correlation in Table 31 appear to be very high, but since they are largely due to similarity of the trends of alcohol consumption and of death rates from alcoholism and cirrhosis, their significance needs to be tested by correlating deviations from those trends. In the case of the relation between total alcohol consumption and the death rate from the two diseases for the period from 1890 to 1920, with deaths lagged one year, the coefficient of correlation between deviations from parabolic trends is .960, indicating that deviations of death rates from the trend of alcohol consumption account for 92 per cent of the deviations from the trend of deaths from alcoholism and cirrhosis.

It is highly probable, of course, that the trends, as well as the deviations from the trends, are causally related. At any rate, in estimating the consumption of alcohol from the death rates, the trends have to be taken into account and the most convenient way of doing this is to make use of the direct relationships between the two variates, without the elimination of trends.

To estimate the consumption of alcohol from death rates in the case of the United Kingdom, the equations are

$$x = 3.568 \log y - 4.56 \text{ (for 1890-1920), and}$$
$$x = 3.245 \log y - 3.79 \text{ (for 1910-1927),}$$

where x is the per capita consumption of alcohol expressed in gallons of proof spirits per capita, and y is the death rate from alcoholism and cirrhosis of the liver per million population. In Table 32 a comparison is made between the estimates of alcohol consumption obtained from these equations and the original estimates of consumption based on imports and taxes on alcoholic beverages.

The deviations given in the last column of Table 32 are the errors involved in estimating the consumption of alcohol from the combined death rate from alcoholism and cirrhosis of the liver. The standard error of the estimates for 1890-1920 is .13, and for 1911-1927 it is .19.[2] That is, there is one chance in three that an error in the computed estimate of consumption will be larger than this. In view of the fact that the causes of death are not always accurately reported, the fact that cirrhosis of the liver does not invariably occur with the use of alcohol, and the fact that it may occur without the use of alcohol, the smallness of these errors is remarkable.[3] The largest errors

[2] The standard error of estimate used here and in later pages is the corrected standard error: that is, adjusted for the number of observations, so that it is the standard error of estimate which is most probably true for the universe from which the statistics used are samples. (Cf. Mordecai Ezekiel, *Methods of Correlation Analysis,* pp. 121-124).

[3] Since the computations in Table 32 were made, the figures of deaths from alcoholism and cirrhosis of the liver in Great Britain have been published for 1928 and 1929: 50 per million population in 1928 and 48 per million in 1929. Applying the equation given above, the estimate of alcohol consumption is 1.73 gallons in 1927 and 1.66 gallons in 1928. The estimates given in the *Alliance Year Book* for 1931 are 1.71 for 1927 and 1.65 for 1928. The errors of estimate for these two years are thus .02 and .01, respectively. The equation is thus as valid for the years since 1927 as for the years to which the curve was fitted.

TABLE 32

CONSUMPTION OF ALCOHOL AND THE ALCOHOLIC DEATH RATE IN GREAT BRITAIN AND IRELAND

Year	Consumption of alcohol	Death rate from alcoholism and cirrhosis a	Death rate from alcoholism and cirrhosis b	Consumption computed from the death rate a	Consumption computed from the death rate b	Deviations from original estimate of consumption a	Deviations from original estimate of consumption b
1890	3.52	171		3.43		—.09	
1891	3.55	173		3.38		—.17	
1892	3.51	168		3.43		—.08	
1893	3.44	173		3.29		—.15	
1894	3.42	158		3.35		—.07	
1895	3.46	165		3.42		—.04	
1896	3.58	172		3.54		—.04	
1897	3.63	185		3.53		—.10	
1898	3.68	185		3.68		.00	
1899	3.79	204		3.83		.04	
1900	3.74	224		3.67		—.07	
1901	3.64	203		3.56		—.08	
1902	3.56	189		3.45		—.11	
1903	3.45	176		3.41		—.04	
1904	3.32	171		3.39		.07	
1905	3.19	169		3.35		.16	
1906	3.21	165		3.32		.11	
1907	3.18	162		3.17		—.01	
1908	3.05	147		3.05		.00	
1909	2.82	136		2.87		.05	
1910	2.79	121		2.93	2.86	.14	.07
1911	2.89	126	113	2.97	2.86	.08	—.03
1912	2.86	129	113	3.08	2.96	.22	.10
1913	2.95	138	120	3.12	2.76	.17	—.19
1914	2.86	142	104	2.97	2.89	.11	.03
1915	2.61	129	114	2.62	2.60	.01	—.01
1916	2.29	103	94	2.15	2.21	—.14	—.08
1917	1.44	76	71	1.27	1.76	—.17	.32
1918	1.17	43	51	1.47	1.60	.30	.43
1919	1.90	49	46	1.70	1.79	—.20	—.11
1920	2.17	57	53		1.83		—.34
1921	1.91		54		1.79		—.12
1922	1.66		53		1.69		.03
1923	1.74		49		1.63		—.11
1924	1.82		47		1.73		—.09
1925	1.81		50		1.73		—.08
1926	1.73		50		1.66		—.07
1927	1.71		48				

SOURCES OF DATA:

Consumption of alcohol: 1890-1910, George B. Wilson, *op. cit.*, *Journal of the Royal Statistical Society*, January, 1912, p. 244; 1911-1927, *The Alliance Year Book*, 1930, p. 321, with beer and wine converted to the equivalent spirits of proof strength. For 1915-1918 population estimates are taken from the Brewers' Almanac, official estimates by the Registrars-General not being available. All figures for alcohol consumption expressed in gallons of proof strength (British proof) per capita.

Death rates from alcoholism and cirrhosis of the liver: 1890-1909, George B. Wilson, *op. cit.*, *Journal of the Royal Statistical Society*, January, 1912, p. 213; 1910-1920-a, computed from population estimates and from reports of the Registrars-General of England and Wales, Scotland and Ireland; 1911-1927-b, computed from population estimates and from reports of the Registrars-General of England and Wales, Scotland and Ireland. Rates are per million population.

For both consumption of alcohol and death rates the figures since 1923 exclude the Irish Free State. Figures in column "a" are based on the old classification of deaths; those in column "b" on the new classification adopted in 1910.

Consumption computed from the death rate: computed from the equations, $x = 3.568 \log y - 4.56$ for the 1890-1920 period, and $x = 3.245 \log y - 3.79$ for the 1910-1927 period.

are for the war years and the period of demobilization, for which the estimates of population are not very reliable.

It might be supposed that the death rate from cirrohsis of the liver, and perhaps alcoholism also, is affected by the causes underlying the general death rate; and therefore that the decline in the combined death rate from these two diseases since 1890 is to be attributed to the decline in the general death rate rather than to the decline in the consumption of alcoholic liquors. This hypothesis has been tested by using the method of multiple correlation; the combined death rate from the two diseases being correlated with both the consumption of alcohol per capita and the general death rate. The resulting Beta coefficients and coefficients of part determination are given in Table 33.[4]

[4] In this correlation the logarithm of the combined death rate from

TABLE 33

COEFFICIENTS OF RELATIONSHIP IN RESPECT TO THE DEATH RATE FROM ALCOHOLISM AND CIRRHOSIS OF THE LIVER

The death rate from alcoholism and cirrhosis of the liver related to	1890-1920 Beta coefficients	1890-1920 Coefficients of part determination	1910-1927 Beta coefficients	1910-1927 Coefficients of part determination
The consumption of alcohol per capita .	1.025	.772	.882	.967
The general death rate	— .250	.168	.242	.688

SOURCES OF DATA:

Death rate from alcoholism and cirrhosis of the liver: same as Table 32, *supra*, p. 79.

Consumption of alcohol per capita: same as Table 32, *supra*, p. 79.

The general death rate: *Statistical Abstract of the United Kingdom.*

Beta coefficients and coefficients of part determination: computed by means of the formulas given by Ezekiel, *op. cit.*, pp. 182-184.

These coefficients indicate that both for the period 1890-1920 and the period 1910-1927 variations in the death rate from alcoholism and cirrhosis of the liver are accounted for very largely by variations in the consumption of alcohol, and to a much smaller degree by variations in the general death rate. This conclusion is supported by the fact that the coefficient of multiple determination in respect to these two independent variables is only slightly greater than the coefficient of determination in respect to the consumption of alcohol alone: .968 compared with .964 for the period from 1890 to 1920, and .973 compared with

the two diseases was considered the dependent variable, and the consumption of alcohol per capita and the logarithm of the general death rate considered independent variables. That is, it was assumed that absolute changes in the consumption of alcohol are accompanied by percentage changes in the death rate from alcoholism and cirrhosis of the liver, but that percentage changes in the general death rate are accompanied by percentage changes in the death rate from alcoholism and cirrhosis of the liver. For the statistical significance of Beta coefficients and coefficients of part determination, see Ezekiel, *op. cit.*, pp. 181-185.

.886 for the period from 1910 to 1927.[5] That is, for the period from 1890 to 1920, 96.4 per cent. of the variations in the death rate from alcoholism and cirrhosis of the liver are accounted for by variations in the consumption of alcohol, but 96.8 per cent. of such deaths are accounted for when variations in the general death rate are also considered a cause; and for the period from 1910 to 1927, 88.6 per cent. of the variations in the death rate from alcoholism and cirrhosis of the liver are accounted for by variations in the consumption of alcohol, and 96.4 per cent accounted for both by variations in alcohol consumption and variations in the general death rate.

ALCOHOL CONSUMPTION AND THE DEATH RATE IN DENMARK

For Denmark annual figures of alcohol consumption and of deaths from alcoholism and from cirrhosis of the liver are available for the period since 1911.[6] The coefficient of correlation between alcohol consumption and deaths from these causes for the period from 1911 to 1927 is .967 with no lag, and .944 with a lag of one year in the death rate. It will be noted that the closer correlation in this case is with no lag in the death rate, while in Great Britain the closer correlation is with a lag of a year in the death rate. This is explained by the fact that in Denmark, for most of the years between 1911 and 1927, the death rate

[5] All these coefficients of determination have been adjusted for the number of observations.

[6] Annual figures can doubtless be obtained for a much longer period than this, since the sources consulted gave figures of five-year averages back to 1891 in the case of alcohol consumption and to 1876 in the case of deaths. While the reliability of the coefficient of correlation increases with the number of cases, the coefficient for the period since 1911 is so high and its standard error so small that additional cases would not appreciably increase the accuracy of the correlation coefficient or of estimates made from the regression equations.

from alcoholism is somewhat greater than that from cirrhosis of the liver, while in the United Kingdom the death rate from cirrhosis is much greater than that from alcoholism. The equations of relationship, with no lag in the death rate, are

$$\log y = .14x + 1.38, \text{ and } x = 6.66 \log y - 8.93$$

where y is the death rate from alcoholism and cirrhosis of the liver, and x is the per capita consumption of pure alcohol in liters.

The data for this analysis, together with the estimates of consumption of alcohol derived from the equation of relationship, are given in Table 34.

TABLE 34

CONSUMPTION OF ALCOHOL AND THE ALCOHOLIC DEATH RATE IN DENMARK

Year	Consumption of alcohol x	Death rate from alcoholism and cirrhosis of the liver y	Consumption computed from the death rates	Deviations from original estimate of consumption
1911	7.18	243	6.96	—.22
1912	6.50	211	6.55	.05
1913	6.12	165	5.84	—.28
1914	6.16	182	6.12	—.04
1915	6.23	166	5.86	—.37
1916	6.68	206	6.48	—.20
1917	3.35	113	4.74	1.39
1918	1.67	54	2.61	.94
1919	2.52	57	2.76	.24
1920	3.03	62	3.00	—.03
1921	2.66	51	2.45	—.21
1922	2.60	51	2.45	—.15
1923	2.81	51	2.45	—.36
1924	2.88	50	2.39	—.49
1925	2.86	54	2.61	—.25
1926	2.66	50	2.39	—.27
1927	2.46	50	2.39	—.07

SOURCES OF DATA:

Consumption of alcohol: Department of Statistics of Denmark. Figures in liters of pure alcohol per capita.

Death rate from alcoholism and cirrhosis: Department of Statistics of Denmark. Figures are per million inhabitants, and refer to the urban population of Denmark.

Consumption computed from the death rate: computed from the equation, $x = 6.66 \log y - 8.93$.

It may be noted that the only two years in which the estimate of consumption of alcohol derived from the death rate differs appreciably from the original estimate of consumption are the war years, 1917 and 1918. The reason for these deviations is doubtless the fact that during those years the consumption of alcohol was rapidly declining, with a lag in the decline in the death rate from alcoholism and cirrhosis of the liver.[7]

During this period the general death rate fell steadily and as in the case of the United Kingdom, it might be supposed that a part of the reduction in the death rate from alcoholism and cirrhosis of the liver is associated with that decline rather than with the reduction in alcohol consumption. When multiple correlation is applied to these variates, the coefficient of multiple determination is .970, only slightly greater than the coefficient of determination with respect to the consumption of alcohol alone, which is .935. The Beta coefficient with respect to the consumption of alcohol is .852 and with respect to the general death rate .368; while the coefficient of part determination with respect to the consumption of alcohol is .961 and with respect to the general death rate .820. Just as in the United Kingdom, the death rate from alcoholism and cirrhosis of the

[7] Since the above calculations were made, data have been made available for the years 1928 and 1929. The consumption of alcohol estimated from the death rate was 2.55 and 2.76 liters per capita for these years, respectively, compared with 2.33 and 2.58 liters reported by the Department of Statistics. The errors of estimates are thus .22 and .18 liters, indicating that the equation of relationship holds for these years as well as for the years from which it is derived.

liver is more closely related to the consumption of alcohol than to the forces underlying the general death rate.[8]

ALCOHOL CONSUMPTION AND THE DEATH RATE IN THE UNITED STATES

The type and degree of relationship between deaths and the consumption of alcohol shown by statistical analyses to exist in the United Kingdom and in Denmark are also revealed in the United States despite certain inadequacies in the statistics. Records in the United States are deficient for two reasons: first, death rates from alcoholism and from cirrhosis of the liver are available only for the registration area of the United States which varies in extent from year to year and does not yet include the entire United States. Second, estimates of per capita consumption of American-made wine are in reality estimates of production, and doubtless are more variable from year to year than the actual consumption.

Because of the changing extent of the registration area it is desirable to use death rates in the registration states of 1900 or in the registration states of 1910 for correlation with the consumption of alcohol. If the former area, which covers 11 states with 40 per cent. of the population, is used, the coefficient of correlation for the twenty years from 1900 to 1919, between the consumption of alcohol and the combined death rate from alcoholism and cirrhosis

[8] In making this analysis it was assumed that any cause resulting in a certain percentage change in the general death rate would result in a percentage change in the death rate from alcoholism and cirrhosis of the liver, but that absolute changes in the consumption of alcohol result in percentage changes in the death rate from these two diseases. That is, the logarithms of the death rate from alcoholism and cirrhosis of the liver, as the dependent variable, were correlated with the consumption of alcohol in liters per capita and the logarithms of the general death rate as independent variables.

of the liver, is .937. If the latter area, covering 21 states and 58 per cent. of the population is used, the corresponding coefficient of correlation for the ten-year period from 1910 to 1919 is .966. In both cases the type of relationship is the same as in Great Britain and in Denmark: that is, the logarithm of the death rate is a linear function of the per capita consumption of alcohol. Other coefficients of correlation between the consumption of alcoholic liquors and death rates from alcoholism and cirrhosis of the liver are given in Table 35.

TABLE 35

ALCOHOLIC DEATHS AS RELATED TO ALCOHOL CONSUMPTION IN THE UNITED STATES, 1910 TO 1919

Correlation between Consumption of	Death rate from	Correlation coefficient
Spirits	alcoholism	.915
Spirits	cirrhosis of the liver	.880
Spirits	both causes	.921
Beer	alcoholism	.903
Beer	cirrhosis of the liver	.976
Beer	both causes	.954
Alcohol	alcoholism	.931
Alcohol	cirrhosis of the liver	.963
Alcohol	both causes	.966

SOURCES OF DATA:

Statistics of consumption: Table 1, *supra*, p. 24.

Statistics of deaths: Bureau of the Census, rates for the Registration States of 1910.

Correlation coefficients: computed by the usual method for linear correlation, using the logarithms of the death rates.

As noted in the case of the United Kingdom, there is a tendency for the consumption of beer and of spirits to vary together, and this may introduce a spurious correlation when they are separately related to the death rates; so that the most significant of these coefficients is that between the consumption of alcohol and the death rate from both alcoholism and cirrhosis of the liver. In this case the equations of relationship are

$$\log y = .029\,x + 2.191, \text{ and}$$
$$x = 3.229 \log y - 5.724$$

where y is the death rate from alcoholism and cirrhosis of the liver per million population, and x is the consumption of alcohol in gallons per capita. It should be noted that the death rates are for calendar years, while the statistics of consumption relate to fiscal years ending June 30. This makes a half-year lag in the death rates.

The data for this analysis, and the estimates of consumption of alcohol derived from the death rate from alcoholism and cirrhosis of the liver are given in Table 36.

TABLE 36

CONSUMPTION OF ALCOHOL AND THE ALCOHOLIC DEATH RATE IN THE UNITED STATES, 1910 TO 1919

Year	Alcohol consumption, gallons per capita, years ending June 30	Death rate from alcoholism and cirrhosis per million population, calendar years	Consumption computed from the death rate	Deviations from the original estimate
	x	y		
1910	1.64	188	1.62	—.02
1911	1.70	191	1.64	—.06
1912	1.66	186	1.61	—.05
1913	1.71	197	1.68	—.03
1914	1.67	185	1.60	—.07
1915	1.46	175	1.52	.06
1916	1.51	196	1.68	.17
1917	1.64	185	1.60	—.04
1918	1.13	137	1.18	.05
1919	.80	103	.78	—.02

SOURCES OF DATA:

Consumption of alcohol: Table 1, *supra*, p. 24.

Death rate from alcoholism and cirrhosis of the liver: Bureau of the Census. Rates are for the registration area of 1910.

Consumption computed from the death rate: computed from the equation, $x = 3.229 \log y - 5.724$.

The standard error of estimate, adjusted for the number of observations, of the consumption computed from the death rate is ± .06. The coefficient of correlation, similarly adjusted, between the death rate and the consumption of alcohol, is .961. The probability of obtaining by chance an adjusted coefficient of correlation as high as .961, even with so small a sample as 10 cases, is exceedingly small.[9] In the phraseology of statistics, the equation derived above may be considered a reliable method of estimating the consumption of alcohol, provided all the observations of death rates are drawn from the same *universe* as those used in deriving the equation.

If we assume that observations of death rates since 1919 are drawn from the same *universe* as those from 1910 to 1919, we can use the equation of relationship given above to estimate the consumption of alcohol in the United States since 1919. In this case, the phrase "drawn from the same universe" is simply the assumption that alcoholic beverages consumed since the adoption of prohibition have the same effect on the death rate as those consumed before the adoption of prohibition. This assumption may not, of course, be valid, and there is no way of determining the degree of its validity.

There are a number of reasons why it may be supposed that the relationship between the consumption of alcoholic beverages and death rates from alcoholism and cirrhosis of the liver has been changed by the advent of prohibition. The quality of liquor and the presence of other ingredients than alcohol may be in part responsible for the effect

[9] This is based on the value of t, which is 10.5. The letter t is used to designate an equation developed by R. A. Fisher to judge the probability of the occurrence of correlation coefficients by chance. For its exact significance readers are referred to Ezekiel, *Methods of Correlation Analysis*, pp. 20 and 256, or to R. A. Fisher, *Statistical Methods for Research Workers*, pp. 159-162.

which those liquors have on the death rate, and those other ingredients may be present in different proportions in the liquors sold under prohibition than in those sold before prohibition. The quality of alcoholic beverages sold under prohibition is doubtless in large part inferior, but so was that sold prior to prohibition.[10] Then the fact that annual changes in the consumption of alcoholic beverages were commonly not very great may conceal an effect on the death rate which is delayed more than the half-year assumed in the analysis. If this is the case, the estimates of consumption during the early years of prohibition would not show as much curtailment as actually occurred, nor would a later rise in consumption be revealed as promptly as it actually occurred. Further, the effects of alcoholic beverages may depend, and in some respects are known to depend, on the percentage of alcohol in the solution drunk. The adoption of prohibition has necessarily produced changes in the drinking habits of the people. It may be argued on the one hand that since alcoholic beverages are now legally contraband, they will be sold, and hence consumed, in the most condensed and harmful forms; and on the other, that alcoholic beverages are now consumed at home rather than at saloons, and probably used in more dilute forms. It may also be argued that in recent years there has been less industrial and misery drinking, and more convivial drinking, than in pre-war years; and that convivial drinking is less likely than misery and industrial drinking to result in alcoholism.[11] It may further be argued, without any basis for

[10] Bert Park, "The Bootlegger and His Forerunners," *The American Mercury*, July, 1926; and The Hearst Temperance Committee, *Temperance—or Prohibition*, pp. 14-15.

[11] That convivial drinking has less influence on alcoholism than other types of drinking appears to be borne out by statistics in Stockholm. In that city alcoholism decreases during the winter, and drunkenness

judging the merit of the argument, that the distribution of alcohol consumption about the per capita average has been different since prohibition from what it was before, and that, if drinking is more or less concentrated among certain sections or age-groups of the population than it was in pre-prohibition years, the character of the relation between per capita consumption and death rates may have changed.[12]

These considerations should be kept in mind in connection with the estimates in Table 37 of the consumption of alcohol since 1919, derived from the equation of relationship used in the preceding table.

TABLE 37

CONSUMPTION OF ALCOHOL IN THE UNITED STATES, 1920–1931, ESTIMATED FROM THE DEATH RATE

Year	Death rate from alcoholism and cirrhosis per million population, (calendar years)	Consumption of alcohol computed from the death rate, gallons per capita, (years ending June 30)	Consumption of alcohol, gallons per capita (calendar years)	Probable limits of alcohol consumption, (calendar years) a		b	
1920	88	.55	.64	.58	.70	.46	.82
1921	99	.72	.82	.76	.88	.64	1.00
1922	109	.89	.92	.86	.98	.74	1.10
1923	117	.95	.97	.91	1.03	.79	1.15
1924	119	.98	1.02	.96	1.08	.84	1.20
1925	125	1.05	1.07	1.01	1.13	.89	1.28
1926	128	1.08	1.11	1.05	1.17	.93	1.29
1927	133	1.13	1.15	1.09	1.21	.97	1.33
1928	136	1.17	1.13	1.07	1.19	.95	1.31
1929	129	1.09	1.09	1.03	1.15	.91	1.27
1930	128	1.08	1.09	1.03	1.15	.91	1.27
1931	130	1.10					

drops during the Christmas season, despite a decided increase in the consumption of alcohol during the holidays (Gunter Schmolders, *Prohibition im Norden*, p. 95).

[12] It is also possible that death rates are less reliably recorded in recent years, on account of the unwillingness of physicians to certify deaths as due to alcoholism. However, any tendency of this sort has probably been offset by a general tendency in recent years toward greater accuracy in reporting the causes of death.

SOURCES OF DATA:

Death rate from alcoholism and cirrhosis of the liver: 1920-1929, Bureau of the Census; 1930-1931, estimated from the rate among the industrial policy holders of the Metropolitan Life Insurance Co. Rates refer to the Registration States of 1910.

Consumption of alcohol computed from the death rate: computed from the equation, $x = 3.229 \log y - 5.724$.

Consumption of alcohol, calendar years: average of successive fiscal years.

Probable limits of consumption of alcohol: derived from the preceding column by subtracting and adding (a) the standard error of estimate, and (b) three times the standard error. There is about one chance in three that the consumption for any one year is greater or less than the limits given in (a), and about one chance in 62 that the consumption for any one year is greater or less than the limits given in (b).

TABLE 38

DEATH RATES IN THE UNITED STATES

	Death rate from alcoholism per million population	Death rate from cirrhosis of the liver per million population	General death rate per 10,000 population
1910	55	133	150
1911	52	139	142
1912	55	131	139
1913	63	134	141
1914	53	132	136
1915	47	128	136
1916	66	130	140
1917	63	122	143
1918	34	103	181
1919	19	84	129
1920	12	76	130
1921	20	79	116
1922	30	79	117
1923	39	78	122
1924	39	80	117
1925	45	80	118
1926	48	80	123
1927	50	83	114
1928	50	86	121
1929	47	82	119

SOURCE OF DATA:

Bureau of the Census. Rates for alcoholism and cirrhosis of the liver refer to the Registration States of 1910, and the general death rate to the entire registration area.

To find, if possible, the relative influence of spirits, wine, beer and the causes underlying the general death rate upon the death rates from alcoholism and from cirrhosis of the liver, the method of multiple correlation has been used. That is, the logarithms of the death rate from alcoholism and of the death rate from cirrhosis of the liver were separately correlated with the four independent variables: the consumption of spirits, the consumption of beer, the consumption of wine, and the logarithms of the general death rate. The death rates used in these analyses are given in Table 38, and the results of the analyses, expressed in partial regression coefficients and coefficients of part determination, in Table 39.

TABLE 39

MEASURES OF RELATIONSHIP BETWEEN ALCOHOLISM, CIRRHOSIS OF THE LIVER, THE GENERAL DEATH RATE AND THE CONSUMPTION OF ALCOHOLIC BEVERAGES, UNITED STATES, 1910-1919

	Coefficients of partial regression	Coefficients of part determination	Coefficients of multiple determination
Death rate from alcoholism correlated with			
The consumption of spirits	.968 ± .350	.839	
The consumption of beer	.030 ± .025	.489	
The consumption of wine	—.546 ± .404	.182	.879
The general death rate	.813 ± .539	.278	
Death rate from cirrhosis of the liver correlated with			
The consumption of spirits	.018 ± .117	.018	
The consumption of beer	.038 ± .008	.943	
The consumption of wine	—.002 ± .136	.00002	.933
The general death rate	—.161 ± .182	.137	

SOURCES OF DATA:

Death rates and consumption of alcoholic liquors: same as Table 37, *supra*.

Coefficients: computed by methods given in Ezekiel, *op. cit.*, *passim*.

Coefficients of multiple determination have been corrected for the number of observations and variables.

The coefficients of partial regression in the above table are computed so as to show, in the case of the consumption of alcoholic beverages, the percentage change in the death rate from alcoholism or cirrhosis of the liver accompanying a change of .01 gallon per capita in the consumption of spirits, beer or wine; and in the case of the general death rate, the percentage change in the death rate from alcoholism or cirrhosis of the liver accompanying a change of one per cent. in the general death rate. The coefficients of part determination measure the proportion of variations in the death rate from alcoholism or cirrhosis of the liver accounted for by variations in the consumption of spirits, beer or wine, or the general death rate. The coefficients of multiple determination give the total percentage of the variations in the death rates from each of these diseases accounted for by variations in all four of the other factors.

The standard errors of the partial regression coefficients, however, are so large that great caution must be used in interpreting their significance. This is because there is a high correlation between the consumption of spirits and that of beer, and some of the effects of one type of beverage may be allocated, statistically, to the other; because the death rates from alcoholism and cirrhosis may in part be the joint effect of consumption of both kinds of liquor; and because the data cover only the short period of ten years.[13] In fact, the only relationships shown by this

[13] It may be noted also that the validity of these coefficients of partial regression, and of the coefficients of determination in this and previous tables, depends on whether we are considering the ten years from 1910 to 1919, or are considering their applicability to other years. So far as this one decade is concerned, the sample consists of the

table to be important are those between the consumption of spirits and the death rate from alcoholism and between the consumption of beer and the death rate from cirrhosis of the liver.

An increase or decrease of one-tenth of a gallon per capita in the consumption of spirits was accompanied during the decade from 1910 to 1919, according to the regression coefficient, by an increase or decrease, respec-

entire universe. For this decade, therefore, the standard errors are meaningless in respect to their primary purpose of showing what coefficients might be obtained from other samples drawn from the same universe. But we know that the data are subject to chance errors of reporting, and probably also to biased errors. That is, while the sample consists of the entire universe, it is a distorted picture of that universe. If we assume that the difference between the true universe and the description of that universe given by the data is no greater than the difference between a random sample and the universe from which the sample is drawn, standard errors may be used to indicate the reliability of coefficients as descriptions of the true relations between the variables involved.

But if we apply the results obtained for the decade 1910 to 1919 to other years, we are assuming that that decade is a random sample of the universe consisting of all the years under consideration. In the present case we would like to apply the results to another decade, so that the total universe consists of 20 or 21 years. Ten years constitute half the universe, which is a relatively large, though an absolutely small sample. It is not, however, a random sample, since all the data are drawn from one section of the universe. If we assume that the large relative size of the sample increases the reliability of the coefficients of relationship as much as the fact that it is a 'spot" sample decreases such reliability, we may use the computed standard errors as measures of the reliability of those coefficients when applied to the rest of the universe: that is, to years in the second decade, 1920 to 1930.

These considerations are apart from the possibility previously discussed (*supra*, p. 87) that the last decade before prohibition and the first decade after prohibition should not be considered parts of the same universe, on the ground that alcoholic beverages consumed since the adoption of prohibition do not have the same effects as those consumed before prohibition.

tively, of 9.7 per cent. in the death rate from alcoholism. There is about one chance in three, however, that the true change in the death rate from alcoholism per tenth of a gallon change in per capita consumption was only 6.2 per cent., and one chance in three that it was as high as 13.2 per cent. There is about one chance in 35 that this regression coefficient has no meaning whatsoever, and that there is no relationship of the type assumed between the per capita consumption of spirits and the death rate from alcoholism.[14] However, the coefficient of part determination indicates that 84 per cent. of the variations in the death rate from alcoholism not accounted for by the other three factors are accounted for by variations in the consumption of spirits.

An increase or decrease of one gallon per capita in the consumption of beer was accompanied, during this decade, by an increase or decrease, respectively, of 3.8 per cent. in the death rate from cirrhosis of the liver. However, there is one chance in three that the true change was only 3 per cent. or as great as 4.6 per cent., and one chance in 250 that there was no true relationship. The coefficient of part determination shows that variations in the consumption of beer accounted for 94 per cent. of the variations in the death rate from cirrhosis of the liver not accounted for by the other factors.

We may also assume that the relative size of the regression coefficients gives some idea of the relative effect of the various liquors upon deaths from these two causes. Neglecting the standard errors, they indicate that a gallon of beer, though averaging about one-twelfth the alcoholic

[14] This, and other expressions in this chapter, regarding the probability that the observed relationships might be due to chance are based on the table regarding the reliability of constants computed from small samples given in Ezekiel, *Methods of Correlation Analysis*, p. 20.

strength of a gallon of proof spirits, has only about 1/53 as much effect on the death rate from alcoholism and 1½ times as much effect on the death rate from cirrhosis, as a gallon of proof spirits.[15] The consumption of wine appears to have no measurable effect on the death rate from cirrhosis of the liver, and a slight tendency to decrease the death rate from alcoholism. The latter effect may be explained on the theory that when American production of wine is large, the price is low, consumers drink wine instead of spirits, and do not so frequently become victims of alcoholism; or it may be considered a chance relationship, for there is one chance out of five that the true relationship is zero.

The death rate from alcoholism seems also to be somewhat related to the general death rate, since a change of one per cent. in the general death rate is accompanied by a corresponding change of .8 per cent. in the death rate from alcoholism: though this conclusion is not very reliable, there being one chance in three that the change in the death rate from alcoholism is only .5 per cent or as great as 1.3 per cent., and about one chance in five that there is no relationship at all. The death rate from cirrhosis of the liver is probably not related at all to the general death rate, since the standard error of the regression coefficient is larger than that coefficient, and both are small.

But, however unreliable the coefficients of partial regression may be, the coefficients of multiple determination show that variations in the four factors listed in Table 39 account for 88 per cent. of the variations in the death rate from alcoholism and 93 per cent. of the variations

[15] The size of the standard errors of these partial regression coefficients and the values obtained for t (*cf.* footnote 8, *supra*, p. 87) indicate that this statement of the relative effects of spirits and of beer is not very reliable.

in the death rate from cirrhosis of the liver. These coefficients are high enough for the regression equations to be applied to data other than that included in the sample analyzed, with a high degree of confidence in the approximate accuracy of estimates derived therefrom.[16]

These regression equations in their complete form are as follows:

$$y_1 = .42053x + .01294z - .23692w + .81303t, \text{ and}$$
$$y_2 = .00774x + .01646z - .00068w - .16062t$$

where y_1 is the deviation from the 1910-19 mean of the logarithm of the death rate from alcoholism per million population,
y_2 is the deviation from the 1910-19 mean of the logarithm of the death rate from cirrhosis of the liver per million population,
x is the deviation from the 1910-19 mean consumption of spirits in gallons per capita,
z is the deviation from the 1910-19 mean consumption of beer in gallons per capita,
w is the deviation from the 1910-19 mean consumption of wine in gallons per capita, and
t is the deviation from the 1910-19 mean of the logarithm of the general death rate per thousand population.[17]

To estimate the consumption of each kind of alcoholic beverage use may be made of the corresponding regression equations:

[16] "If the regression equation is to be used solely as a basis for making new estimates of the values of the dependent factor to be expected for given values of the independent factors, then it does not make such a great difference as to the accuracy of the several regression coefficients. Any deficiency in one will tend to be compensated for by an excess in another, and the whole set will provide estimates of the accuracy indicated by the standard error of estimate." Ezekiel, *op. cit.*, p. 261. As noted above, this is true only on the assumption that the "other" data are drawn from the same *universe* as those in the sample.

[17] The regression coefficients in these equations differ from those in Table 39, *supra*, p. 91, because in that table they have been converted to the basis of natural logarithms and expressed in percentages.

$$x = 1.415\ y_1 + .436\ y_2 - 1.845t$$
$$z = .256\ y_1 + 56.823\ y_2 + 10.279t$$

with all the terms having the same meaning as before.[18]

In Table 40 these equations have been used to estimate the consumption of spirits and the consumption of beer for the years from 1910 to 1919, so that they may be compared with the original estimates derived from tax reports. It will be noted that there is very little difference in the estimates for most years.

TABLE 40

ESTIMATES OF THE CONSUMPTION OF SPIRITS AND OF BEER, 1910-1919, DERIVED FROM DEATH RATES

(gallons per capita)

Year ending June 30	Consumption of spirits: Estimate from the death rates	Estimate from tax records	Difference	Consumption of beer: Estimate from the death rates	Estimate from tax records	Difference
1910	1.38	1.42	—.04	20.25	19.77	.48
1911	1.40	1.46	—.06	21.08	20.69	.39
1912	1.44	1.45	—.01	19.53	20.02	— .49
1913	1.51	1.51	.00	19.60	20.72	—1.12
1914	1.44	1.44	.00	19.62	20.69	—1.07
1915	1.28	1.26	.02	18.84	18.40	.44
1916	1.54	1.37	.17	19.39	17.78	1.61
1917	1.49	1.62	—.13	17.92	18.17	—.25
1918	.89	.85	.04	14.72	14.87	—.15
1919	.76	.77	—.01	8.11	8.00	.11

SOURCES OF DATA:

Estimates from the death rates: computed from the equations $x = 1.415y_1 + .436y_2 - 1.845t$ and $z = .256y_1 + 56.823y_2 + 10.279t$.

Estimates from tax records: Table 1, *supra*, p. 24.

The standard error of estimate, for the estimates derived from death rates, is .07 gallons per capita in the case of spirits and .77 gallons per capita in the case of

[18] No equation has been derived for wine, since wine appears to have no significant connection with death rates from alcoholism and cirrhosis of the liver.

beer. But in applying these equations to other years than those from 1910 to 1919, these standard errors should be corrected for the number of observations and variables. When this is done, they are .09 gallons per capita in the case of spirits and .99 gallons per capita in the case of beer.

These standard errors should be kept in mind in interpreting the estimates in Table 41, in which the above equations are applied to the years since the adoption of prohibition. Furthermore, the pre-prohibition tendency for the consumption of spirits and that of beer to fluctuate together may result in making the estimates for one type of beverage too large and for the other too small. This is especially true if, as is very probable, weak solutions of spirits have under prohibition been substituted for beer.

TABLE 41

ESTIMATES OF CONSUMPTION OF SPIRITS AND OF BEER, 1920-1929, DERIVED FROM DEATH RATES

(gallons per capita)

Year ending June 30	Spirits	Beer
1920	.45	5.63
1921	.87	6.13
1922	1.01	6.21
1923	1.23	6.12
1924	1.27	6.55
1925	1.35	6.61
1926	1.36	6.80
1927	1.45	7.37
1928	1.41	8.52
1929	1.38	7.26

SOURCES OF DATA:

Same as Table 40, *supra*, p. 97.

CHAPTER FOUR

The Consumption of Alcoholic Beverages Under Prohibition:

Estimate from Arrests for Drunkenness

One of the most conspicuous effects of the excessive use of alcoholic beverages is public drunkenness, and it may be presumed that there is some relationship between the number of persons arrested for intoxication and the

TABLE 42

Consumption of Spirits and Convictions for Drunkenness England and Wales, 1891-1914 and 1919-1928

Year	Consumption of spirits, gallons per capita	Convictions for drunkenness per 10,000 population	Year	Consumption of spirits, gallons per capita	Convictions for drunkenness per 10,000 population
1891	.89	58	1908	.75	52
1892	.90	53	1909	.61	46
1893	.87	50	1910	.58	44
1894	.85	52	1911	.59	46
1895	.88	48	1912	.58	49
1896	.90	53	1913	.59	50
1897	.91	54	1914	.59	48
1898	.93	57	1919	.42	16
1899	.97	59	1920	.42	25
1900	.99	56	1921	.34	20
1901	.98	58	1922	.31	19
1902	.94	58	1923	.29	19
1903	.88	63	1924	.29	20
1904	.85	62	1925	.29	19
1905	.81	59	1926	.26	17
1906	.79	56	1927	.26	16
1907	.80	55	1928	.25	14

Sources of Data:
The Alliance Year Book, 1931, pp. 322 and 329.

consumption of liquor. That this is the case in England and Wales, where records of convictions for drunkenness and of the consumption of alcoholic spirits are available back to 1891, is obvious from examination of the figures in Table 42.

The coefficient of correlation between the consumption of spirits and the convictions for drunkenness for the period covered in this table is +.963. This is sufficient to make it possible to estimate the consumption of spirits from the convictions for drunkenness with a high degree of accuracy.

Similar records are not available in the United States for a long enough period before the adoption of prohibition to determine the relation between public drunkenness and the consumption of alcoholic beverages with nearly as much confidence in the results as in England and Wales. There are no compilations in the United States of convictions for drunkenness, and those for arrests go back only to 1910. For the decade from 1910 to 1919, however, arrests for drunkenness were very closely related both to the consumption of spirits and to the total consumption of pure alcohol. The coefficient of correlation between the arrests for drunkenness and the consumption of spirits, corrected for the number of observations, is +.913; and that between arrests for drunkenness and the consumption of pure alcohol, similarly corrected, is +.928. The equations of relationship are

$$x_1 = .0111\,y - .6381 \text{ and}$$
$$x_2 = .0127\,y - .7417$$

where x_1 is the consumption of spirits in gallons per capita,
x_2 is the consumption of pure alcohol in gallons per capita, and
y is the number of arrests per 10,000 population in 383 cities and towns.

In Table 43 there are given, for each year from 1910

to 1919, the arrests for drunkenness in 383 places, the consumption of spirits and of pure alcohol as estimated from arrests, and the consumption as estimated from tax records.

TABLE 43

ARRESTS FOR DRUNKENNESS AND THE CONSUMPTION OF ALCOHOLIC BEVERAGES, UNITED STATES, 1910-1919

Year	Arrests for drunkenness per 10,000 population, 383 cities	Consumption of spirits (gallons per capita)		Consumption of alcohol (gallons per capita)	
		Estimate from arrests	Estimate from tax records	Estimate from arrests	Estimate from tax records
	y	x_1		x_2	
1910	175	1.30	1.44	1.48	1.67
1911	179	1.35	1.46	1.53	1.68
1912	185	1.42	1.48	1.61	1.69
1913	191	1.48	1.48	1.68	1.69
1914	187	1.44	1.35	1.63	1.57
1915	182	1.38	1.32	1.57	1.49
1916	192	1.49	1.50	1.70	1.58
1917	180	1.37	1.24	1.56	1.39
1918	138	.89	.81	1.01	.97
1919	102	.49	.52	.55	.53

SOURCES OF DATA:

Arrests for drunkenness: 1914 to 1919, computed by Mr. John C. Gebhart, Director of Research, Association Against the Prohibition Amendment, from figures collected by the Moderation League; 1910-1913, estimated from arrests in 514 places, reported by Mr. Robert E. Corradini, in U. S. Congress, Senate, Subcommittee of the Committee on the Judiciary, *The National Prohibition Law*, p. 1504. (The former of these two series, though referring to a smaller number of places, is used in preference to the latter, so far as available, because population estimates since 1920 are based on the 1930 as well as the 1920 census.)

Estimates of the consumption of spirits and of pure alcohol from arrests for drunkenness: computed from the equations, $x_1 = .0111y - .6381$, and $x_2 = .0127y - .7417$.

Estimates of the consumption of spirits and of pure alcohol from tax records: computed from Table 1, *supra*, p. 24, by averaging successive fiscal years. Figures for spirits are given in proof gallons, and those for alcohol in gallons of pure alcohol.

The standard errors of the estimates of consumption, as

derived from arrests for drunkenness in comparison with those derived from tax records, are .10 gallons for spirits and .14 for pure alcohol. These standard errors of estimate are sufficiently small and the coefficients of correlation sufficiently high to permit the use of arrests for drunkenness since 1920 as a means of estimating the consumption of spirits and of pure alcohol, provided it is assumed that arrests bear the same relation to the use of spirits and of alcohol that they did prior to the adoption of prohibition. If this assumption is made, there is about one chance in three that for any given year the estimates in Table 44 differ from the actual consumption by as much as the standard errors of estimate, and about one chance in fifty that they differ from the actual consumption by as much as three times the standard errors of estimate.

TABLE 44

THE CONSUMPTION OF SPIRITS AND OF PURE ALCOHOL, 1920 TO 1929; ESTIMATES FROM ARRESTS FOR DRUNKENNESS

Year	Arrests for drunkenness per 10,000 population, 383 cities	Estimate of consumption of spirits, proof gallons per capita	Estimate of consumption of pure alcohol, gallons per capita
1920	71	.15	.16
1921	92	.38	.43
1922	122	.72	.81
1923	141	.93	1.05
1924	141	.93	1.05
1925	142	.94	1.06
1926	146	.98	1.11
1927	149	1.02	1.15
1928	157	1.10	1.25
1929	151	1.04	1.18

SOURCES OF DATA:
Same as Table 43, *supra*, p. 101.

It is not, however, reasonable to suppose that arrests

bear exactly the same relation to the use of spirits and of alcohol since the adoption of prohibition as before prohibition. On the one hand, it may be argued that under prohibition, especially during its early years, police have been more strict in making arrests, and that a larger proportion than formerly of persons appearing on the streets under the influence of liquor are arrested.[1] But on the other hand, when the sale of liquor is illegal and it cannot be obtained in public saloons, and when the police are more strict in arresting intoxicated persons, it is reasonable to suppose that drinking is less public and that fewer drunken persons appear on the streets relative to the quantity of liquor consumed. When drinking takes place largely at homes, clubs and speakeasies, it is probable that friends keep most of those intoxicated off the streets until they have had time to sober up.

Because of these uncertainties, the estimates of the consumption of spirits and of alcohol derived from arrests for drunkenness should be considered less reliable than those derived from the sources of production or from the death rates from alcoholism and cirrhosis of the liver.

[1] There are great variations in police severity regarding drunkenness in the various cities, and great changes of policy in some cities from time to time, both before and since prohibition. (Cf. John C. Gebhart, "Prohibition: Statistical Studies of Enforcement and Social Effects," *Statistics in Social Studies*, pp. 114-25.) These differences are probably averaged out in the figures of arrests in 383 cities, except perhaps for a general increase in strictness during the early years of prohibition and a possible relaxation in recent years.

CHAPTER V

The Consumption of Alcoholic Beverages under Prohibition: Comparison of Estimates

In the foregoing chapters estimates have been made by three methods, completely independent of each other, of the consumption of alcoholic beverages since the adoption of prohibition. In Table 45 the results of these three methods in respect to the consumption of pure alcohol are brought together.

TABLE 45

Estimates of the Consumption of Pure Alcohol in the United States, 1920 to 1930

(gallons per capita)

Year	Estimate from sources of production	Estimate from death rates	Estimate from arrests for drunkenness	Final estimate	Index of consumption of alcohol 1911-14 = 100
1920	—	.64	.16	—	
1921	.26	.82	.43	.54	32.0
1922	.90	.92	.81	.91	53.8
1923	1.17	.97	1.05	1.07	63.3
1924	1.08	1.02	1.05	1.05	62.1
1925	1.13	1.07	1.06	1.10	65.1
1926	1.24	1.11	1.11	1.18	69.8
1927	1.08	1.15	1.15	1.12	66.3
1928	1.23	1.13	1.25	1.18	69.8
1929	1.31	1.09	1.18	1.20	71.0
1930	1.03	1.09		1.06	62.7

Sources of Data:

Estimate from sources of production: Table 30, *supra*, p. 72.

Estimate from death rates: Table 37, *supra*, p. 89.

Estimate from arrests for drunkenness: Table 44, *supra*, p. 102.

Final estimate: average of the estimate from sources of production and the estimate from death rates.

The inadequacies of these estimates, and the doubtful character of some of the assumptions underlying them, have been pointed out in the preceding pages. In view of these inadequacies, it is extremely remarkable that the agreement is so close for the years since 1923. Of the three estimates, that from arrests for drunkenness is the least reliable. Because of this, it is best to take the average of the estimate from sources of production and the estimate from death rates as the final estimate of the consumption of beverage alcohol in the United States under prohibition; though the final estimate would not be appreciably different were the estimate from arrests for drunkenness to be included.

During the early years of prohibition there is less agreement among the estimates, which, however, is readily understood. The estimate from sources of production is doubtless too low during those years, on account of the consumption of private stocks accumulated before the passage of the Volstead Act; while the estimate from the death rates is probably too high, due to the delayed effect of beer upon the death rate from cirrhosis of the liver.

It has been pointed out in the preceding pages that these various estimates are subject to a very high degree of reliability, provided it is assumed that alcoholic beverages used since the adoption of prohibition have the same effect upon the death rate from alcoholism and cirrhosis of the liver as those used before prohibition. The fact that the three estimates, totally independent of one another, differ so little, may be considered evidence that this assumption is correct, and that there is little difference, in its effects upon deaths from these two causes, between the liquor sold now and that sold in pre-war times.

TABLE 46

ESTIMATES OF THE CONSUMPTION OF ALCOHOLIC BEVERAGES IN THE UNITED STATES, 1920 TO 1930

(gallons per capita)

	Spirits			Beer		Wine
Year	Estimate from sources of production	Estimate from death rates	Estimate from arrests	Estimate from sources of production	Estimate from death rates	Estimate from sources of production
1920	. . .	.45	.15	. . .	5.63	. . .
1921	.30	.87	.38	1.26	6.13	.44
1922	1.54	1.01	.72	1.71	6.21	.57
1923	1.96	1.23	.93	2.24	6.12	.95
1924	1.75	1.27	.93	2.84	6.55	.90
1925	1.80	1.35	.94	3.46	6.61	.86
1926	1.91	1.36	.98	4.21	6.80	1.05
1927	1.53	1.45	1.02	5.03	7.37	1.08
1928	1.75	1.41	1.10	6.05	8.52	1.07
1929	1.86	1.38	1.04	7.11	7.26	.89
1930	1.33			6.90		.87

SOURCES OF DATA:

Estimates from sources of production: Table 29, *supra*, p. 71.

Estimates from death rates: Table 41, *supra*, p. 98. Estimates for successive fiscal years averaged to convert to calendar years.

Estimate from arrests: Table 44, *supra*, p. 102.

All estimates of spirits in proof gallons.

There have also been given, in connection with some of the preceding estimates, figures representing the probable minimum and maximum limits of consumption, based on standard errors. It is not possible to compute such maximum and minimum limits in the case of the final estimate of consumption. The close agreement of the three estimates is open to only two explanations: either they are substantially accurate or agreement is due to an extraordinary coincidence.

In respect to the various kinds of alcoholic beverages consumed in recent years there is not as much agreement among the estimates. This is due to the fact that for many years prior to prohibition there was a marked tendency for annual changes in the consumption of spirits and of beer to be similar in direction and amount, and even with the very best statistical technique factors related to the consumption of one kind of beverage cannot be accurately isolated from those connected with the other kind. In respect to the consumption of beer, the estimate from death rates appears to be considerably too high for most of the prohibition period. This makes it probable that the estimate of the consumption of spirits is too low. For wine it has been possible to make an estimate only from sources of production. All of these estimates are given in Table 46.

In Table 47 comparison is made between the pre-war consumption of alcoholic beverages, the estimated consumption in 1921-22, during the early period of prohibition, and that in the more recent period from 1927 to 1930.

TABLE 47

THE CONSUMPTION OF ALCOHOLIC BEVERAGES IN THE UNITED STATES BEFORE AND AFTER THE ADOPTION OF PROHIBITION

(gallons per capita)

Period	Spirits	Beer	Wine	Pure Alcohol
1911-14	1.47	20.53	.59	1.69
1921-22	.92	1.49	.51	.73
1927-30	1.62	6.27	.98	1.14

SOURCES OF DATA:

1911-14: Table 2, *supra*, p. 26.

1921-22 and 1927-30: Table 45, *supra*, p. 104, and Table 46, *supra*, p. 106. Figures for spirits, wine and beer taken from the estimates from sources of production.

These estimates indicate that during the early years of prohibition the per capita consumption of spirits was reduced approximately to two-fifths, and that of beer to one-fifteenth the pre-war level. In the four years from

1927 to 1930, however, the per capita consumption of spirits averaged about 10 per cent and of wine about 65 per cent greater than from 1911 to 1914, while the consumption of beer was about 30 per cent as great. The total consumption of liquor, expressed in terms of its content of pure alcohol, dropped during the early years of prohibition to one-third the pre-war level, but in recent years has been two-thirds as great as prior to the World War.

PART TWO

The Effect of Prohibition Upon Expenditures

CHAPTER VI

Pre-Prohibition Expenditures for Alcoholic Beverages

One of the most important of the economic aspects of prohibition is the extent to which expenditures for alcoholic beverages have been modified thereby. To estimate such changes in expenditure it is necessary first to estimate the amounts spent for liquor prior to prohibition, both by the entire nation and by important groups in the population.

THE NATIONAL LIQUOR BILL

There is no way of ascertaining exactly what the American public spent for its alcoholic beverages before prohibition. The total liquor bill may, however, be estimated from retail prices and records of consumption.

Pre-Prohibition Prices of Alcoholic Beverages. As shown in Table 48, wholesale prices of alcoholic beverages were comparatively stable from 1891 to 1916, lager beer ranging from $5 to $7 per barrel and whisky from $1.15 to $1.40 per gallon.

Retail prices, according to the testimony of persons living throughout this period, were still more stable than wholesale prices. Precise data, however, on retail prices are not obtainable, and the accompanying estimates (Table 49) are the best available.

TABLE 48

WHOLESALE PRICES OF ALCOHOLIC BEVERAGES IN THE UNITED STATES, 1890 TO 1918

Year	Ale barrel	Lager Beer barrel	Porter barrel	Whisky gallon (a)	Whisky gallon (b)
1890	7.00–8.00	5.00–7.00	7.00–8.00	1.043	1.092
1891	7.00–8.00	5.00–7.00	7.00–8.00	1.151	1.210
1892	7.00–8.00	5.00–7.00	7.00–8.00	1.158	1.157
1893	7.00–8.00	6.60	7.00–8.00	1.154	1.156
1894	7.00–8.00	6.00	7.00–8.00	1.199	1.120
1895	7.00–8.00	6.00	7.00–8.00	1.225	1.212
1896	7.00–8.00	5.75	7.00–8.00	1.205	1.203
1897	7.00–8.00	5.60	7.00–8.00	1.189	1.183
1898	7.00–8.00	6.60	7.00–8.00	1.229	1.222
1899	7.00–8.00	6.60	7.00–8.00	1.250	1.234
1900	7.00–8.00	6.30	7.00–8.00	1.248	1.245
1901	7.50	6.30	7.50	1.286	1.265
1902	7.50	6.30	7.50	1.310	1.314
1903	7.50	6.30	7.50	1.281	1.282
1904	7.50	6.30	7.50	1.270	1.263
1905	7.50	6.30	7.50	1.264	1.261
1906	7.50	6.30	7.50	1.288	1.288
1907	7.50	6.30	7.50	1.312	1.313
1908	7.50	6.00	7.50	1.358	1.358
1909	7.50	6.00	7.50	1.358	
1910	7.50	6.00	7.50	1.325	
1911	8.00	6.00	8.00	1.340	
1912	8.00	6.00	8.00	1.340	
1913	8.00	6.00	8.00	1.316	
1914	8.27	6.27	8.25	1.367	
1915	8.27	6.25	8.50	1.390	
1916	8.50	6.50	8.50	1.404	
1917		7.25	9.00	2.444	
1918		10.50	10.50	5.460	

SOURCES OF DATA:

Ale, lager beer, porter and whisky (a): annual reports of the Cincinnati Chamber of Commerce.

Whisky (b): Massachusetts, House, *Report of the Commission on the Cost of Living* (Boston, 1910), pp. 673-682.

TABLE 49

ESTIMATED RETAIL PRICES OF ALCOHOLIC BEVERAGES IN THE UNITED STATES PRIOR TO 1915

	Price per gallon (a)	Price per gallon (b)
Distilled liquors, domestic.......	$5.00	$4.50
Distilled liquors, imported......	8.00	Twice the declared value, including duty
Malt liquor, domestic	.50	.50
Malt liquor, imported	1.00	1.00
Wine, domestic	2.00	2.00
Wine, imported	4.00	Twice the declared value, including duty

SOURCES OF DATA:

(a) George B. Waldron, "Economics of the Drink Traffic," *The Chautauquan*, v. 51, pp. 96-107.

(b) *The American Grocer*, July 12, 1911, pp. 6-7, and June 9, 1915, pp. 4-5.

The Annual Liquor Bill Prior to Prohibition. The stability of retail prices and the records of consumption make it possible to estimate the total amount spent for alcoholic beverages. This is done in Table 50, using the price estimates of *The American Grocer,* except in the case of domestic distilled liquors, in which the higher estimate of Mr. Waldron has been used.

During the entire period between the Civil War and the adoption of prohibition alcoholic beverages were an important source of government revenue, and in recent years other sources have been necessary to take their place. Since this revenue, from whatever source derived, reduces the share of the national income available for spending by individuals, the actual gain in purchasing power through complete abstention from alcoholic liquors is not the total expenditure upon alcoholic drinks, but such expenditure less the government revenue derived therefrom. For this reason there is also given in Table 50 the estimated total national, state and municipal revenue from liquor, and the net annual liquor bill of the country. Since the revenues of local governments, aside from cities over 30,000 population, obtained from liquor are not obtainable, the estimate of the net annual liquor bill tends to be larger than the true figure. On the other hand, however, the estimate does not include "moonshine" and home-made drinks, on which no Federal tax was paid.

TABLE 50

ESTIMATED EXPENDITURES ON ALCOHOLIC BEVERAGES IN THE UNITED STATES, 1890-1916

(millions of dollars)

Year ending June 30	Spirits	Wine	Beer	Total	Government revenue	Net liquor bill
1890	442	75	429	946	141	805
1900	496	75	613	1,184	222	962
1910	677	141	929	1,747	283	1,464
1911	704	142	987	1,834	279	1,555
1912	710	132	970	1,812	281	1,531
1913	754	130	1,019	1,903	291	1,612
1914	732	123	1,032	1,887	287	1,600
1915	647	76	929	1,652	284	1,368
1916	714	110	910	1,734	305	1,429

SOURCES OF DATA:

Expenditure on spirits, wine and beer: computed from price data in Table 49, *supra*, p. 113, and data of production and imports from *Statistical Abstract of the United States*, 1912, 1920 and 1922.

Government revenue: Table 115, *infra*, p. 249. Liquor revenue of states and cities estimated by interpolation for years not available.

Just as we have taken the years from 1911 to 1914 as representative of the pre-prohibition consumption of alcoholic beverages, we may take them as typical of pre-prohibition expenditures upon those beverages. The average annual expenditure during these four years amounted to $1,859,000,000, of which $725,000,000 was for spirits, $132,000,000 for wine, and $1,002,000,000 for beer.

It will be noted from the preceding tables that the

expenditure for alcoholic beverages, both in total and per capita, increased during the decade from 1890 to 1900, and also from 1900 to 1910. This increase, however, was at a much slower rate than the increase of the national income, so that the percentage of the national income spent on alcoholic beverages decreased about one per cent during each of these decades. The estimated national income and the relation of liquor expenditure thereto are given in Table 51.

TABLE 51

ESTIMATED PERCENTAGE OF THE NATIONAL INCOME SPENT FOR ALCOHOLIC BEVERAGES IN THE UNITED STATES

Year	Total national income (millions)	Spent for alcoholic beverages (millions)	Per cent. for alcoholic beverages	Spent for alcoholic beverages, tax deducted (millions)	Per cent. for alcoholic beverages, tax deducted
1890	$12,082	$946	7.8	$805	6.7
1900	17,965	1,184	6.6	962	5.4
1910	31,400	1,747	5.6	1,464	4.7
1911-14 average	32,950	1,859	5.6	1,575	4.8
1915	36,000	1,652	4.6	1,368	3.8

SOURCES OF DATA:

National income: 1890 and 1900, Willford I. King, *The Wealth and Income of the People of the United States,* (New York, 1915), p. 129; 1910-1915, National Bureau of Economic Research, *Income in the United States,* (New York, 1921), v. 1, p. 64.

Spent for alcoholic beverages, Table 50, *supra,* p. 114.

Business Fluctuations and the Liquor Bill. Prior to the adoption of prohibition, the consumption of alcoholic beverages, and the amount spent upon them, varied with business fluctuations, rising in times of prosperity and falling in times of depression. In Table 52 there are given for a period of thirty-five years prior to the World War the per capita consumption of spirits and of beer, the deviations in the consumption of spirits and of beer from the trend

TABLE 52

Business Fluctuations and the Consumption of Alcoholic Beverages

Year ending June 30	Consumption of spirits (gallons per capita)	Consumption of beer (gallons per capita)	Deviations in Consumption: Of spirits from average	Of beer from trend	Combined deviations	Business fluctuations, per cent. deviation from normal
1880	1.27	8.26	—.11	—1.21	—.21	— 5
1881	1.38	8.65	.00	—1.18	—.10	11
1882	1.40	10.03	.02	— .15	.01	16
1883	1.46	10.27	.08	— .26	.06	14
1884	1.48	10.74	.10	— .15	.09	5
1885	1.27	10.62	—.11	— .62	—.16	—11
1886	1.28	11.21	—.10	— .39	—.13	—18
1887	1.21	12.24	—.17	— .29	—.19	— 4
1888	1.26	12.78	—.12	.48	—.08	2
1889	1.32	12.73	—.06	.07	—.05	— 2
1890	1.39	13.57	.01	.56	.06	4
1891	1.42	14.72	.04	1.35	.15	12
1892	1.48	15.07	.10	1.35	.21	7
1893	1.51	16.04	.13	.87	.20	12
1894	1.33	15.17	—.05	.74	.01	— 3
1895	1.13	14.99	—.25	.21	—.23	—17
1896	1.00	15.71	—.38	.57	—.33	— 3
1897	1.01	14.82	—.37	— .67	—.43	—11
1898	1.11	15.84	—.27	.00	—.27	—10
1899	1.17	15.19	—.21	—1.01	—.29	— 4
1900	1.28	16.06	—.10	— .49	—.14	4
1901	1.31	15.95	—.07	— .96	—.15	— 1
1902	1.34	17.15	—.04	— .11	—.05	3
1903	1.43	17.64	.05	.03	.05	4
1904	1.44	17.88	.06	— .09	.05	1
1905	1.41	17.99	.03	— .33	.00	— 6
1906	1.47	19.51	.09	.83	.16	5
1907	1.58	20.53	.20	1.50	.33	10
1908	1.39	20.23	.01	.85	.08	10
1909	1.32	19.04	—.06	— .70	—.12	—17
1910	1.42	19.77	.04	— .32	.01	1
1911	1.46	20.69	.08	.24	.11	3
1912	1.45	20.02	.07	— .78	.00	— 5
1913	1.51	20.72	.13	— .43	.09	5
1914	1.44	20.69	.06	— .82	—.01	3

SOURCES OF DATA:

Consumption of spirits and beer: *Statistical Abstract of the United States*, 1922, pp. 692-697.

Deviation of spirits from average: computed from the consumption of spirits. Deviations are computed from the average, in view of the absence of a significant trend.

Deviation of beer from trend: computed from the consumption of beer, using the straight line trend, y=35.4t, with t=o at the mid-year.

Combined deviations: deviation of spirits plus one-twelfth the deviation of beer from the trend, thus reducing the beer deviations to the same alcoholic strength as spirits.

Business fluctuations, per cent deviation from normal: *The Annalist*, January 16, 1931, p. 162. Figures are for calendar years just preceding the fiscal years, with monthly index numbers averaged and expressed as deviations from 100.

of consumption, the combined deviations of spirits and beer, and the deviations of business from normal, as indicated by the Axe-Houghton index of business activity. The figures relating to the consumption of spirits and beer are for fiscal years, while those relating to business are for the preceding calendar years. The coefficients of correlation between variations in the consumption of alcoholic beverages and fluctuations in business are higher with this half-year lag than with no lag in consumption.

It will be noted that the years of good business were generally the years of the highest consumption of alcoholic beverages, for example, in 1882-83, 1890-92 and 1906; while the lowest consumption of liquor occurred in the depression years of 1885-86, 1895-98 and 1908. By no means all of the variations in consumption are accounted for by business fluctuations, however. The coefficient of correlation between the deviations in consumption of spirits from the average and deviations in business from normal is .621; that between deviations from trend in the consumption of beer and deviations of business from normal is .406; while that between the combined deviations in the consumption of spirits and beer is .663. The reason why the last of these is greater than the other two is because there is a tendency for consumption to shift from spirits to beer in times of business depression. The significance of these coefficients may be expressed by saying that during the period from 1880 to 1914 business fluctuations accounted for between 35 and 55 per cent of the annual variations in the consumption of spirits and beer.

The Influence of Price Changes. Retail prices of alcoholic beverages were too stable for a quarter of a century prior to the World War to provide any evidence regarding the influence of price changes upon consumption. From 1917 to 1919 prices advanced and consumption declined, but it is not possible to separate the influence of rising prices from that of new state prohibitory laws and war-time restrictions.

In Great Britain, with the retail price of spirits four times and that of beer three times as high in recent years as just before the war, expenditures are about 80 per cent greater per capita. However, the consumption of alcoholic beverages has been reduced not only by higher prices, but also by restrictions on the hours of sale.[1] In Denmark and Germany and other European countries, higher prices in recent years have accompanied lower rates of consumption than in pre-war years. Lack of price data makes more precise comparisons impossible. In France the price of ordinary wine dropped about 60 per cent during the first decade of the present century, at a time when general retail prices were rising, and this was accompanied by an increase in the per capita consumption of approximately 35 per cent.[2]

[1] *The Alliance Year Book*, 1931, pp. 321 and 324. Retail prices were computed from figures of consumption and expenditure.

[2] Statistique General de la France, *Salaires et Coût de l'Existence à diverses époques, jusqu'en 1910* (Paris, 1910), pp. 56 and 66.

Thus the evidence indicates that the consumption of alcoholic beverages is quite responsive to price changes, but it is not possible to determine just how responsive.

FAMILY AND GROUP EXPENDITURES FOR LIQUOR

Expenditures for alcoholic beverages are not distributed evenly among the entire population, for some groups of persons spend much more for liquor than other groups.

Average Per Capita and Per Family Expenditure. The average expenditure on alcoholic beverages per capita, both in the United States and in the United Kingdom, is given in Table 53.

TABLE 53

ESTIMATED EXPENDITURES PER CAPITA FOR ALCOHOLIC BEVERAGES, 1890-1916

Year	Spirits	Wine United States	Beer	All alcoholic beverages United States	 United Kingdom
1890	$7.01	$1.19	$6.80	$15.00	$20.98
1900	6.52	.98	8.05	15.55	22.76
1910	7.34	1.52	10.07	18.93	16.86
1911	7.51	1.52	10.53	19.58	17.49
1912	7.47	1.38	10.20	19.05	17.22
1913	7.81	1.35	10.56	19.72	17.62
1914	7.47	1.27	10.54	19.27	17.23
1915	6.51	.77	9.36	16.63	19.20
1916	7.09	1.09	9.03	17.21	21.57

SOURCES OF DATA:

United States: computed from figures in Table 50, *supra*, p. 114, and estimates of population.

United Kingdom: *The Alliance Year Book*, 1931, p. 325. Figures are converted from pounds to dollars at the par of exchange.

Utilizing census data in respect to the average size of families, and interpolating for intercensal years, we obtain the estimated expenditure per family on alcoholic beverages in pre-prohibition days. This estimate is given in Table 54.

TABLE 54

ESTIMATED EXPENDITURE PER FAMILY FOR ALCOHOLIC BEVERAGES IN THE UNITED STATES, 1890-1916

Year	Spirits	Wine	Beer	Total
1890	$34.35	$5.83	$33.32	$73.50
1900	30.64	4.61	37.84	73.09
1910	33.03	6.84	45.32	85.19
1911	33.64	6.81	47.17	87.72
1912	33.32	6.15	45.49	84.96
1913	34.68	5.99	46.89	87.56
1914	33.02	5.61	46.59	85.17
1915	28.64	3.39	41.18	73.17
1916	31.05	4.77	39.55	75.38

SOURCES OF DATA:

Computed from Table 53, *supra*, p. 119, and census data on the size of families *(Statistical Abstract of the United States)*, intercensal years being interpolated.

Regional Expenditures. That drinking habits differ in various parts of the country is well known, and confirmed by the budget studies of the United States Department of Labor in 1890-91, 1901-02 and 1918-19. During the last of these studies war-time restrictions and, in several states, prohibitory laws, were in force, and the reported expenditures may be nearer the actual expenditures in some sections than in others. These investigations, however, indicate that family expenditures for liquor are higher in the industrial regions of the east and north central than in other sections of the country, though the reported expenditures in some states differ considerably from the regional averages. Expenditures on liquor by regions, as reported in these three budget studies, are given in Table 55.

It is probable that differences in expenditures on alcoholic beverages among various regions are not of primary significance. Liquor habits vary according to the nationality of workingmen, and also according to their occupation; and it is because samples vary in these and other respects that the differences in geographic regions appear.

TABLE 55

REPORTED EXPENDITURE FOR LIQUOR BY WORKINGMEN'S FAMILIES IN GEOGRAPHICAL REGIONS

Region	1890-91	1901-02	1918-19
North Atlantic	$9.25	$23.72	$11.51
South Atlantic	3.89	19.48	2.64
North Central	33.27	30.38	8.25
South Central	1.55	14.09	2.74
Western		11.91	3.51
All United States	12.65	22.28	7.18

SOURCES OF DATA:

1890-91: Sixth and Seventh Annual Reports of the United States Commissioner of Labor. Computations made by the author.

1901-02: Eighteenth Annual Report of the United States Commissioner of Labor.

1918-19: *Cost of Living in the United States,* Bulletin of the United States Bureau of Labor Statistics No. 357.

The Influence of Urban Life. It is probable that people living in urban centers spend more for alcoholic beverages than those living in rural regions. But since local records of sales of liquor are not available in the United States for the pre-prohibition period, the only statistical evidence that can be cited in this respect is the fact that death rates from alcoholism and from cirrhosis of the liver are lower in rural than in urban areas.

In Table 56 there are given the death rates in the cities and in the rural parts of the Registration States for the three years from 1910 to 1920. The cities include only those with more than 10,000 population, all places with less than this population being classed as rural.

The Influence of Age, Sex and Marital Status. Since adult males are heavier drinkers than women and children, a change in the proportion of adult males in the population is likely to be reflected in the per capita consumption of alcoholic beverages. In 1880 males fifteen years of age and older constituted 31.5 per cent of the population,

TABLE 56

URBAN AND RURAL DEATH RATES FROM ALCOHOLISM AND CIRRHOSIS OF THE LIVER

(Rates per 100,000 population)

Year	Alcoholism Urban	Alcoholism Rural	Cirrhosis of the liver Urban	Cirrhosis of the liver Rural
1910	6.7	4.1	16.1	10.2
1911	5.8	3.8	16.7	10.5
1912	6.4	4.1	15.9	10.1
1913	7.5	4.4	16.2	9.7
1914	6.2	3.7	15.4	9.7
1915	5.4	3.4	14.5	9.8
1916	7.9	3.8	15.1	8.9
1917	7.1	3.5	14.0	8.3
1918	3.5	2.0	11.8	7.5
1919	2.2	1.1	9.4	6.5
1920	1.3	0.7	8.1	6.1

SOURCE OF DATA:

Bureau of the Census, *Mortality Rates, 1910-1920*, pp. 344 and 372.

while in 1910 they were 35.3 per cent, and in 1920 34.9 per cent. That is, a per capita consumption of liquor 10 per cent greater in 1910 than in 1880 would indicate approximately the same consumption per adult male.

Marital status also affects the consumption of liquor. It is generally recognized that unmarried men drink more heavily than married men, but no statistical evidence of this is available in the United States.[3]

The Influence of Nationality. In the report of the Commissioner of Labor respecting family budgets in 1890, all budgets are published in detail. This has made it possible to compute the reported expenditures by nationalities and by industries. When classified by nationalities,

[3] It is interesting to note that among workingmen in Bombay, single men spend 87 per cent more for liquor than the average family, and 65 per cent more than the average "normal" family, consisting of husband, wife and two children. The liquor expenditures of workingmen in Bombay in various income groups are given in Table 57.

TABLE 57

EXPENDITURES FOR LIQUOR BY ALL FAMILIES, BY "NORMAL" FAMILIES, AND BY SINGLE MEN, IN BOMBAY

	All Families		Normal Families		Single Men	
Size of income Rs.	Spent for liquor Rs.	Per cent. for liquor	Spent for liquor Rs.	Per cent. for liquor	Spent for liquor Rs.	Per cent. for liquor
Below 360	15.31	5.0	10.81	3.3	25.88	8.3
360- 480	13.69	3.3	13.87	3.3	28.44	8.9
480- 600	21.56	4.0	22.94	4.4	36.32	7.1
600- 720	22.62	3.6	26.12	2.1	41.94	6.6
720- 840	29.37	3.9	28.69	3.9	52.19	6.9
840- 960	33.31	3.8	39.87	4.6	62.69	7.2
960-1080	38.50	3.8			68.32	6.4
All incomes	23.81	3.8	24.38	4.3	37.19	7.1

SOURCE OF DATA:

Shirras, *Report on an Enquiry into Working Class Budgets in Bombay*, pp. 50-53, 124-25. Monthly figures have been converted into yearly figures, and annas and pice into fractions of a rupee.

families of Belgian, French, German and Southern European origin report larger expenditures for liquor than those of English, Scotch, Irish, Welsh or Scandinavian origin. All European families, both those residing in Europe and those in the United States, report expenditures for liquor about 50 per cent greater than American families.

There is a greater difference between the expenditures for liquor by those in the higher and the lower income groups among American families than among European families. This indicates that in Europe and among European families in the United States alcoholic drinks tend to be classed by workingmen's families among the necessities, while among American families they partake more of the nature of luxuries, to be purchased when families are prosperous.

The reported liquor expenditures by workingmen's families of various nationalities are given in Table 58 and of

European and American families in various income classes in Table 59.

TABLE 58

REPORTED EXPENDITURES FOR LIQUOR BY NATIONALITIES: WORKINGMEN'S FAMILIES, 1890

Nationality	In the United States	In Europe
Canadian	$7.67	
American	10.92	
English	11.25	$13.15
Irish	11.90	15.88
Welsh	13.51	14.01
Scandinavian	13.79	
Scotch	14.35	8.84
German	21.33	11.29
Southern European	23.29	
Belgian and French	29.64	21.74
Central European	31.24	
All European	15.43	14.94

SOURCE OF DATA:

Sixth and Seventh Annual Reports of the United States Commissioner of Labor. Computations by the author. Southern European families include Italian, Spanish and Portuguese; and Central European families include Bohemian, Austrian, Hungarian and Polish.

TABLE 59

REPORTED EXPENDITURES FOR LIQUOR BY INCOME CLASSES: EUROPEAN AND AMERICAN WORKINGMEN'S FAMILIES, 1890

Size of income	European Families In Europe	European Families in the United States	American families	All families in the United States
$150-$300	$10.07			
300- 450	12.86	$7.54	$4.92	$5.78
450- 600	14.33	10.89	5.54	7.70
600- 800	20.41	16.00	8.63	11.63
800-1000	22.57	15.04	16.50	15.62
1000-1200	29.16	21.91	21.75	21.06
1200-1500	38.30	35.60	40.60	37.11
Over 1500		36.95	43.82	38.24
All families	14.94	15.43	10.92	12.65

SOURCE OF DATA:

Same as Table 58.

The Influence of Occupation. That expenditures for liquor vary also with the occupation of workingmen is shown by the budgets collected in Europe and in the United States in 1890. At that time the reported expenditure by workers in the iron ore industry was only $8.58 per family, while that in the glass industry was $54.84 per family. Other industries included in this study—cotton, pig iron, bituminous coal, woollen, coke, bar iron and steel—showed expenditures per family ranging from $15.98 to $26.25 per year. It is significant that the same differences appear in the European budgets. So striking is the similarity that the conclusion seems inescapable that there are definite causes of drinking connected with the nature of occupations. The reported expenditures by industries are given in Table 60.

TABLE 60

REPORTED EXPENDITURES FOR LIQUOR BY WORKINGMEN'S FAMILIES IN VARIOUS INDUSTRIES, 1890

Industry	Average family expenditure In the United States	In Europe
Iron ore	$8.58	$7.53
Cotton	15.98	16.56
Pig iron	17.61	20.00
Bituminous coal	18.09	21.76
Woollen	18.39	26.34
Coke	20.25	20.85
Bar iron	25.10	25.26
Steel	26.25	26.19
Glass	54.84	39.18

SOURCE OF DATA:

Same as Table 58, *supra*, p. 124.

The Influence of Permanent Poverty and Economic Status. Not only does the consumption of alcoholic beverages by workingmen vary with nationality and with occupation; it appears also to vary with the attitude taken by wage-earners as to their economic status and the possibility of improving that status. Workingmen who feel that there is a reasonable chance of rising to better-paid or more desirable jobs, or of becoming owners or business men, find a certain enthusiasm in working for promotion or in saving to purchase property or to enter business on their own account. But workmen who consider themselves low in the social scale, who believe they can never hope to improve their economic status, and who live in undesirable surroundings and assume that they will remain there, are likely to find the use of alcohol the easiest method of psychological compensation. Alcohol, in turn, tends to make such workers satisfied with their conditions, and to stultify what efforts might be practicable by way of improving their economic status.

It is quite possible that part of the variation in liquor consumption among geographic regions is due to varying attitudes of workingmen as to the permanence of their economic circumstances. To examine this possibility would require figures of consumption of alcoholic beverages and data regarding economic conditions in local areas, for there is obviously local as well as regional variation in workingmen's attitudes. These data are not available for any community in the United States.

The extreme amount, however, which may be spent by workingmen under especially unfavorable living conditions may be illustrated by one of the working class districts of London. In the borough of Bermondsey housing conditions are appalling. There is overcrowding, with three-fourths of a room per person; sanitary facilities are inadequate, with only 150 bathrooms in all the 18,146 houses and tenements in the district, and the dwellings are in bad condition, it being necessary in 1928 to invoke legal aid in more than a fourth of the houses to get the owners to make necessary repairs. The principal field of employment in the region is the transport service connected with docks, wharves and railways. In 1925 the average weekly wage for a fully employed man was less than $14, or $700 per year. Yet the expenditure on liquor amounted to $58 per capita, which must have been about $250 per family. Over seven times as much was spent on drink as on milk, though nearly a third of the population of Bermondsey are children under twelve years of age; and the expenditure for drink amounted to more than the total expenditure on bread, milk, house rent and taxes.[4]

The Influence of Family Incomes. It might be assumed from the foregoing discussion of the effect of poverty and economic status upon liquor expenditure that families with small incomes generally spend more for liquor than families with large incomes. This is not the case, however. All workingmen's budget studies in the United States and foreign countries in which expenditures for alcoholic beverages are separately listed show that the larger the income the greater the amount spent for liquor. In Table 61 there are given the reported expenditures for alcoholic drinks by families with various levels of income in three budget studies in the United States. In two of these investigations, those of the United States Bureau of Labor, there is obviously a large degree of under-reporting of the money spent for liquor. The reported expenditures for liquor in the 1890 study were only about one-sixth, and in the 1918-1919 study about one-tenth of the expenditures per family for the country as a whole, as computed from prices and the total consumption. While it is doubtless true that the average for all families in the country is larger than that

[4] George B. Wilson, "Bermondsey: A Study in Drink Consumption," *The Alliance Year Book*, 1930, pp. 98-112.

for workingmen's families, it is hardly conceivable that it is six times as great.

In Chapin's study a serious effort was made to obtain a full statement of expenditures for liquor. His study, however, refers only to New York City. Workingmen in New York probably spend more for liquor than workingmen in the country as a whole, but, on the other hand, there is probably some under-reporting even in Chapin's study.

TABLE 61

WORKINGMEN'S FAMILY INCOMES AND EXPENDITURES FOR LIQUOR IN THE UNITED STATES

UNITED STATES BUREAU OF LABOR

1890–91			1918–19		
Size of income	Spent for liquor	Per cent. for liquor	Size of income	Spent for liquor	Per cent. for liquor
$300- 450	$5.78	1.5	Under $900	$4.41	0.5
450- 600	7.70	1.5	$900-1200	6.55	0.6
600- 800	11.63	1.7	1200-1500	6.73	0.5
800-1000	15.52	1.8	1500-1800	7.37	0.5
1000-1200	21.05	2.0	1800-2100	6.65	0.4
1200-1500	37.11	2.8	2100-2500	9.21	0.4
Over 1500	38.24	2.2	Over 2500	15.82	0.6
All incomes	12.65	1.8	All incomes	7.18	0.5

CHAPIN

1908—NEW YORK CITY

Size of income	Spent for liquor	Per cent. for liquor
$400- 600	$18.47	2.7
600- 700	27.25	4.2
700- 800	32.52	4.4
800- 900	37.65	4.4
900-1000	36.56	3.9
1000-1100	50.67	4.9
Over 1100	59.96	5.2
All incomes	35.17	4.3

SOURCES OF DATA:

1890-91: Sixth and Seventh Annual Reports of the United States

Commissioner of Labor. Computations made by the author from budgets printed in these reports.

1918-19: *Cost of Living in the United States*, Bulletin No. 357 of the Bureau of Labor Statistics, p. 453.

1908, New York City: R. C. Chapin, *Standard of Living Among Workingmen's Families in New York City*, (New York, 1909), p. 149.

Not many budget studies in foreign countries include expenditures for liquor as a separate item. Among those that do, there are two of especial significance, one made by the United States Bureau of Labor in northwestern Europe in 1890 and 1891, and one made by the Bombay Labour Office, in Bombay, in 1921. The expenditures on liquor reported in these studies are given in Table 62.

TABLE 62

WORKINGMEN'S FAMILY INCOMES AND EXPENDITURES FOR LIQUOR IN FOREIGN COUNTRIES

Northwestern Europe—1890-91			Bombay—1921		
Size of income	Spent for liquor	Per cent. for liquor	Size of income (rupees per annum)	Spent for liquor (rupees per annum)	Per cent. for liquor
$150- 300	$10.07	4.1	Under 360	15.31	5.0
300- 450	12.86	3.5	360- 480	13.69	3.3
450- 600	14.33	2.8	480- 600	21.56	4.0
600- 800	20.41	3.0	600- 720	22.62	3.6
800-1000	22.57	2.6	720- 840	29.37	3.9
1000-1200	29.16	2.7	840- 960	33.31	3.8
1200-1500	38.30	2.6	960-1090	38.50	3.8
All incomes	14.94	3.1	Over 1080	37.12	3.1
			All incomes	23.81	3.8

SOURCES OF DATA:

Northwestern Europe: Sixth and Seventh Annual Reports of the United States Commissioner of Labor. Computations made by the author from budgets printed in these reports.

Bombay: G. Findlay Shirras, *Report on an Enquiry into Working Class Budgets in Bombay*, (Bombay, 1923), p. 51. Monthly figures have been converted into yearly figures, and annas and pice into fractions of a rupee.

There is doubtless an understatement of expenditures for liquor in these studies as well as in those in the

United States. They agree, nevertheless, with investigations in the United States that it is the better-paid workmen and the families with the larger incomes which spend the most money on alcoholic beverages.

LIQUOR EXPENDITURES BY ECONOMIC CLASSES

It is sometimes said that though wealthy persons may be drinking as much liquor and spending as much on it as before prohibition, that the members of the working class are spending less.[5] To examine thoroughly the validity of this contention it would be necessary to know what part of the pre-war expenditure for liquor was incurred by the working class and what part by other classes of the population. Unfortunately, there seems to be no reliable estimate of pre-war liquor expenditures by any considerable group of persons, either in one locality or scattered throughout the nation, with the exception of Chapin's study of workingmen's families in New York City. Furthermore, there are no definite figures available regarding the number of persons, especially of males over fifteen years of age, in the various economic classes of the nation.

The Distribution of Population Among the Principal Economic Classes. Despite these difficulties, an attempt has been made to allocate the liquor bill in 1910 among the single men and families of the three principal economic classes: the wage-earning class, the business, professional and salaried class, and the farming class. To do this it has been

[5] Samuel Crowther, for example, who estimates that there has been an annual diversion of spending due to prohibition of between two and six billion dollars, and declares that this diversion was primarily responsible for the prosperity of the nation between 1922 and 1929, rests his entire argument on the alleged smaller expenditures of workingmen for drink. (Samuel Crowther, *Prohibition and Prosperity*, pp. 23, 51 and 58.)

necessary to estimate the number of unmarried men and of families in each of these classes. The method of making these estimates is given in Table 63.

TABLE 63

AN ESTIMATE OF THE NUMBER OF UNMARRIED MALES AND OF FAMILIES IN THE PRINCIPAL ECONOMIC CLASSES IN THE UNITED STATES, 1910

	Per cent.	Millions
AGRICULTURAL CLASS		
Number of persons normally occupied in agriculture (1)		8.81
Percentage of total number of persons engaged in agriculture and related occupations who are males (2)	85.7	
Number of males in agriculture, computed from above figures		7.55
Number of males in agriculture under 15 years of age (3)		1.02
Number of males in agriculture over 15 years of age		6.53
Percentage of males in rural areas who are unmarried (3)	37.5	
Estimated number of unmarried males in agriculture, assuming the same percentage as in all rural areas		2.45
Estimated number of married and widowed males in agriculture		4.08
BUSINESS, PROFESSIONAL AND SALARIED CLASS		
Estimated total number of persons in the business, professional and salaried class: that is, entrepreneurs plus salaried employees outside of agriculture (1)		8.19
Percentage of persons in trade and in public and professional service who are males (2)	78.9	
Number of males in business, professional and salaried class, assuming same proportion to total as in above occupations		6.46
Percentage of males over 15 years of age in urban areas who are unmarried (3)	40.0	
Estimated number of unmarried males in the business, professional and salaried class, assuming the same percentage as in urban areas		2.58
Estimated number of married and widowed males in the business, professional and salaried class		3.88

WAGE-EARNING CLASS

Estimated number of wage-earners outside of agriculture (1)		18.10
Percentage of persons engaged in mining, manufacturing, transportation, domestic and personal service and clerical work who are males (2)	74.4	
Estimated number of male wage-earners outside of agriculture, assuming same percentage as in above occupations		13.47
Number of male wage-earners under 15 years of age outside of agriculture (3)		.33
Estimated number of unmarried male wage-earners over 15 years of age, outside of agriculture, assuming same percentage as in urban areas		5.26
Estimated number of married and widowed male wage-earners over 15 years of age, outside of agriculture		7.88

SOURCES OF DATA:

(1) Willford I. King, *The National Income and Its Purchasing Power* (New York, 1930), pp. 50, 56, 60, 62.

(2) *Statistical Abstract of the United States*, 1930, p. 50.

(3) *Thirteenth Census of the United States*, 1910.

Class Consumption of Alcoholic Beverages. It was recognized in pre-prohibition discussions of the liquor problem that members of the urban wage-earning class were heavy consumers of beer, that the more expensive types of liquor were consumed almost exclusively by the business, professional and salaried class, and that the farming class drank less than either the urban wage-earning or the business, professional and salaried class. There is no reason to doubt the accuracy of this opinion. The only statistical evidence which can be presented in its support, however, is the differences in death rates from alcoholism and cirrhosis of the liver among these three classes.

In Table 56, *supra*, figures were given regarding death rates in the urban and rural parts of the registration States. In 1910 and the following years the death rates from these two diseases in the rural parts of the registration States were slightly less than two-thirds the rates in the urban parts. Since the rural parts of the registration States include all towns of less than 10,000 population, we cannot see this difference in death rates as a precise measure of the difference in the consumption of alcoholic beverages between the farming class and the rest of the population. The difference gives strong support, however, to the conclusion that the members of the farming class consumed considerably less liquor, both spirits and beer, than members of the urban population.

In 1911 the death rate from alcoholism among the industrial policyholders of the Metropolitan Life Insurance Company, comprising a large proportion of the urban wage-earning population, was 4.0 per 100,000 persons.[6] This may be compared with 3.8 per 100,000 in the rural parts of the registration States, with 5.8 in the urban parts, and with 4.9 in the entire registration area. Substantially these same differences appear in other years.[7] Since deaths from alcoholism are associated primarily with the consumption of spirits, this supports the opinion that wage-earners were less heavy drinkers of spirits than the business, professional and salaried class, which constitute the non-wage earning part of the urban population.

The death rate from cirrhosis of the liver among the industrial policyholders of the Metropolitan Life Insurance Company in 1911 was 16.3 per 100,000, which compares with 10.5 in the rural parts of the registration States, with 16.7 in the cities of the Registration States, and with 14.0 in the entire registration area. Substantially the same differences

6 The industrial policyholders of the Metropolitan Life Insurance Company include about a third of the entire urban population, and consist mainly of wage-earners. (Letters from the statistician of the Company.) These policyholders may not, however, be a random sample of the entire wage-earning class. Full reliance cannot, therefore, be placed upon the following comparisons of these policyholders with the general population.

7 See Table 56, *supra*, p. 122, and 101, *infra*, p. 213.

appear in other years.[8] We have noted that cirrhosis of the liver appears, in the United States, to be more closely associated with the consumption of beer than with that of spirits. These figures therefore support the opinion that members of the wage-earning class consumed, prior to prohibition, more beer than did the population as a whole. These death rates provide no evidence, however, that the urban wage-earning class consumed more beer than the rest of the urban population: though this may have been the case, since the relatively heavy consumption of spirits by the business, professional and salaried class may have contributed to the apparently high death rate from cirrhosis of the liver among the non-wage earning part of the urban population.

Class Expenditures upon Alcoholic Beverages. When we turn to the average expenditures by individuals and families in each of the three principal economic classes, the evidence is still less satisfactory. In Table 54 the average expenditure for alcoholic beverages in 1910 was estimated at about $85 per family. The average expenditure per adult male was considerably less than this, for there were about a third more adult males than families. The average expenditure per adult male in that year was about $65, of which $35 was for beer, $25 for spirits and $5 for wine.

The adult male members of the farming class, since they consumed considerably less alcoholic beverages of all kinds than did the members of the other classes, must have spent much less than $65 each. An estimate of about half that much is arbitrary, but not unreasonable.

It may be presumed that the average adult male wage-earner, drinking somewhat more beer but considerably less spirits than the average adult male in the entire population, spent somewhat less, certainly not more, than the average adult male. Again, it is arbitrary but not unreasonable to estimate the amount at $50 per year.

[8] See Table 56, *supra*, p. 122, and 101, *infra*, p. 213.

Another estimate of liquor expenditure among members of the wage-earning class may be made from workingmen's family budgets. It has been noted above that in Chapin's study, which is the only budget investigation in the United States in which sufficient care was taken to prevent gross under-reporting of expenditures on liquor, the average expenditure for liquor among 361 workingmen's families in New York City in 1908 was $35.17.[9] On the assumption that there was some under-reporting even in these cases, and that New York families spent about the same amount for liquor as families in other industrial regions, $40 a year may be considered a reasonable estimate of the pre-war average expenditure by workingmen's families. This is about twice the average expenditure reported in the workingmen's budgets collected by the Bureau of Labor in 1901-02, and three times that reported in the budgets collected in 1890-91. In view of the larger expenditures for liquor by unmarried than by married men, this is in substantial agreement with the estimate of $50 per year per adult wage-earner.

We have already noted that the apparent death rates from alcoholism and cirrhosis of the liver among the non-industrial part of the urban population indicate that, prior to prohibition, the members of the business, professional and salaried class were the principal consumers of alcoholic spirits, and apparently also fairly heavy consumers of beer. There is no doubt that the more expensive types of alcoholic beverages, both of spirits and of beer, were consumed almost exclusively by members of this class; and that this class paid higher average prices for its alcoholic beverages than did the wage-earning class. The average adult male in the business, professional and salaried class must therefore have spent far

[9] See Table 61, *supra*, p. 128.

more for alcoholic beverages than the average adult male in the entire population. Again, it is arbitrary, but not unreasonable, to estimate the average expenditure of adult males among this class at twice the average for the entire population, which would amount to $130 per year.

Another estimate of the average expenditure for liquor by members of the business, professional and salaried class may be made by assuming that such expenditures increase with increases in family incomes, as they do in the working class; and assuming also that such expenditures by the lower income groups of the business, professional and salaried class are about the same as by the higher income groups of the wage-earning class.

Among the workingmen's families in New York city studied by Chapin in 1908, the average family income was $810 and the average family expenditure for liquor about $35 per year. The families in the lowest income group among these, with 60 per cent as much income as the average family, spent only about half as much for liquor; while the families in the upper income group, with incomes 40 per cent above the average, spent 70 per cent more for liquor. That is, the expenditure for liquor increased at a rate at least 50 per cent greater than the rate of increase in income. A similar relation between incomes and liquor expenditure is shown in other budget studies.

Since there is not a sharp line of demarkation between the wage-earning class and the business, professional and salaried class, family incomes in the lower income groups of the latter class are probably about the same as in the upper income groups of the wage-earning class, that is, about $1000 to $1200 in 1910; and if liquor expenditures are about the same, they must have been about $50 or $60 per year at that time. The average income of all income-receiving members of the business, professional and salaried class amounted in 1910 to

$1870.[10] This indicates that the average income of families in this class was between $2000 and $2500, since many families have more than one income-recceiver. If we take the lower figure of $2000, in order to avoid the effect upon the average of a few enormously large incomes, and assume that the amount spent on liquor increases at a rate 50 per cent greater than the rate of increase in income, then $120 or $125 is a minimum estimate of the expenditure for liquor in 1910 by the average family of the business, professional and salaried class.

Allocation of the Liquor Bill in 1910 among the Principal Economic Classes. In Table 64 the total liquor bill for the year 1910, estimated in a preceding table at $1,747,000,000, is allocated among the families and unmarried men of the three principal economic classes in the nation, in accordance with these assumptions regarding family and individual expenditures for alcoholic beverages. While it was generally recognized, prior to prohibition, that unmarried men spent more for liquor than married men, how much more is unknown. The estimates of liquor expenditures by the unmarried and the married members of each of the principal economic classes are therefore less reliable that the total spent by each of these classes.

Perhaps some allowance ought also to be made for expenditures by unmarried women not attached to families. Judging from pre-war temperance literature, however, it does not appear probable that this amounted to a great deal, partly because few women used alcoholic beverages, and partly because what they did drink was in many cases paid for by their gentlemen escorts.

There is thus much that is arbitrary about the estimates in Table 64, and this should be borne in mind in connection

[10] Computed from estimates in King, *The National Income and Its Purchasing Power*, pp. 60, 62, 108 and 138.

with the estimates presented therein. However, any allocation of the total liquor bill in 1910 differing substantially from that made in this table would involve assumptions which appear less reasonable than those used in making that allocation.

TABLE 64

ESTIMATED DIVISION OF THE LIQUOR BILL AMONG ECONOMIC CLASSES IN 1910

7,900,000 married wage-earners' families at $40 per year	$316,000,000	
5,300,000 unmarried male wage-earners at $60 per year	318,000,000	
Total by the wage-earning-class		$634,000,000
3,900,000 families of the business, professional and salaried class at $120 per year	468,000,000	
2,600,000 unmarried male members of the business, professional and salaried class at $150 per year	390,000,000	
Total by the business, professional and salaried class		858,000,000
4,100,000 farm families at $25 per year	103,000,000	
2,500,000 unmarried male agricultural workers at $35 per year	87,000,000	
Total by the agricultural class		190,000,000
Balance, representing errors of estimate and expenditures by single women not attached to families		65,000,000
		$1,747,000,000

SOURCES OF DATA:

Number of members of each class: Table 63, *supra*, pp. 131-32.

Rate of expenditure per year: see text, *supra*.

Total liquor bill: Table 50, *supra*, p. 114.

It thus appears probable that prior to the World War the business, professional and salaried class was responsible for about half the total liquor bill, the urban and village wage-earning class for from a third to two-fifths of it, and the farming class for not more than an eighth of it.

CHAPTER VII

Expenditures for Alcoholic Beverages Under Prohibition

The effect of prohibition upon the nation's expenditure for alcoholic beverages can be determined only by comparing the actual liquor bill today with the liquor bill as it would have been without prohibition. Neither of these can be arrived at exactly; even the best possible estimates are only approximations, and subject to considerable error.

THE PROBABLE LIQUOR BILL IN THE ABSENCE OF PROHIBITION

Let us first estimate the amount that the American public would probably be spending for alcoholic beverages without national prohibition. In this estimate no allowance will be made for the effect of the growing movement toward state-wide prohibition, a movement which was making rapid headway during the last decade preceding the adoption of the Eighteenth Amendment. The reason for neglecting this influence is that data are unavailable regarding the degree of enforcement of these laws, and of the extent to which the consumption of alcoholic drinks was actually restricted by them. No state had absolute prohibition prior to 1913, for previous to the passage of the Webb-Kenyon Act any resident could obtain liquor directly from other states.

There is but little statistical evidence regarding the effect of state prohibition laws in the budget studies referred to in the preceding chapter. In Maine, which was the only state covered by these studies to have a prohibition law in 1890, the reported average expenditure for liquor of workingmen's families was much lower than that for the entire country, but not greatly different from that in "wet" states like Rhode Island and New Jersey, and southern states like the Carolinas. In 1901-02, the reported family expenditures for liquor were more than twice as great in "dry" Maine as in "wet" New Jersey.[1] However, the number of family budgets obtained in each state was not large, and there is no assurance that these figures actually represent state-wide conditions.

The 1921-1930 Liquor Bill as Predicted from Conditions of 1911-1914. It has been noted in previous chapters that the consumption of alcoholic drinks was fairly stable during the years from 1911 to 1914, and that the price of liquor at retail had been fairly stable for a quarter of a century. If we assume that the per capita consumption in recent years, without prohibition, would have been the same as in 1911-1914, and if we also assume that the prices of alcoholic liquors would have been the same, and, further, that liquor taxes would have been unchanged, the drink bill since 1921, as it would have been without prohibition, is given in Table 65.

The assumptions underlying the estimates in the above table are readily challenged. We should, for example, expect an increased consumption in recent years on account of larger family and individual incomes, especially during those years in which business activity was above normal. Between 1914 and 1928 the per capita income, after allowing for changes in the price level, increased approximately 25 per cent, and this, on the basis of the relation between

[1] Sixth, Seventh and Eighteenth Annual Reports of the United States Commissioner of Labor.

TABLE 65

THE LIQUOR BILL AS PREDICTED FROM CONDITIONS OF 1911-1914
(millions of dollars)

Year	Spirits	Wine	Beer	Total	Liquor taxes	Net liquor bill
1921	819	149	1,132	2,100	321	1,779
1922	832	152	1,149	2,133	326	1,807
1923	844	154	1,166	2,164	331	1,833
1924	857	156	1,184	2,197	336	1,861
1925	869	158	1,201	2,228	341	1,887
1926	882	161	1,218	2,261	346	1,915
1927	894	163	1,236	2,293	351	1,942
1928	907	165	1,253	2,325	356	1,969
1929	919	168	1,270	2,357	361	1,996
1930	932	170	1,288	2,390	366	2,024

SOURCES OF DATA:
Computed from population estimates and from pre-war per capita expenditures (*cf.* Table 53, *supra*, p. 119).

the size of incomes and the use of liquor shown by workingmen's family budgets, should cause an appreciable increase in expenditures for liquor.[2] To offset this, however we should note that the per capita consumption of spirits was no greater during the 1911-1914 period than during periods of high business activity thirty and forty years earlier, despite the fact that per capita income, in terms of purchasing power, had more than doubled. The consumption of beer had been increasing steadily from 1880 to 1907, but there had been little change after the latter year, both the steady increase up to 1907 and the lack of it after that date being accounted for largely by the number of immigrants from beer-using countries. It is, therefore, by no means certain that the larger per capita incomes since the World War would have meant larger expenditures upon alcoholic beverages.

[2] Mr. Willford I. King estimates the per capita realized income, expressed in 1913 dollars, at $452 in 1928, and at an average of $360 for the years from 1911 to 1914. (King, *The National Income and Its Purchasing Power*, p. 67).

Consideration should also be given to the development of substitutes for alcoholic beverages, and to the psychological conditions associated with drinking.

For many years prior to the adoption of prohibition the trend of per capita consumption of milk and of carbonated beverages, and probably also of fresh fruit juices, had been upward. But the use of these beverages, and also that of coffee, was accelerated after the World War, in part, probably as substitutes for beer.[3] Since it is highly probable that the growing realization of the importance of milk and of the healthfulness of fresh fruit juices would have caused increases in their use, apart from prohibition, it is possible that they might have been substituted for beer to some extent, even without national prohibition.

In the period of intense temperance and prohibition agitation it was recognized that the saloon was the "poor man's club" and that some substitute for its social atmosphere would be necessary. That substitute has come in ways then impossible. Shorter work weeks, longer weekends, automobiles and surfaced highways, have all contributed to more ready contacts with other people. New elements in common life also provide to a considerable degree the same psychological effects as alcohol. The movies and talkies, especially, take their audiences out of the drabness of factory and home, and offer the escape from reality which might otherwise be obtained by drinking. Moreover, larger family incomes, more outdoor life, better food and medical service, improved sanitation, and better transportation facilities have operated to raise the standard of health, to increase the mobility of individuals, and to make wider friendships possible. These changes have tended to make less " compen-

[3] *Cf.* chapter eight, *infra*, pp. 184-92.

sation" necessary, and thus to reduce the craving for alcoholic euphoria as a means of escape from the world of reality. Opposed to these factors are the growing complexity, tension and insecurity of modern life and especially the restrictions of individual opportunity attending the passing of the frontier and the growing concentration of wealth and industrial control, all of which tend to intensify the need for escape from reality and thus to increase the use of alcohol.

There has also been an increase in convivial drinking during the past decade, and in the use of alcoholic beverages by both men and women at social gatherings. This is a general adoption by a large section of society of drinking customs formerly restricted chiefly to the wealthy class. This change in drinking habits may, like other changes in manners and morals after the World War, have been due primarily to the psychological repercussions of that conflict, to the larger incomes received by a considerable section of the population and an accompanying emulation of the wealthier class, and to the cumulative effect of changed attitudes toward religion and former social standards. The increase in convivial drinking may thus not have been primarily due, as is usually supposed, to prohibition, and might have occurred without the Eighteenth Amendment and the Volstead Act.

These various factors are not amenable to statistical measurement, and it is not possible to arrive at reliable conclusions as to their combined effect upon the consumption of alcoholic beverages.

The assumptions that prices of alcoholic beverages and taxes upon them, would, without prohibition, be the same as in 1911-14, may also be challenged. The extreme price fluctuations since 1914 could hardly fail to affect the price of alcoholic drinks, and it is not likely that taxes would have been permitted to revert to the pre-war rates.

The probable effect of changes in the general level of prices upon the prices of alcoholic beverages may be estimated in two ways: (1) by comparing the pre-prohibition prices of materials entering into the production of liquors with the prices of those materials in recent years; and (2) by assuming that prices of alcoholic beverages, aside from taxation, would have followed approximately the courses of other prices.

In Table 66 there are given the prices of the principal materials entering into the production of alcoholic beverages for the year 1914-15 and the year 1928-29.

TABLE 66

PRICES OF PRINCIPAL MATERIALS USED IN PRODUCING ALCOHOLIC BEVERAGES

Material	Average pre-war price (1913-14 unless otherwise stated)	Average prices 1928-29	Weighted ratio of 1928-29 prices to 1913-14 prices
	Materials used in producing beer		
Barley	$ .51 per bushel	$ .65 per bushel	
Rice	3.62 per 100 lbs.	3.92 per 100 lbs.	
Corn	.70 per bushel	.92 per bushel	1.179
Hops	.28 per pound	.26 per pound	
Sugar	.045 per pound	.053 per pound	
	Materials used in producing wine		
Wine grapes	$.30 per lug	$.98 per lug	3.266
	Materials used in producing spirits		
Barley	$.51 per bushel	$.65 per bushel	
Wheat	.89 per bushel	1.29 per bushel	
Rye	.58 per bushel	.95 per bushel	1.360
Corn	.70 per bushel	.92 per bushel	
Oats	.40 per bushel	.44 per bushel	

SOURCES OF DATA:

Cereals and grains: *Yearbook of Agriculture*, 1930. Pre-war price of barley is taken for the year 1914-15.

Hops: Wm. A. Schoenfeld, *A Compendium of Hop Statistics*, p. 11. Pre-war price is for 1915, and post-war for 1928 only.

Sugar: United States Beet Sugar Association.

Wine grapes: Shear, *Economic Status of the Grape Industry*, p. 94, and *Yearbook of Agriculture*, 1930, p. 733. Pre-war price is the 1910-1916 average, estimated from ratio of farm prices during that period to farm prices in 1925 and 1926.

Weighted ratio of 1928-29 to 1913-14 prices: computed from the preceding prices, using as weights the quantities of these materials taken by producers of fermented liquors and of spirits in 1913-14.

In Table 67 the above relative costs of materials are utilized with other data to make comparative estimates of the average cost of production of malt, vinous and distilled liquors in 1914 and in 1929, assuming the use of the same methods with the same efficiency.

TABLE 67

ESTIMATED COMMERCIAL COSTS OF PRODUCING ALCOHOLIC BEVERAGES 1914 AND 1929, TAXES EXCLUDED

Item	Total cost 1914	Cost per barrel 1914	Estimated cost per barrel, 1929
Malt liquors			
Materials	$129,724,000	$1.960	$2.311
Wages	53,244,000	.804	1.834
Other costs and profit	184,170,000	2.782	7.736
Total cost (wholesale value)		$5.546	$11.981
Total cost (wholesale value) per gallon		.179	.386
Vinous liquors		Cost per gallon 1914	Estimated cost per gallon 1929
Materials	$9,489,000	$.211	$.689
Wages	1,194,000	.027	.062
Other costs and profit	5,935,000	.132	.591
Total cost (wholesale value)		$.370	$1.342
Distilled liquors			
Materials	$40,997,000	$.225	$.306
Wages	3,994,000	.022	.050
Other costs and profits	14,527,000	.080	.221
Total cost (wholesale value)		$0.327	$.577

SOURCES OF DATA:

Total cost, 1914: *Census of Manufactures.* Other costs and profit computed from "value added by manufacture" by deducting wages and taxes.

Cost per barrel (beer) and per gallon (wine and spirits), 1914: computed from total cost and from production for fiscal year 1913-14.

Estimated cost per barrel, and per gallon, 1929, materials: computed by applying the price ratios from Table 66 to 1914 cost.

Estimated cost per barrel and per gallon, 1929, wages: computed by multiplying the 1914 cost by 2.281, this being the 1929 to 1914 ratio of average wages in all industries (calculated from total wages and number of wage-earners reported by the Census of Manufactures).

Estimated cost per barrel and per gallon, 1929, other costs and profits: computed on the assumption that the ratio between these costs and wages increased between 1914 and 1929 in the same proportion as in all manufacturing industries.

On the basis of these estimates the wholesale value of beer (taxes excluded) would have been in 1929, without prohibition, more than twice that in 1914, the wholesale value of spirits somewhat less than twice as great, and that of wine more than three and a half times as great. It should be borne in mind, however, that the prices of some of the materials used in producing alcoholic beverages may have been affected by prohibition, and that improvements in methods of production might have reduced costs.

It is thus probably as reasonable to assume that without prohibition the prices of alcoholic beverages would have followed approximately the course of general commodity prices as to assume that they would have changed in accordance with the above estimates. From 1921 to 1929 the price level of commodities at wholesale was approximately 50 per cent above that of the pre-war period, and about 30 per cent below that of 1918.[4]

The Federal tax rates on beer were increased in 1917 from

[4] See the index number of the United States Department of Labor, in the *Monthly Labor Review, Federal Reserve Bulletin,* or the *Survey of Current Business.*

$1.50 per barrel to $3, and in 1919 to $6, and those on spirits from $1.10 per gallon to $3.20 in 1917, and to $6.40 in 1919. The rate on wines, which previously had borne no Federal tax, was made to vary with the alcoholic content, probably averaging about $0.20 per gallon in 1917, the rate for those with an alcoholic content of from 14 to 21 per cent. In view of the fiscal needs of the federal government and the growing temperance sentiment it is highly improbable that the tax rates on alcoholic beverages would have been reduced, without prohibition, to the pre-war rates. On the other hand, there would probably have been some reduction from the 1919 rates, along with other post-war tax reductions. This is especially true in view of the effect of the 1919 rates upon attempts to sell liquor without paying the Federal tax.[5] While it is impossible to tell what would have been the exact post-war taxes upon alcoholic beverages had prohibition not been adopted, it seems likely that they would have been approximately the same as those in force from 1917 to 1919.

On the assumption that the 1917-19 tax rates would have been retained since the War, and the assumption that the prices of liquor, aside from the direct effect of taxes, would have followed the direction of the general price level, it is possible to estimate the probable prices of alcoholic beverages in recent years, had prohibition not been adopted. Four methods of making this estimate for beer and for spirits, and one for wine, are given in Table 68.

In Table 69 an estimate is made of the probable liquor bill from 1921 to 1930, without prohibition, on the assumptions: (1) That the per capita consumption would have been substantially the same as in 1911-14; (2) that

[5] *Cf.* chapter 12, *infra*, pp. 248-54.

retail prices of alcoholic beverages, aside from taxation, would have followed approximately the course of other prices, and (3) that the 1917-19 rates of taxation would have been in force.

TABLE 68

ESTIMATED PROBABLE POST-WAR PRICES OF ALCOHOLIC BEVERAGES HAD PROHIBITION NOT BEEN ADOPTED

Method 1	Beer per barrel	Spirits per gallon	Wine per gallon
Pre-war wholesale price	$7.00	$1.34	
Pre-war wholesale price, less tax	5.50	.24	
Pre-war wholesale price, less tax, raised 50 per cent.	8.25	.36	
1917-19 tax, to be added	3.00	3.20	
Estimated post-war wholesale price	11.25	3.56	
Pre-war retail price	15.00	5.00	
Ratio pre-war retail to wholesale price	2.5	3.73	
Estimated post-war retail price, assuming pre-war ratio to wholesale price	28.13	13.28	
Method 2			
1918 wholesale price	10.50	5.46	
1918 wholesale price, less tax	7.50	2.26	
1918 wholesale price, less tax, reduced 30 per cent	5.25	1.58	
Estimated post-war wholesale price, tax added	8.25	4.78	
Estimated post-war retail price, assuming pre-war ratio to wholesale price	20.63	17.83	
Method 3			
Pre-war retail price	15.00	5.00	$2.00
Pre-war retail price, less tax	13.50	3.90	2.00
Pre-war retail price, less tax, raised 50 per cent	20.25	5.85	3.00
Estimated post-war retail price, including 1917-19 rate of tax	23.25	9.05	3.20
Method 4			
Estimated 1929 cost of production, tax omitted (*cf.* Table 67)	11.98	.58	1.34

Estimated post-war wholesale price, including 1917-19 rate of tax	14.98	3.78	1.54
Estimated post-war retail price, assuming pre-war ratio to wholesale price	37.45	14.10	
Final Estimate			
Estimated post-war retail price, average of the four methods	27.37	13.57	
Ratio to pre-war retail price	1.8	2.7	1.6
Estimated post-war per capita expenditures for liquor	$18.83	$20.44	$2.21

Sources of Data:

Pre-war and 1918 wholesale prices: Table 48, *supra*, p. 112.
Pre-war retail prices: Table 49, *supra*, p. 113.
Rates of taxation: Table 114, *supra*, p. 248.
Estimated post-war per capita expenditures: average annual expenditures in 1911-1914 (Table 53, *supra*, p. 119) adjusted by ratio of estimated post-war to pre-war retail prices.

TABLE 69

The 1921-1930 Liquor Bill as Predicted from 1911-14 Consumption, 1921-29 Price Level, and 1917-19 Rates of Taxation
(millions of dollars)

Year	Spirits	Wine	Beer	Total	Liquor taxes	Net liquor bill
1921	2,212	239	2,037	4,488	775	3,713
1922	2,245	243	2,069	4,557	787	3,770
1923	2,279	246	2,100	4,625	799	3,826
1924	2,313	250	2,131	4,694	811	3,883
1925	2,347	254	2,162	4,763	823	3,940
1926	2,381	257	2,193	4,831	835	3,996
1927	2,415	261	2,225	4,901	847	4,054
1928	2,449	265	2,256	4,970	859	4,111
1929	2,483	268	2,287	5,038	871	4,167
1930	2,516	272	2,318	5,106	883	4,223

Sources of Data:

Spirits, wine and beer: computed from population estimates and estimated post-war per capita expenditures (Table 68).

Liquor taxes: estimated liquor taxes at 1911-14 rates (*cf.* Table 65, *supra*, p. 141) plus $4.20 per capita increase. This per capita increase is obtained by applying the differences between the pre-war and the 1917-19 rates of taxation to the 1911-14 average per capita consumption (*cf.* Table 2, *supra*, p. 26, and Table 114, *infra*, p. 248).

It should be noted that in the estimates in the above table no allowance has been made for reduced consumption on account of relatively higher prices (due to tax increases relatively greater than the increase in the general price level), nor for the effects of business fluctuations. Since business activity in 1911-14 averaged slightly above normal, both these factors tend to make the estimates in Table 69 maximum estimates, especially during the years of business depression, 1921, 1927 and 1930.

The 1921-1930 Liquor Bill as Predicted from the Trend in the Proportion of the National Income Spent on Liquor. Another method of estimating the probable expenditure upon alcoholic beverages in recent years, under the conditions of sale prevailing before the World War, is to observe the trend during a long period of years in the percentage of the national income spent for drink. That percentage, as we have already noted, declined constantly from 1890 to 1910 at a rate of approximately 5 per cent per decade. From 1910 to 1914 there was no substantial change in this percentage, but in 1915 it dropped a whole per cent below the 1910 percentage.[6] These contrary tendencies make it difficult to assume either that, without war-time restrictions and prohibition, the trend of percentage of the national income spent for drink would have continued downward, or that it would have tended to flatten out. If we make the former assumption, that without national prohibition the twenty-year trend would have been maintained, and assume, further, that the same percentage of the national income would have been paid out in liquor taxes, we have the estimates of post-war expenditures for liquor given in Table 70. In view of the possibility that the curve of trend of the percentage of the national income spent for liquor would have tended to flatten out, and the probability that taxes

[6] See Table 51, *supra*, p. 99.

would have been higher than in pre-war times, these may be considered minimum estimates of the probable expenditures for alcoholic drinks in recent years, had prohibition not been adopted. It may also be noted that this method of estimating probable post-war liquor expenditures automatically makes allowances for fluctuations in business activity, since such fluctuations are reflected in the national income.

TABLE 70

ESTIMATED PROBABLE NATIONAL EXPENDITURE FOR ALCOHOLIC BEVERAGES 1920 TO 1930, WITHOUT NATIONAL PROHIBITION

Year	National income (millions of dollars)	Probable per cent of the national income spent for liquor: Including taxes	Probable per cent of the national income spent for liquor: Excluding taxes	Probable total liquor bill (millions of dollars)	Probable net liquor bill (taxes excluded) (millions of dollars)
1920	73,999	4.6	3.7	3,404	2,738
1921	66,371	4.5	3.6	2,987	2,389
1922	65,925	4.4	3.5	2,901	2,307
1923	74,337	4.3	3.4	3,196	2,527
1924	77,135	4.2	3.3	3,240	2,545
1925	81,931	4.1	3.2	3,359	2,622
1926	85,548	4.0	3.1	3,422	2,652
1927	88,205	3.9	3.0	3,440	2,646
1928	89,419	3.8	2.9	3,398	2,593
1929	93,500	3.7	2.8	3,460	2,618
1930	78,000	3.6	2.7	2,808	2,106

SOURCES OF DATA:

National income: 1920-1928. King, *The National Income and Its Purchasing Power*, p. 74; 1929-30, rough estimate made from the preceding by considering changes in business activity, employment, earnings and dividends.

Probable per cent. of national income spent for liquor: continuation of the trend shown in Table 51, *supra*, p. 115.

THE ACTUAL LIQUOR BILL UNDER PROHIBITION

There is no authentic information available regarding the actual expenditure of the nation upon alcoholic beverages since the adoption of prohibition. The best method of making an estimate of this expenditure is the same as that used in estimating the pre-prohibition liquor bill, namely:

applying estimated average retail prices to estimates of the consumption of alcoholic beverages.

The Prices of Alcoholic Beverages. Varying degrees of enforcement, varying conditions of production and sale and the absence of openly published quotations make it very difficult to estimate with confidence the average or typical prices of alcoholic beverages since the adoption of prohibition. There are available, however, three collections of price quotations in various parts of the United States in 1929 and 1930.

One of these collections was published in December, 1929. Most of these prices are given in Table 71, liquors of presumably similar quality being grouped together. Aside from the prices given in this table, beer was quoted in Chicago at $85 per barrel, champagne in New York at $90 to $135 a case, cognac in New York at $11 to $15 a quart, and cognac in New Orleans at $4.50 to $5 a quart.

TABLE 71

PRICES OF ALCOHOLIC BEVERAGES IN FOURTEEN CITIES IN DECEMBER, 1929
(dollars per quart)

City	Wines, cordials and brandy	Bourbon, Scotch, Tequila and whisky	Gin, rye rum and Bourbon	Synthetic gin, corn, moonshine and alcohol
Boston	6¼	5½-7	4 -7	
New York	3 -6	4½-12	7	1 -2½
Washington		10-12	3⅛-6	
Buffalo			6	
Chicago		15-20		2½-3¾
Twin Cities		9		3¾-4
Des Moines			2½	
Seattle		7	5	3
Butte	1½	8		3
San Francisco	⅝-3	7½-9½	1¼-5	2 -3
Los Angeles	¾-2½	7 -12	3½	
Dallas		6½-10		4
New Orleans		5	4½-5	
Memphis				2
Average	$3.14	$8.93	$4.66	$2.91

SOURCE OF DATA:

The Atlanta Journal, December 19, 1929. Prices quoted per case, per gallon, per Imperial quart, per short quart, per "fifth," and per pint have all been converted to prices per quart. In only one case, Los Angeles, is Bourbon classed with gin, rye and rum, on account of a price much below that of Scotch, whereas in other cities there is little difference between these two liquors. Quotations in any city between the ranges given are omitted.

TABLE 72

PRICES OF ALCOHOLIC BEVERAGES AT VARIOUS PLACES AND DATES, 1926 TO 1930

	Beer		Spirits		
Place	Per glass	Per quart	Domestic per quart	Imported per quart	Kind of spirits
Burlington, Vt.				$6-$10	whisky
New York City		$2		8	whisky
Mohawk Co., N. Y.			$5		brandy
Wilkes-Barre, Pa.			1¼		corn
Buffalo	$.10			5	Scotch or rye
Philadelphia	.10-.15		2		gin
Virginia			2-5		corn
West Virginia			4-5		corn
South Carolina			¾-2		corn
" "				5	Scotch or rye
Atlanta			1¼-4		corn
Georgia (rural)			½		corn
South Bend, Ind.			4-8		brandy and whisky
Detroit		1		5-6	whisky
Ecorse, Mich.		.20-.60		3-3¾	whisky
Chicago	.25	1		8½-10	Bourbon
Wichita, Kans.			8		whisky
New Mexico			1½-3		rye
" "				5-6	Bourbon
San Francisco	.25-.50			5½-8	Scotch and rye (by the drink)
Average		$1.10	$3.26	$6.21	

SOURCES OF DATA:

Burlington, New York City, Mohawk Co., Buffalo, Philadelphia, South Carolina, South Bend, Detroit, and New Mexico: articles by John P. Kennedy, William G. Shepherd, and others, in *Collier's*, October 27, 1928, and May 4, May 18, and June 1, 1929.

New York and Ecorse: New York Times Magazine, July 27, 1930, and July 14, 1929.

West Virginia: Francis Pridemore, in *The North American Review*, July, 1929.

Georgia (rural): Walter W. Liggett, in *Plain Talk*, May, 1930.

Wichita: *Wichita Eagle*, January 17, 1926.

Wilkes-Barre, Virginia and Atlanta: prices quoted to the author in 1929 and 1930.

Quotations by the case, gallon or pint have been converted to the price per quart.

The second set of price quotations on alcoholic beverages is a collection made by the author from newspaper and magazine articles and from prices quoted him personally, mostly in 1929 and 1930. These quotations are given in Table 72.[7]

The third collection of price quotations was made in July, 1930, and is more extensive than either of the two given above. In order to obtain the best possible sample of liquor prices throughout the country, the author sent a questionnaire to the editors of 130 newspapers in the leading cities, asking if a reporter familiar with conditions could give prevailing quotations in his city. Replies were received from 33 cities, for some of which the data given were rather meagre, but for others quite complete. These quotations are given in Tables 73 to 76 in the form of price ranges for domestic and "imported" beer, wine and spirits. Due to the varying qualities of liquors sold under the same name, and the varying sorts of liquors sold in different parts of the country, it has not been practicable to compute average prices of specific varieties.

Quotations were received in terms of many quantity

[7] No systematic effort has been made to discover price quotations in magazines and newspapers. Were this to be done the list could doubtless be much extended, but it is not believed the average prices thus obtained would vary greatly from those given in Tables 71 to 76.

TABLE 73

PRICES OF ALCOHOLIC BEVERAGES IN JULY, 1930, IN THE UNITED STATES
(cents per glass or drink)

City	Beer	Wine	Spirits
New Bedford	5		15-50
Worcester			15-75
Schenectady	15	25	50
New York	15-50	10-50	25-100
Newark	10-40	10-25	10-100
Baltimore	15-25		15-75
Washington	25-35		25-50
Richmond			25
Charleston			25-50
Miami			50
Atlanta		10-25	15-25
New Orleans		25	25-50
Detroit	25	20	25-50
Flint	25-50	25	25-50
Cincinnati			50
Columbus		10	
Pittsburgh	25	50	15-50
Youngstown	25		10-25
Fort Wayne	20-25	25-50	25-100
Chicago	25	25-50	25-75
St. Paul	25-35		
Oklahoma City			50
Dallas	25		50
Houston			25-50
San Francisco		25-35	25-50

SOURCE OF DATA: newspaper reporters in the various cities.

units: bottles of varying size, pints, quarts, fifths, Imperial quarts, gallons, and cases of varying size, as well as by the glass and the drink. Except for prices per glass or drink, all of these quotations have been reduced to prices per quart. Quarts have been assumed to be United States standard quarts, though some of them are probably short quarts of 25 or 26 ounces. Bottles with the size not specified have been assumed to hold one quart, but some of them, especially in the case of beer, are probably only

TABLE 74

PRICES OF BEER IN JULY, 1930, IN AMERICAN CITIES
(dollars per quart)

City	"Imported"	Domestic
New Bedford	1.00*	
Worcester	1.25-2.00	.15-.20
Schenectady	1.25-1.50*	.25-.40
New York—1	1.10-2.00*	.30
New York—2	.67-1.50	
New York—3		.33-.83
Newark	2.00 up	.50
Baltimore	.25*	.13*
Washington		.40
Charleston		.25*
Jacksonville	.50*	.08*
Miami	1.00*	.25*
Atlanta	.50-.67*	.08-.25*
New Orleans		.25*
Louisville	1.50	.40-1.00
Detroit	.50-.67*	.30
Flint	.50-.67*	.50*
Cincinnati		.40-.50
Columbus	1.00	.25-.50
Pittsburgh	.50	.40
Youngstown	1.00-1.50	.25-.75
Toledo		.15-.75*
Fort Wayne	1.00-1.50	.12-.25
Chicago	.75-1.00*	.45-.50*
St. Paul		.35-1.00
Tulsa		.20-.35*
Oklahoma City		.50-.70
Dallas		.21*
Houston		.21-1.00
San Francisco		.75-1.00*
Spokane	2.00	
Average	1.09	.40

SOURCE OF DATA: newspaper reporters in the various cities. Prices marked (*) are per bottle of unspecified size. Many of these are probably pint or 12-ounce bottles, though assumed to be quarts in computing the average. The three quotations in New York City are from reporters on three newspapers.

TABLE 75

PRICES OF WINE IN AMERICAN CITIES IN JULY, 1930
(dollars per quart)

City	"Imported"	Domestic
Worcester		.75-4.00
Schenectady	2.50-6.00	.50-1.25
New York—1	7.50-12.00*	1.25-5.00
New York—2		.75-1.25
New York—3	5.00-30.00*	
Newark	3.50-10.00	.75-3.50
Baltimore	4.00	1.00-3.00
Richmond		3.00
Charlotte		1.00
Charleston	5.50-6.67	
Jacksonville	5.00-6.00	2.00
Miami	3.00-7.00	1.00-2.00
Atlanta	2.00-3.00	.50
New Orleans		3.00
Louisville	2.50-4.00	1.00-3.75
Detroit	8.33-10.00	1.25
Flint	3.50	
Columbus		1.00
Pittsburg	5.50-6.00	.75
Youngstown		.60-2.00
Toledo	18.00*	
Fort Wayne		.50-10.00
Chicago	Up to 25.00*	.75-2.50
St. Paul		1.00
Tulsa		5.00-7.50
Oklahoma City		.75-1.00
Houston		1.25
San Francisco	7.50-10.00	1.00
Average	$5.37	$1.78

SOURCE OF DATA: newspaper reporters in the various cities. Prices marked (*) are for champagne and not included in the average.

pint or 12-ounce bottles. These assumptions tend to make the quotations given in the table lower than they are in reality. On the other hand, averages for all cities have been computed from the mid-points of the range for each

TABLE 76

PRICES OF BEVERAGE SPIRITS IN AMERICAN CITIES IN JULY, 1930
(dollars per quart)

City	"Imported"	Domestic
New Bedford	5.00- 8.00	
Worcester		2.00-12.00
Schenectady	6.00-10.00	
New York—1	6.00-10.00	1.66- 3.75
New York—2	5.50-15.00	3.33- 6.00
New York—3		2.00- 8.33
Newark	2.00-10.00	2.00- 5.00
Baltimore	8.33	1.50- 6.00
Washington		3.00- 8.00
Richmond	6.67-10.00	1.25- 3.00
Charlotte	5.00-10.00	1.25- 4.00
Charleston	4.00- 4.50	.62- .75
Jacksonville	5.00	.50- 3.00
Miami	4.00- 5.00	1.00
Atlanta	7.00- 9.00	1.50- 3.00
New Orleans		4.00- 8.00
Louisville	6.00-10.00	1.25- 8.00
Detroit	6.00- 8.00	4.00- 8.00
Flint	7.00- 8.00	2.00 up
Columbus	4.00-12.00	4.00- 4.75
Pittsburgh	8.33-10.00	1.00-16.66
Youngstown	7.00-13.00	1.50- 6.67
Toledo	5.50	2.00- 5.50
Fort Wayne	6.66-14.00	.50-11.00
Chicago	10.00-13.00	2.00-10.00
St. Paul		1.00-12.00
Des Moines	8.33-11.67	
Wichita	6.25	3.00
Tulsa	15.00	5.00
Oklahoma City	10.00-14.00	2.00- 4.00
Dallas	10.00-14.00	3.00- 6.00
Houston	3.00- 8.00	2.00
San Francisco	6.25	1.00- 5.00
Spokane		2.50- 8.33
Average	$8.17	$4.01

SOURCE OF DATA: newspaper reporters in the various cities.

city, and since it is probable that more liquor is sold at prices in the lower half of the price range than at prices in the upper half, this tends to raise the computed averages above the true averages.[8] The width of the price range in many cities is notable, and is due partly to widely varying qualities of liquor, partly to the class of patrons making the purchases, and partly to the varying quantity units in which purchases are made.

In Table 77 the price averages from the three sets of quotations are brought together so that they can be readily compared. It may be noted that the agreement is remarkably close, considering the differences in their scope and the methods of collecting them. Since the set collected by the author from newspaper reporters is the most extensive, it will be used for computing, along with estimates of consumption, the national expenditure on alcoholic beverages in recent years. For this purpose we need to obtain an average of the "imported" and domestic spirits. Were the quotations of "imported" spirits those of genuinely imported liquor, we would omit them altogether, since only a small part of the liquor consumed in the United States is actually imported. A number of the reporters sending in quotations stated that the prices given for "imported" liquor were for domestic liquor sold as imported, or of imported liquor "cut" with domestic alcohol. Undoubtedly a considerable quantity of liquor is sold at these "imported" prices, but any estimate of the relative quantity sold thus is arbitrary. To assume that one-tenth of the total is sold at the "imported" prices is, we believe, conservative, and the weighted average in the last column of Table 77 is computed on this basis.

[8] In three cases, domestic wine in Fort Wayne and Tulsa and domestic spirits in Pittsburgh, the highest price has been reduced to that given for other cities, so as to avoid the inclusion in the average of abnormally high prices.

TABLE 77

AVERAGE PRICES OF ALCOHOLIC BEVERAGES IN THE UNITED STATES
1929-1930
(dollars per quart)

	Quotations collected by the New York Times	Quotations mostly from newspapers and journals	Quotations collected from newspaper reporters	Weighted average of quotations from reporters
"Imported" beer		1.10	1.09	
Domestic beer			.40	.47
"Imported" wine			5.37	
Domestic wine	3.14		1.78	2.14
"Imported" spirits	8.93	6.21	8.17	
Domestic spirits	3.79	3.26	4.01	4.43

SOURCES OF DATA:

Averages of sets of quotations: Tables 71-76, *supra*, pp. 152-58. The most expensive class of spirits in Table 71 is assumed to be the same as the "imported" spirits in the other sets of quotations; and the other two classes considered comparable to the domestic spirits of the other sets.

Weighted average of quotations from newspaper reporters: computed from the preceding column by giving "imported" and domestic liquors weights of 1 and 9, respectively.

To estimate annual expenditures on alcoholic beverages we ought to have prices such as the above for each year since the adoption of prohibition, since there have undoubtedly been considerable price changes from time to time. However, it has not seemed feasible at the present time to collect any extensive series of prices for several years past; and only one series of price quotations covering the entire prohibition period has come to the author's attention. This series is the index number of gin in Washington published by the Crusaders. No method is available of testing the reliability of this index, nor of its applicability to other parts of the country, nor to other varieties of alcoholic liquor. Judged, however, in the light of the known relation between supply and price, it does not appear to be an unreasonable estimate of the probable price changes of alcoholic beverages generally since 1920.

In Table 78 this index number is given, together with the weighted average price of liquors in 1930 adjusted by it for each of the preceding years.

TABLE 78

INDEX OF PRICE OF GIN IN WASHINGTON AND ADJUSTED PRICES OF ALCOHOLIC BEVERAGES IN THE UNITED STATES

Year	Index of price of gin in Washington	Adjusted estimate of prices of alcoholic beverages per gallon		
		Spirits	Wine	Beer
1920	315	$10.73	$5.19	$1.14
1921	220	7.50	3.62	.80
1922	190	6.47	3.13	.69
1923	150	5.11	2.47	.54
1924	150	5.11	2.47	.54
1925	150	5.11	2.47	.54
1926	140	4.77	2.30	.51
1927	130	4.43	2.14	.47
1928	150	5.11	2.47	.54
1929	140	4.77	2.30	.51
1930	130	4.43	2.14	.47

SOURCES OF DATA:

Index of price of gin: read from chart distributed by The Crusaders, Washington, D. C. (released for publication April 12, 1931).

Adjusted estimate of prices of alcoholic beverages: 1930 price adjusted in accordance with the index of price of gin.

Retail prices, however, must be modified to take account of liquors produced at home at low cost. At home and in small stills, with little or no wages and little overhead, alcoholic beverages can be produced at lower costs than those estimated in Table 67. The total cost of materials for making five gallons of beer, using hop-flavored malt syrup, yeast, and sugar or sugar and syrup, and including the cost of bottle caps, but not bottles, all purchased at retail, was in 1929 about $1.50. This is 30 cents a gallon.

If wine grapes were purchased at auction in the autumn of 1929 at the average price of $1.17 per lug of about

26 pounds net weight, and a yield of 1.8 gallons per lug obtained, the cost of wine would have been 65 cents per gallon.[9] With grapes purchased at retail, the cost may be estimated at about a dollar a gallon.

Ordinary sugar is probably one of the most expensive, but also one of the most common, materials used in the production of distilled spirits at home and in small stills. At an average retail price of 6.66 cents per pound in 1929 and a yield of 12 gallons, proof strength, per 100 pounds, this cost is 56 cents a gallon.[10] The total cost, where the product is for use at home and for sale to personal friends, and labor involved is not valued highly, can hardly be over a dollar a gallon, especially since most home-made spirits probably contain less alcohol than proof spirits.

The approximate cost of production of beverage spirits may also be estimated from the cost of producing denatured alcohol. The average wholesale price of denatured alcohol No. 5 was 36.6 cents a gallon in 1913, and since 1921 has varied from this price to 57.8 cents a gallon.[11] This generally sells at retail for use in automobiles as an anti-freeze at not over a dollar a gallon, and is 188 proof, containing nearly twice as much alcohol as proof spirits, and probably more than twice as much as most beverage spirits.

In 1930 and 1931 the cost of producing all kinds of

[9] This average price is that of four varieties, Carignane, Mission, Petite Sirah, and Zinfandel, as reported in the *Yearbook of Agriculture*, 1930, p. 733. For the yield, see footnote to Table 8, *supra*, p. 37.

[10] The average retail price of sugar has been computed from the monthly prices reported in the *Monthly Labor Review*. For the yield, see footnote to Table 21, *supra*, p. 62.

[11] *Statistical Abstract of the United States*, 1924, p. 306, and 1930, p. 326.

alcoholic beverages was probably less than in 1929, because of price declines. During most of the period since 1921 prices of materials have not been higher than in 1929, except for grapes, which were sold at $2.26 a lug in 1921, and declined gradually to 98 cents in 1928, and ordinary sugar, which sold for more than 6 cents at wholesale most of the time from 1921 to 1924, and as high as 9.8 cents a pound during a part of 1923. These price fluctuations have not been sufficient to make the average cost of production of alcoholic beverages, at any time since the price deflation of 1920, vary significantly from the estimates given in the preceding pages for 1929, with the exception of wine, which in 1921 cost about twice as much as in 1929.

It is not possible to make a reliable estimate of the proportion of alcoholic beverages consumed which is made at home and the proportion purchased from speakeasies and bootleggers. Doubtless a larger part of the wine used is produced at home than of beer or of spirits, because of the ease with which it is made. The author's own guess would be that the quantity of wine made at home is about equal to that sold through speakeasies and bootleggers; but it is better to under-estimate than over-estimate present day expenditures on liquor, and so we will assume, in the tables that follow, that three-fourths of it are made at home or sold to friends at the approximate cost, and only one-fourth purchased at prevailing retail prices.

During the early years of prohibition, this proportion between home and commercial production may also have been true of beer. In recent years, however, the commercial production of beer appears to be extensive. The President of the Chicago Chamber of Commerce estimates that in Cook County the sales of beer at joints served by professional bootleggers amount to 25 million pints weekly.

This is at the rate of more than 20 gallons per capita per year, and accounts for nearly 10 per cent of the entire consumption of the nation at the present time, as estimated in Chapter II.[12] Probably much more than half of the total beer consumption is now produced commercially, so that if we assume that half of it is produced at home, our estimate of expenditures will be conservative.

In the case of spirits, the proportion produced for sale is probably still larger than in the case of beer, and consequently we are assuming that only one-fourth of the total is produced at home, and three-fourths sold at average prices. Before applying the estimated average cost to the estimates of consumption given in the preceding chapter, an adjustment must be made for the difference between the alcoholic content of liquors as sold and that of proof spirits. In pre-war times the average alcoholic content of gin was placed at 30 per cent, of American common whisky at 35 per cent, of Scotch whisky at 40 per cent, and of the best American whisky at 43 per cent.[13] There is no reason, so far as the author knows, for assuming that liquors are stronger at the present time, and since the lower the actual alcoholic content the higher the price in terms of proof spirits, it makes for conservatism in estimating liquor expenditures to assume that spirits today average 40 per cent alcohol, when they quite likely average somewhat less than this.

The estimate of the average cost to users of alcoholic beverages, based on these assumptions, is given in Table 79.

The preciseness of these estimates, given to the exact cent, is of course a consequence of the method of computation, and has no real significance. It is better, then,

[12] Robert Isham Randolph, *The New York Times*, February 27, 1930; and Table 6, *supra*, p. 33.

[13] Francis Peabody, *The Liquor Problem* (Boston, 1905), p. 18.

TABLE 79

ESTIMATED AVERAGE COST TO USERS OF ALCOHOLIC BEVERAGES, 1929-1930

	Estimated average retail price per gallon	Estimated home cost of production per gallon	Estimated percentage produced at home	Estimated average cost cost to users per gallon
Beer	$1.88	$0.30	50	$1.09
Wine	8.56	1.00	75	2.89
Spirits (proof strength).	22.15	1.00	25	16.86

SOURCES OF DATA:

Estimated average retail price: Table 77, *supra*, p. 160. Figures converted from price per quart to price per gallon, and that of spirits from an assumed average strength of 40 per cent alcohol to 50 per cent, by volume.

Estimated home cost of production: *supra*, pp. 161-62.

Estimated percentage produced at home: see text, *supra*.

in estimates of expenditures for liquor, to reduce them to round numbers. While it would be as reasonable to revise them upward to round numbers as to reduce them, the latter will give us a more conservative estimate of expenditures. We will consider, then, the cost of beer to the user to be $1 per gallon, that of wine $2.50 and that of spirits $16.

The Liquor Bill Under Prohibition. As suggested above, it seems more reasonable, in view of the relative supplies of liquor, to suppose that liquor prices have followed a course such as is indicated by the adjusted prices in Table 78 than that the 1930 prices have prevailed throughout the period since the adoption of prohibition. On the other hand, probably a larger part of the liquor consumed was produced at home in the early days of prohibition than in more recent years. It is better, therefore, in estimating the total liquor bill of the nation, since 1920, to assume that the figures arrived at in Table 79 represent each year the average cost of liquor than to revise them upward.

Using then, the round figures of average cost to users of $1 per gallon for beer, $2.50 per gallon for wine and

$16 per gallon for proof spirits, and the estimates of consumption from Chapter II, we have the estimates of the annual liquor bill since prohibition given in Table 80.[14]

TABLE 80

ESTIMATED EXPENDITURES PER CAPITA UPON ALCOHOLIC BEVERAGES, 1921-1930

Year	Spirits	Wine	Beer	Total
1921	$4.80	$1.10	$1.26	$7.16
1922	24.64	1.43	1.71	27.78
1923	31.36	2.38	2.24	35.98
1924	28.00	2.25	2.84	33.09
1925	28.80	2.15	3.46	34.41
1926	30.56	2.63	4.21	37.40
1927	24.48	2.70	5.03	32.21
1928	28.00	2.68	6.05	36.73
1929	29.76	2.23	7.11	39.10
1930	21.28	2.18	6.90	30.36

SOURCES OF DATA: computed from estimate of consumption, Table 29, *supra*, p. 71, at $16.00 per gallon for spirits, $2.50 per gallon for wine, and $1.00 per gallon for beer.

In Table 81 the total expenditure on liquor for the entire nation, estimated on the same basis, is given for the period since 1920.

In view of the arbitrary character of the assumptions made in these estimates as to the portions of alcoholic beverages made at home and the portions purchased from speakeasies and bootleggers, it may be worthwhile to note what the liquor bill would have been had it all been purchased at the retail prices reported in July, 1930. Applying these prices to the estimates of consumption, the resulting estimates of expenditures upon beer rise from $353,000,000 in 1922 to $1,624,000,000 in 1929; upon wine from $539,000,000 in 1922 to

[14] In these computations, the estimates of consumption used are those derived from the sources of production. This is because these estimates appear to be more reliable, in respect to the consumption of each of the three types of alcoholic beverages, than those obtained from death rates from alcoholism and cirrhosis of the liver, or from arrests for drunkenness.

TABLE 81

ESTIMATED TOTAL EXPENDITURES ON ALCOHOLIC BEVERAGES IN THE UNITED STATES, 1921-1930
(millions of dollars)

Year	Spirits	Wine	Beer	Total
1921	528	120	136	784
1922	2,704	158	188	3,050
1923	3,504	265	250	4,019
1924	3,168	255	321	3,744
1925	3,312	248	398	3,958
1926	3,568	305	490	4,363
1927	2,896	320	595	3,811
1928	3,360	320	726	4,406
1929	3,616	270	864	4,750
1930	2,624	268	850	3,742

SOURCES OF DATA: same as Table 80.

$924,000,000 in 1929; and upon spirits from $3,743,000,000 in 1922 to $5,006,000,000 in 1929. The total liquor bill would have been $4,635,000,000 in 1922 and $7,554,000,000 in 1929. If, on the other hand, all the liquor consumed since prohibition had been produced at home at the costs estimated above, the total liquor bill would have been only $288,000,000 in 1922 and $583,000,000 in 1929.[15]

These estimates may be considered maximum and minimum limits to liquor expenditures under prohibition, with no probability that the actual expenditures were close to either limit. It is possible, however, that the actual liquor bill may have departed considerably from the estimates given in Table 81. If, for example, it is assumed that only one-fourth of the wine and beer, as well as of spirits, is produced at home, the estimate of expenditure for liquor in 1929 would be about $900,000,000 greater than the figure given in the table; while if it is assumed that only half of the spirits

[15] Computed from estimates of retail prices and of home costs given in Table 79, and estimates of the consumption of alcoholic beverages, given in Table 29, *supra*, p. 71.

is purchased at the average reported retail price and the rest obtained at the home cost of production, the estimate of the total liquor bill in 1929 would be about a billion dollars less than that given in Table 81. The differences in other years would be somewhat less than this.

THE EFFECT OF PROHIBITION UPON EXPENDITURES FOR LIQUOR

These estimates of liquor expenditure under prohibition may be compared with the estimates of probable expenditure had there been a post-war reversion to the conditions of sale of 1911-1914, or to those conditions with somewhat higher taxation. This comparison is made in Table 82.

TABLE 82

THE EFFECT OF PROHIBITION UPON THE LIQUOR BILL

(millions of dollars)

	Estimated probable expenditure for liquor without prohibition				Estimated actual expenditure with prohibition
	Total		Net		
Year	Maximum	Minimum	Maximum	Minimum	
1921	4,488	2,987	3,713	2,389	784
1922	4,557	2,901	3,770	2,307	3,050
1923	4,625	3,196	3,826	2,527	4,019
1924	4,694	3,240	3,883	2,545	3,744
1925	4,763	3,359	3,940	2,622	3,958
1926	4,831	3,422	3,996	2,652	4,363
1927	4,901	3,440	4,054	2,646	3,811
1928	4,970	3,398	4,111	2,593	4,406
1929	5,038	3,460	4,167	2,618	4,750
1930	5,106	2,808	4,223	2,106	3,742

Probable expenditure without prohibition: maximum, Table 69, *supra*, p. 149; minimum, Table 70, *supra*, p. 151. "Net" expenditures are with liquor taxes deducted.

Estimated actual expenditure: Table 81, *supra*, p. 167.

The most striking feature about this comparison is the similarity, since 1922, between the estimated probable expenditure for liquor without prohibition and the estimated actual expenditure with prohibition. Without prohibition the average annual liquor bill in recent years would probably have been between three and five billion dollars, most likely about four billion dollars (assuming the two estimates to have equal validity); while the estimated actual expenditure has also been about four billion dollars, rising from three billion dollars in 1922 to four and three-fourths billions in 1929. Since 1923 the estimated actual expenditure has been very close to the maximum estimate, and far beyond the minimum estimate, of the net liquor bill without prohibition.

The conclusion to which these estimates point is that prohibition, except for the first three years, has not substantially affected the total expenditure of the nation for alcoholic drinks. Since, however, the alcoholic beverage industry no longer contributes to the support of government, there has been a net loss to consumers and taxpayers of approximately the amount of the taxes which, without prohibition, would have been collected from the industry.

The actual liquor expenditure estimated in Table 82 for 1921 is only about a fourth of the estimated probable expenditure without prohibition. This estimate is probably considerably too low, since the estimate of consumption derived from sources of production is too low for that year.[16] Nevertheless, there was probably a release of purchasing power in that year of about two billion dollars. In 1920 and the latter half of 1919, for which no estimate of actual liquor expenditure has been made, this release may have been still greater.

A considerable change has occurred in the relative expenditure on spirits and beer. In 1911-1914 the amount spent for beer was about 40 per cent greater than that spent for spirits. On the assumption of a greater increase

[16] *Cf. supra*, p. 105.

in taxes on spirits than on beer, we have estimated that in recent years there would have been, without prohibition, little difference between the amount spent for spirits and that spent for beer, each being somewhat over two billion dollars in years of business prosperity. Prohibition has raised the amount spent for spirits to three or three and a half billion dollars, and reduced that for beer to less than a billion dollars. The amount spent for beer, however, is growing, having increased, according to the estimates, from a quarter of a billion dollars in 1923 to more than four-fifths of a billion in 1929.

Upon the expenditure for wine prohibition appears to have had little effect, both the estimated probable expenditure without prohibition and the estimated actual expenditure with prohibition being from a quarter to a third of a billion dollars per year.

TABLE 83

THE EFFECT OF PROHIBITION UPON THE AMOUNT SPENT FOR SPIRITS, FOR WINE AND FOR BEER

(millions of dollars)

Year	Probable maximum expenditure without prohibition			Estimated actual expenditure		
	Spirits	Wine	Beer	Spirits	Wine	Beer
1921	2,212	239	2,307	528	120	136
1922	2,245	243	2,069	2,704	158	188
1923	2,279	246	2,100	3,504	265	250
1924	2,313	250	2,131	3,168	255	321
1925	2,347	254	2,162	3,312	248	398
1926	2,381	257	2,193	3,568	305	490
1927	2,415	261	2,225	2,896	320	595
1928	2,449	265	2,256	3,360	320	726
1929	2,483	268	2,287	3,616	270	864
1930	2,516	272	2,318	2,624	268	850

SOURCES OF DATA:

Probable maximum expenditure without prohibition: Table 69, *supra*, p. 149.

Estimated actual expenditure: Table 81, *supra*, p. 167.

It may be noted that business depression appears to have as much effect upon the expenditure for liquor since the adoption of prohibition as before. Especially has the depression beginning in 1929 reduced the consumption of spirits and the expenditure upon them. The reduction in the amount spent in 1930, as compared with 1929, was probably close to a billion dollars, since there have been price declines for which no allowancce has been made.[17]

Finally, in considering the amount spent for alcoholic beverages, we should not ignore completely the rapid spread of state prohibition laws from 1914 to 1919. Opinions doubtless differ as to whether or not these laws would have been more effective than national prohibition in checking the consumption of alcoholic beverages and expenditures upon them. If we assume that state laws would have been moderately well enforced, we must conclude that the adoption of national prohibition has failed to reduce the use of alcoholic beverages and has increased the sum spent on them.

[17] Prices of alcoholic beverages may not have been appreciably reduced in 1930, but they quite certainly were in 1931. See the *New York Times*, April 12, 1931, and May 31, 1931.

CHAPTER EIGHT

Prohibition and the Shifting Pattern of Consumption

That the habits of consumption of the American people are constantly changing is a fact well known to business men, for such changes in habits are reflected in the decay of some industries and the growth of others. The causes of changes in the pattern of consumption are varied: among them are new inventions, advertising, the tenets of religious and social organizations, political activity, and modifications of the economic status and income levels of individuals and classes. The years since the adoption of the Eighteenth Amendment and the passage of the Volstead Act have been a period when forces such as these have been especially strong.

Prohibition is thus one among many causes operating to modify the extent and character of goods purchased by the American public. Many of its supporters have believed it to be the most important of these causes, and have claimed that prohibition was chiefly responsible for the marked increases between 1920 and 1929 in the sales of automobiles, electric refrigerators, radios, bathroom fixtures, household appliances and other home equipment.[1] It is evident from

[1] This argument has appeared in many places. See especially the following: Ernest H. Cherrington, "A Study of the Social Effect of National Prohibition," Congressional Record, November 19, 1929; Samuel Crowther, *Prohibition and Prosperity,* ch. 2; statistics presented by *The Christian Science Monitor,* June 10, 1930, under the headline, "From

the preceding analysis that prohibition has had a much smaller effect upon the national patterns of consumption and expenditure that its supporters have supposed. It did result, nevertheless, during its early years, in the release of about two billion dollars of purchasing power per year, and during more recent years has reduced the national expenditure upon beer and increased that upon distilled spirits.

In order to put these changes in their proper perspective we need to compare their magnitude with that of other changes in the patterns of consumption and expenditure occurring before and since the adoption of prohibition. Besides, we would like to know what was the effect of the purchasing power released during the early years of prohibition, what goods were substituted for liquors in the national economy. To deal with these problems thoroughly we should know the quantities consumed and money spent for all the goods, or main classes of goods, used in the United States. Unfortunately, such comprehensive data are not available, and we have only the evidence from limited samples of the changes in our national patterns of consumption and expenditure.

Consumption of and Expenditure Upon Selected Articles. In Table 84 there is given for selected years the apparent consumption per capita of a number of commodities for which it is possible to make reasonable estimates both of consumption and expenditures for several years prior to the World War. Upon these commodities the American public spends from a fourth to a fifth of its entire income.

Vacuum Cleaners to Bathtubs People Have Bought More in Dry Era"; Deets Pickett, *Why I Am For Prohibition;* and *Prohibition Prosperity,* and *The Facts About Prohibition—Illustrated—Trust Your Eye,* both prepared by the Research Department, Board of Temperance, Prohibition and Public Morals, Methodist Episcopal Church.

TABLE 84

APPARENT CONSUMPTION PER CAPITA OF SELECTED ARTICLES

Article	Unit	1909	1914	1921	1925	1929
Beer	gal.	19.04	20.69	1.26	3.46	7.11
Wine	gal.	.67	.53	.44	.86	.89
Spirits	gal.	1.32	1.44	.30	1.80	1.86
				1920		
Meat and lard	lb.	169	150	158	165	158
Wheat flour	lb.	211	203	175	177	171
Corn meal	lb.	58	41	25	23	24
Sugar	lb.	82	91	93	113	114
Manufactured ice	lb.	314	430	558	696	718
Tea	lb.	1.24	.92	.83	.86	.73
Coffee	lb.	11.45	10.14	11.70	10.92	12.15
Cigars	no.	85	84	85	60	51
Cigarettes	no.	58	147	297	642	911
Manufactured tobacco	lb.	4.7	4.4	3.8	3.5	3.1
Boots and shoes	pr.	3.1	2.9	2.8	2.8	3.0
Hosiery	pr.	7.6	8.4	8.4	10.1	9.9
Pianos	1/1000	4.0	3.3	2.5	2.5	1.0
Phonographs	1/1000	3.6	5.0	12.9	4.9	2.6
Carriages and wagons	1/1000	16.7	11.4	3.3	1.4	.4
Motor vehicles	1/1000	1.5	5.5	19.3	33.8	39.1
Auto tire casings	1/1000	20	82	283	495	552
Gasoline	gal.	6	15	40	81	129

SOURCES OF DATA:

Beer, wine and spirits: 1909 and 1914, *Statistical Abstract of the United States*, 1922, pp. 692-97; 1921, 1925 and 1929, Table 46, *supra*, p. 106, using estimates from sources of production.

Meat and lard, wheat flour, corn meal and sugar, 1909 to 1925: Working, "The Decline in Per Capita Consumption of Flour in the United States," *Wheat Studies of the Food Research Institute*, vol. ii, pp. 278-79, and vol. iv, p. 86. Figures for 1929 estimated from data from the following sources: meat and lard, Table 426, *Yearbook of Agriculture*, 1929, p. 887; wheat flour and corn meal, *Census of Manufactures*; sugar, United States Beet Sugar Association.

Tea and coffee: net imports, *Statistical Abstract of the United States*.

Cigars, cigarettes and manufactured tobacco: annual reports of the Commissioner of Internal Revenue, and *Statistical Abstract of the United States*.

Ice, boots and shoes, hosiery, pianos, phonographs, carriages and wagons, motor vehicles, and auto tire casings: *Census of Manufactures*, and *The Growth of Manufactures, 1899 to 1923*, Census Monographs, VIII. Figures are for domestic production, less exports and plus imports. For some items foreign trade figures are not available for 1909 and 1914, and it has been assumed that the same proportion of the total was exported or imported as in later years. In some cases, figures given in the various reports of the census of manufactures are not strictly comparable, on account of changes in classification, and have been modified in the best manner to make them comparable. Auto tire casings in 1909, not reported by the census, are estimated from the ratio of the number of casings to automobiles in 1914. All figures for these items in the 1920 column are averages of census reports and foreign trade for 1919 and 1921. These are the best available estimates of consumption for the year 1920; they are used rather than figures for the year 1919 because prohibition came into force in the middle of that year, and rather than 1921, because of the severe business depression.

Gasoline: 1909 and 1914, *Industrial and Engineering Chemistry Journal*, 1917, p. 529; 1920, 1925 and 1929, *Statistical Abstract of the United States*.

In Table 85 there are given the average annual percentage changes in the consumption of these selected articles for four periods: (1) the pre-war pre-prohibition period from 1909 to 1914; (2) the war-time period, 1914 to 1920, during which about half the states adopted prohibitory laws and during which the War Prohibition Act and the Volstead Act came into force; (3) the early post-war prohibition period, 1920 to 1925, when the consumption of alcoholic beverages was most greatly reduced; and (4) the late prohibition period, 1925 to 1929, with the consumption of alcoholic beverages fairly stable.

If prohibition had made any decided change in the national pattern of consumption, at least in respect to the items listed in this table, the percentages in the 1914-20 period would differ appreciably from those for the other periods and from the trend throughout the entire two decades. The only item in which this is the case is that of phonographs. It may be that during the early years of prohibition

TABLE 85

APPARENT AVERAGE ANNUAL PERCENTAGE CHANGE IN PER CAPITA CONSUMPTION OF SELECTED ARTICLES

Article	1909 to 1914	1914 to 1921	1921 to 1925	1925 to 1929
Beer	1.7	—13.4	43.7	26.4
Wine	— 4.2	— 0.5	23.9	.9
Spirits	1.8	—11.3	125.0	.8
		1914 to 1920	1920 to 1925	
Meat and lard	— 2.2	.9	.9	— 1.1
Wheat flour	— .8	— 2.3	.2	.8
Corn meal	— 5.7	— 6.4	— 2.3	1.1
Sugar	2.1	.4	4.3	.2
Manufactured ice	7.4	5.0	5.0	.8
Tea	— 5.2	— 1.6	.7	— 3.8
Coffee	— 2.5	2.6	1.3	2.8
Cigars	— .2	.2	— 4.7	— 3.8
Cigarettes	30.7	17.0	23.2	10.5
Manufactured tobacco	— 1.3	— 2.3	— 1.6	— 2.9
Boots and shoes	— 1.3	— .6	0	1.8
Hosiery	2.1	0	4.0	— .5
Pianos	— 3.7	— 4.0	0	—15.0
Phonographs	7.8	26.3	—12.4	—11.7
Carriages and wagons	— 6.3	—11.8	—11.5	—17.9
Automobiles	53.3	41.8	15.0	3.9
Auto tire casings	62.0	40.9	15.0	2.9
Gasoline	30.0	27.8	20.5	14.8

SOURCE OF DATA:

Table 84, *supra*, p. 174. Average annual percentage changes have been computed by dividing the change during the period by the number of years in the period, and are thus slightly greater than the actual year to year percentage changes. In most cases they are not accurate to within half a per cent, on account of the smallness of the units in Table 84.

people purchased phonographs instead of liquor; but on the other hand the large purchases of phonographs from 1919 to 1921 may have been due entirely to the increasing national income; while the marked decline since that time is obviously

TABLE 86

ESTIMATED TOTAL CONSUMER EXPENDITURE FOR SELECTED ARTICLES
(millions of dollars)

Article	1909	1914	1921	1925	1929
Beer	880	1,032	136	398	864
Wine	140	123	120	248	270
Spirits	616	732	528	3,312	3,616
			1920		
Meat and lard	2,622	3,313	6,835	6,962	7,549
Wheat flour	681	683	1,510	1,241	1,059
Corn meal	141	131	176	129	154
Sugar	433	525	1,907	929	914
Manufactured ice	52	73	178	224	235
Tea	55	51	64	75	69
Coffee	202	256	585	649	724
Cigars and cigarettes	395	473	1,151	1,304	1,466
Other tobacco	231	266	437	321	403
Boots and shoes	648	726	1,442	1,369	1,418
Hosiery	114	147	417	585	680
Pianos	86	82	113	129	52
Phonographs	17	37	189	89	20
Carriages and wagons	185	159	92	36	11
Automobiles	247	561	2,557	3,789	4,052
Auto tires	50	210	810	1,118	902
Total (omitting liquors)	6,237	7,904	19,708	20,820	24,463
Total national income	31,890	35,600	74,000	81,900	93,500
Per cent of national income spent for above goods	19.5	22.2	26.6	25.4	26.2

SOURCES OF DATA:

Beer, wine and spirits: 1914, Table 50, *supra*, p. 114; 1909, computed in the same manner; 1921, 1925 and 1929, Table 81, *supra*, p. 167.

Meat and lard, wheat flour, corn meal, sugar, tea and coffee: computed from the average retail price reported by the Bureau of Labor Statistics and the estimates of total consumption from which estimates of per capita consumption in Table 84 were derived (see footnote to Table 84, *supra*, p. 174). Retail prices of tea and coffee estimated for 1909 by assuming the same relation to the declared import value as in 1913-15.

Automobiles: all years except 1929 computed from the estimated number sold in each price class, and the average price of cars in the class (from Epstein, *The Automobile Industry,* Chicago, 1928, pp. 335-45); 1929 estimated by multiplying the wholesale value by 1.315, the ratio of estimated retail to wholesale value in 1925.

Gasoline: computed from average retail price (from Minerals and Transportation Division, Chamber of Commerce, and *Facts and Figures of the Automobile Industry,* 1930) and estimates of total consumption used in deriving per capita consumption (see footnote to Table 84, *supra,* p. 174).

Other items computed by raising the wholesale value reported by the Census of Manufactures, corrected for the value of foreign trade, by arbitrary percentages, as follows: cigars and cigarettes, other tobacco, boots and shoes, hosiery, pianos, phonographs, and carriages and wagons, 50 per cent; auto tires, 40 per cent; and manufactured ice, 20 per cent. The reasonableness of these arbitrary increases has been tested in most cases by the Harvard surveys of retail trade (Bulletins of the Bureau of Business Research, Harvard University Graduate School of Business Administration), by the *Census of Distribution,* or by data from trade sources.

to be attributed to the substitution of radios rather than to the increased use of beverage alcohol.

In Table 86 the estimated total national expenditure for these selected articles is given, thus making possible a comparison of the magnitude of the decline in liquor expenditure during the early years of prohibition and the magnitude of other changes in the national pattern of expenditure. Assuming that prohibition reduced the liquor bill by two billion dollars per year in 1920 and 1921, it is clear that this could have accounted for only a minor part of the increased expenditures on other things: for compared with 1914 the increased cost of meat products alone was three and a half billion dollars, of wheat flour and sugar more than two billions, of tobacco and footwear nearly two billions, and the increased expenditure on automobiles, tires and gasoline over three and a half billions. These increases were due primarily to the growth of population (nine per cent. from

1914 to 1920) and to the inflation of prices and the doubling of the national income in terms of dollars. In fact, the saving from a reduction in the liquor bill appears to have been lost in price inflation.

TABLE 87

TOTAL SAVINGS DEPOSITS IN THE UNITED STATES, 1910 TO 1930

Year	Total savings deposits, June 30 (millions of dollars)	Total savings deposits, dollars per capita	Annual per cent. increase in savings deposits per capita	National income of preceding year (millions of dollars)	Percentage of national income added to savings deposits
1910	6,835	74.08		27,661	
1911	7,963	85.00	14.7	29,345	3.8
1912	8,404	88.38	4.0	29,660	1.5
1913	8,548	88.57	0.2	31,755	0.5
1914	8,712	88.96	0.4	33,393	0.5
1915	8,807	88.66	— 0.3	33,227	0.3
1916	9,459	93.88	5.9	34,690	1.9
1917	10,876	106.44	13.4	40,585	3.5
1918	11,535	111.35	4.6	48,314	1.4
1919	13,040	124.19	11.5	56,658	2.7
1920	15,314	143.90	15.9	61,628	3.7
1921	16,501	153.02	6.3	68,442	1.7
1922	17,579	160.91	5.2	58,271	1.8
1923	19,727	176.61	9.8	61,187	3.5
1924	21,189	186.31	5.5	69,295	2.1
1925	23,134	200.51	7.6	71,905	2.7
1926	24,696	210.83	5.1	76,561	2.0
1927	26,091	219.94	4.3	80,284	1.7
1928	28,413	236.75	7.6	82,921	2.8
1929	28,218	232.35	— 1.9	84,119	— 0.2
1930	28,485	234.53	0.9	88,000	0.3

SOURCES OF DATA:

Total savings deposits: Savings Bank Division, American Bankers Association, *Savings Deposits and Depositors,* 1930, p. 7.

National income: 1910 to 1928, King, *The National Income and Its Purchasing Power,* p. 74; 1929 estimated by the author. "Imputed" income is excluded.

Other columns: computed by the author.

The Relation of Prohibition to Savings. It has also been argued that due to prohibition savings deposits have increased, more life insurance has been taken out, and larger investments have been made in building and loan associations.[2]

In Table 87 there are given the total savings deposits in the United States each year since 1910, together with the increase in such deposits per capita and the proportion of the national income each year represented by such savings deposits. Total savings deposits include time certificates of deposit payable in thirty days and over, and postal savings re-deposited in banks, as well as accounts classified by banks as "savings accounts," both at savings banks and at other banks.

In Table 88 a summary comparison is made for total savings deposits between the pre-prohibition and post-prohibition periods.

TABLE 88

SAVINGS DEPOSITS BEFORE AND SINCE PROHIBITION

	Pre-prohibition period 1910 to 1919	Post-prohibition period 1919-20	Post-prohibition period 1920 to 1930
Average annual per cent increase in per capita savings	6.0	15.9	5.0
Average annual per cent of the national income added to savings deposits	1.8	3.7	1.8

SOURCE OF DATA:
Table 87, *supra*, p. 179.

There is thus no reason, so far as total savings deposits are concerned, for believing that prohibition has had a permanent effect upon savings. The first year after prohibition went into effect, however, showed the largest percentage growth in total and in per capita savings deposits

[2] For this argument also see the references in footnote 1, p. 172.

TABLE 89

LIFE INSURANCE ISSUED AND IN FORCE, 1910 TO 1930

Year	Issued (millions of dollars)	In force at end of year (millions of dollars)	Issued (dollars per capita)	In force at end of year (dollars per capita)	Ratio of insurance in force to national income (per cent)
1910	2,557	16,404	28	178	.56
1911	2,870	18,003	31	192	.61
1912	3,082	19,265	32	202	.61
1913	3,400	20,564	35	213	.62
1914	3,315	21,589	34	220	.65
1915	3,595	22,784	36	229	.66
1916	3,212	24,679	31	245	.61
1917	4,891	27,189	48	266	.56
1918	5,131	29,870	50	288	.53
1919	8,315	35,880	79	342	.58
1920	10,105	42,281	95	397	.62
1921	8,730	45,983	81	425	.79
1922	9,774	50,291	99	458	.82
1923	12,070	56,804	108	509	.82
1924	13,195	63,780	117	563	.89
1925	15,473	71,690	135	624	.94
1926	16,461	79,644	141	683	.99
1927	17,136	87,022	145	736	1.05
1928	18,673	95,206	156	794	1.13
1929	19,267	103,146	158	849	1.17
1930	19,020	107,948	154	876	1.20

SOURCES OF DATA:

Issued (millions of dollars): 1910 to 1929, *Statistical Abstract of the United States*, 1931, pp. 308; 1930, The Spectator Company. The amount issued is that written and paid for.

Ratio of insurance in force to national income: computed from insurance in force and estimates of the national income. For 1910-1028 estimates of the national income are from King, *op. cit.* p. 74; for 1929 and 1930, made by the author on the basis of annual changes in production, trade and income tax returns.

of any year since 1910. In part this may be attributed to prohibition; but how large a part is uncertain, as the increase in per capita savings deposits was also very great in earlier years of business prosperity, 1911 and 1917.

TABLE 90

ASSETS OF BUILDING AND LOAN ASSOCIATION

Year	Millions of dollars	Dollars per capita
1910	946	10
1911	1,040	11
1912	1,138	12
1913	1,248	13
1914	1,358	14
1915	1,484	15
1916	1,599	16
1917	1,769	17
1918	1,898	18
1919	2,127	20
1920	2,534	24
1921	2,891	27
1922	3,343	31
1923	3,943	35
1924	4,766	42
1925	5,509	48
1926	6,334	54
1927	7,156	61
1928	8,016	67
1929	8,695	73
1930	8,829	72

SOURCES OF DATA:

Assets in millions of dollars: *Statistical Abstract of the United States*, 1931, p. 279.

Dollars per capita: computed from the preceding column and population estimates.

It is possible, furthermore, that the total savings deposits reported by the banks exaggerate the actual amount of savings in recent years in comparison with former years. With the passage of the Federal Reserve Act and amendments thereto, legal reserve requirements for time deposits were reduced to a greater extent than for demand deposits, and this may have resulted in the transfer of funds from demand accounts to time or savings accounts. Time deposits of Federal Reserve member banks have increased from 16.6 per cent of their total deposits in 1915 to 41.2 per cent in 1928, and time and savings deposits in all banks were in 1928, 1929 and 1930 56 per cent of all deposits, whereas from 1918 to 1920 they were only 46 or 47 per cent of all deposits.

In Table 89 figures are given regarding the amount of life insurance issued and in force; and in Table 90 regarding the assets of building and loan associations.

In Table 91 the growth in life insurance issued and in force and in the assets of building and loan associations are summarized for pre-prohibition, early prohibition and the late prohibition periods.

TABLE 91

LIFE INSURANCE ISSUED AND IN FORCE, AND ASSETS OF BUILDING AND LOAN ASSOCIATIONS, BEFORE AND SINCE PROHIBITON

	Pre-prohibition period 1910-1918	Early prohibition period 1920-1922	Late prohibition period 1923-1930
Average amount of life insurance issued per year, dollars per capita	36	92	139
Average amount of life insurance in force, dollars per capita	226	427	704
Average ratio of life insurance in force to the national income (per cent)	.60	.74	1.02
Average assets of building and loan associations, dollars per capita	14	27	57

SOURCES OF DATA:
Tables 89 and 90, *supra*, pp. 181 and 182.

It is evident from Tables 89 to 91 that from 1910 to 1930 there was a steady increase in the amount of life insurance issued and in force, and in the assets of building and loan associations. It is evident also that the rate of increase has been higher since the adoption of prohibition than before. Much more insurance is issued, and much more carried, in recent years, than in pre-prohibition days. It is especially noteworthy that the amount issued increased by three-fifths in 1919, the year in which prohibition went into effect.

But whether or not prohibition is the chief, or an important contributing cause of these increased investments in life insurance and building and loan associations is debatable. The issuance of government life insurance to millions of men in the army popularized insurance more than ever before; in recent years business concerns have greatly increased the amount of insurance carried on executives and working forces; and the rapid rise of the price level in 1919 made the carrying of greater amounts of insurance necessary to provide the same protection to dependents as in former years. The growth of assets of building and loan associations is largely the result of suburban development and housing construction in new areas accessible by automobile from urban centers. These influences are sufficient to account for the growth of investments in life insurance and in building and loan associations; and in view of the fact that such investments have continued to increase since 1923 at a rapid rate, despite the large liquor bill, it is reasonable to conclude that they have been more important than prohibition.

The Substitutes for Beer. The foregoing analyses justify the conclusion that prohibition has made no significant change in the general pattern of consumption or of expenditure of the American people. Nevertheless, since prohibition has drastically reduced the consumption of beer, it is pertinent to inquire whether there have been definite substitutes for this beverage, or whether the money formerly spent upon it has been diffused over the entire range of commodities and services purchased. Definite substitutes for beer may have been other alcoholic beverages, non-alcoholic drinks, or goods providing a nervous reaction akin to alcoholic euphoria.

In chapter five it was estimated that the per capita consumption of beer was in 1927-1930 about 14 gallons less than in 1911-1914, while the per capita consumption of spirits was about .15 of a gallon and that of wine .4 of a gallon greater than during the former period. The alcoholic content of the increased amount of spirits and wine is about one-fifth of that of the decreased amount of beer. It is quite possible that the consumption of wine might have increased without prohibition, due to the changing racial composition of the American nation and to the rapid growth of grape production in California. Spirits, however, have probably been a partial substitute for beer, and naturally so, for contraband goods tend to be sold in their most concentrated forms.

In Table 92 there is given the per capital consumption of the principal non-alcoholic drinks for which it has been possible to obtain statistics, the chief omissions being fresh fruit drinks and fountain carbonated beverages.

Since the adoption of prohibition the per capita consumption of tea has been about a fourth of a pound less, and that of coffee two pounds more, than during the decade prior to 1917. At the rate of one teaspoonful of tea or one tablespoonful of coffee per cup, only half a pound of the increased coffee consumption is a direct substitute for tea.[3] The other pound and a half, at eighty

[3] The amount of coffee per cup recommended by experts varies. Thus Alice Foote MacDougall (*The Encyclopedia Britannica*, 14th edition, vol. 5, p. 976, recommends one dessert-spoonful per cup, while Fannie Farmer (*The Boston Cooking-School Cook Book*, Boston, 1923, p. 33) recommends one cup of coffee to 7 cups of water.

TABLE 92

PER CAPITA CONSUMPTION OF NON-ALCOHOLIC BEVERAGES

Year	Tea (pounds)	Coffee (pounds)	Carbonated beverages (gallons)		Grape juice and other still beverages (gallons)	Cereal beverages (gallons)	Milk New York metropolitan area (gallons)
			Bottled	Coca-Cola			
1890	1.33	7.83	0.4	Less than .01			21.4
1891	1.29	8.00					22.3
1892	1.38	9.67					23.6
1893	1.33	8.31		..			23.3
1894	1.36	8.30		..			23.5
1895	1.40	9.33		..			23.7
1896	1.33	8.11		..			23.6
1897	1.58	10.12		..			23.6
1898	.94	11.68		..			24.1
1899	.98	10.79	0.7	..			25.5
1900	1.10	9.81		..			25.3
1901	1.12	10.45		..			25.6
1902	.92	13.34		.01			26.0
1903	1.27	10.82		.01			27.0
1904	1.31	11.68	0.9	.01			28.0
1905	1.19	12.00		.02			29.5
1906	1.06	9.74		.02			31.1
1907	.96	11.17		.03			30.8
1908	1.03	9.84		.03			29.7
1909	1.24	11.45	1.3	.04			30.4
1910	.89	9.33		.05			31.8
1911	1.06	9.29		.05			33.5
1912	1.06	9.26		.06			33.6
1913	97	8.90		.07			34.2
1914	.92	10.14	1.7	.07			34.1
1915	.93	10.62		.08			34.9
1916	1.08	11.20		.10			35.0
1917	1.01	12.38		.12			34.4
1918	1.42	10.43		.10			35.5
1919	.62	11.89	3.6	.18	.08		37.6
1920	.83	11.70		.18			40.9
1921	.69	12.02	3.2	.15	.07	2.65	42.8
1922	.85	11.04		.14		1.80	45.6
1923	.91	12.36	4.3	.15	.07	1.46	46.8
1924	.80	12.17	4.4	.15		1.33	47.7
1925	.86	10.92	4.9	.17	.06	1.38	47.6

TABLE 92—*Continued*

PER CAPITA CONSUMPTION OF NON-ALCOHOLIC BEVERAGES

1926	81	12.54	5.4	.18		1.29	48.7
1927	.74	11.97	5.8	.19	.08	1.15	50.1
1928	.75	12.01	6.3	.20		1.08	50.4
1929	.73	12.09	6.7	.22	.07	.99	50.4
1930	.68	12.80	6.6	.23		.93	49.3

SOURCES OF DATA:

Tea and coffee: *Statistical Abstracts of the United States,* 1910 to 1930. Figures for 1930 from *Foreign Commerce of the United States* (net imports).

Bottled carbonated beverages: 1919 and 1924 to 1930, estimates by American Bottlers of Carbonated Beverages; other years computed from value of products, mineral and carbonated waters, by calculating the ratio to the value of carbonated beverages in 1925 (value of products from *Census of Manufactures*). Up to and including 1914 non-carbonated soft drinks, aside from malt drinks, are included.

Coca-Cola: the Coca-Cola Company. A considerable part of the Coca-Cola sold is bottled and included in the figures of the preceding column.

Grape juice and other still beverages: computed from the value of products, *Census of Manufactures,* by assuming an average wholesale value of one dollar per gallon, except in 1919, when an average value of one and one-half dollars per gallon is assumed, on account of the high price of grapes. Grape juice constitutes the major part of the beverages in this class. Poor's and Moody's industrial manuals report the output of the Welch Grape Juice Company to have been about two million gallons per year from 1916 to 1919, and about three million gallons since 1927. The gross sales of this company, according to the Standard Statistics Corporation Records, amounted approximately to two million dollars in 1917 and 1918, to three million in 1919, and also to three million dollars in 1922 and in 1923.

Cereal beverages; *Statistics Concerning Intoxicating Liquors,* 1930, p. 61. Figures are for fiscal years ending June 30. Cereal beverages are frequently called "near beer".

Milk: computed from milk and cream receipts at the New York market and the population of eighteen counties in the New York City area (intercensal years interpolated). Figures of milk and cream receipts are derived from the *Milk Recorder,* and supplied to the author by Mr. M. P. Catherwood, of the New York State College of Agriculture.

tablespoonfuls per pound and three cups per pint, would

indicate an increase in the consumption of coffee, aside from substitution for tea, of about five gallons per capita per year. However, the average consumption of coffee since 1920 has been practically the same as it was during the years from 1901 to 1905, and the increase since the adoption of prohibition cannot therefore be definitely attributed to prohibition.

The use of bottled carbonated beverages was apparently increasing slowly prior to the World War. Consumption in recent years is about four gallons per capita per year greater than it would have been had the trend from 1904 to 1914 been continued. Coca-Cola, grape juice, root beer and other non-carbonated non-cereal beverages have never sold in sufficient quantities to be significant as substitutes for beer. Cereal beverages, or "near beer," were growing in popularity before the adoption of prohibition, but no statistics are available of the actual output.[4] Since 1921 their use has gradually declined, so that it is now less than one gallon per capita.

There is little evidence available regarding carbonated drinks sold at soda fountains, nor of the sale of fresh fruit drinks. The total retail sales in 1929 of drug stores having fountains and of soda fountains and soft-drink stands was about twice the retail value of bottled carbonated beverages sold.[5] When allowance is made for the drugs, toilet articles, ice cream and confectionery, and

[4] The most popular non-alcoholic cereal beverage prior to the adoption of prohibition was Bevo, produced by the Anheuser-Busch Company. At the time prohibition went into effect, this company was shipping three-fourths as much Bevo as beer. (Feldman, *Prohibition: Its Economic and Industrial Aspects*, p. 62).

[5] Sales of drug stores and fountains from the Bureau of the Census, *Census of Distribution, 1930, United States Summary of Retail Distribution*. Retail value of bottled carbonated beverages computed at five cents per half-pint bottle, which is a little more than three times the wholesale value reported by manufacturers to the Census of Manufactures.

other articles sold at these drug stores and fountains, the value of beverages sold at fountains must be less than that of bottled beverages; and since a considerable part of fountain beverages are sold at higher prices, the quantity sold is probably a minor fraction of the quantity of bottled carbonated beverages sold. Among fresh fruit drinks, orange juice is probably the most popular. The production of oranges in 1909, less exports, amounted approximately to one-fifth of a box per capita, while since 1922 the rate has been one-fourth of a box per capita except in years of an abnormally large crop, as in 1928. This is an increase of about 25 per cent.[6]

The most notable change in the consumption of non-alcoholic beverages since the adoption of prohibition has been an increase in the use of milk. The per capita consumption of milk in the New York metropolitan area, which is probably typical of urban areas in this respect, increased steadily, aside from moderate cyclical fluctuations, from 1885 to 1918 at an average annual rate of half a gallon. From 1918 to 1923, however, the annual rate of growth mounted to two and a half gallons, since which time the rate of increase of half a gallon has been resumed. The rapid increase between 1918 and 1923 was sufficient to make the consumption of milk in recent years about nine gallons per capita greater than it would have been had the rate increase prior to 1918 been undisturbed.

If we were to assume that all of the changes in the consumption of non-alcoholic beverages since 1918 have been due to the substitution of those drinks for beer, we would say that fourteen gallons of beer per capita have been replaced by nine gallons of milk, five gallons of coffee,

[6] *Yearbook of Agriculture*, 1930, p. 727; *and the Monthly Summary of Foreign Commerce of the United States*, December, 1930.

four gallons of carbonated beverages and one gallon of cereal and fruit beverages. These are in addition to three-twentieths of a gallon of spirits, equivalent in alcoholic content to one and three-fourths gallons of beer. To what extent the non-alcoholic beverages have actually been substitutes for beer, and to what extent their use would have increased without prohibition, is a question regarding which it is not possible to form a definite conclusion. It is reasonable to suppose that with an increasing percentage of the population living in urban areas, with more leisure time, more travel, greater indulgence in sports and attendance at amusement and summer resorts, and with better understanding of the healthful qualities of milk and fresh fruits, the use of the non-alcoholic drinks would have increased, apart from prohibition. This is especially probable, when we bear in mind the fact that these non-alcoholic drinks are used to a great degree by children, youths and women, while beer is consumed principally by adult men.

Other drinks, moreover, are not the only possible substitutes for beer. Sugar preparations may serve as a substitute, since there is considerable similarity between the physiological effects of concentrated doses of sugar and those of light doses of alcohol. Still another possible substitute is tobacco, which has a slight narcotic effect similar to that of alcohol; and another the moving picture, which may be a means of psychological "compensation."

The available figures regarding the consumption of ice cream, confectionery and tobacco and attendance at moving pictures are given in Table 93.

The rate of increase in the consumption of ice cream has been less since the adoption of prohibition than during the years from 1910 to 1916. Judged by its value,

TABLE 93

PER CAPITA CONSUMPTION OF ICE CREAM, CONFECTIONERY, AND TOBACCO AND ATTENDANCE AT MOTION PICTURES

Year	Ice Cream (gallons)	Confectionery (index number, 1914=100)	Tobacco (pounds)	Motion picture attendance (times per year)
1899		61	4.9	
1900			5.0	
1901			5.1	
1902			5.4	
1903			5.5	
1904		69	5.4	
1905			5.4	
1906			5.6	
1907			5.6	
1908			5.4	
1909		86	5.6	
1910	1.0		5.7	
1911			5.7	
1912			5.8	
1913			5.8	
1914	1.7	100	5.7	
1915			5.6	
1916	2.1		6.0	
1917	2.1		6.4	
1918	2.1		6.4	
1919	2.2	120	5.6	
1920	2.4		5.7	
1921	2.3	116	5.3	
1922	2.4		5.6	19
1923	2.6	128	6.2	20
1924	2.5		6.1	21
1925	2.8	125	6.2	22
1926	2.8		6.2	22
1927	2.8	136	6.2	25
1928	2.9		6.2	28
1929	3.0	130	6.3	40

SOURCES OF DATA:

Ice cream: Bureau of Agricultural Economics, United States Department of Agriculture.

Confectionery: computed from the *Census of Manufactures*, on the assumption that prices of confectionery have followed the general level of wholesale prices.

Tobacco: 1923 to 1929, *Statistical Abstract of the United States*, 1930, p. 849; 1918 to 1922, *Statistical Abstract of the United States*, 1924, p. 783; 1899 to 1917, computed from the total consumption of leaf tobacco by manufacturing plants, *Statistical Abstract of the United States*, 1919, p. 557. The figures for the period up to 1917 make no allowance for imports and exports of manufactured tobacco, but the error on this account is slight. The apparent sudden increase in consumption in 1923, and the higher level since that date are due in part to differences in methods of computation. Figures given in the various issues of the *Statistical Abstract* do not agree.

Motion picture attendance: Motion Picture Producers and Distributors of America.

the rate of increase in the consumption of confectionery has been less since 1919 than before that year. Tobacco was used to no greater extent during the first three years after the adoption of prohibition than during the decade prior to the World War. The increased consumption since 1922, insofar as it is real and not due to a change in the method of computation, is amply accounted for by smoking by women. In fact, the enormous increase in cigarette consumption in recent years has been a substitution for other forms of tobacco, rather than a growth in the use of tobacco. There is thus no statistical evidence that prohibition has led to increased use of ice cream, confectionery or tobacco, and these products have not, apparently, been substitutes for beer. Figures regarding motion picture attendance are not available for pre-prohibition years.

PART THREE

Other Economic Phases of Prohibition

CHAPTER IX

Prohibition and Industrial Efficiency

One of the two principal economic arguments made in favor of prohibition is that it has greatly increased industrial efficiency.[1] Even though prohibition has, since the first three years, had little direct effect upon the expenditures of the nation, it is possible that through its effect upon industrial efficiency, prohibition has increased the national income, and therefore, enlarged the purchases of many commodities. Unfortunately, there is little definite data available regarding the relation of prohibition to economic productivity.

The Effect of Drinking Upon Efficiency. Prohibition, if it actually resulted in the cessation of use of alcoholic beverages, might be expected to affect the efficiency of industry in several ways. The principal effect of alcohol is on the central nervous system, and experiments show that a decrease in the consumption of alcohol during, or immediately preceding, working hours is accompanied by greater skill at work. The finer co-ordination made possible by the absence of alcohol tends to reduce the accident rate. The elimination of drinking bouts should tend to eliminate absenteeism, especially on Monday, and irregularity in reporting at work. The impossibility of drinking to excess should result in less sickness and absence on account

[1] This argument, like others in respect to the economic effects of prohibition, has appeared in many places. See especially Irving Fisher, *Prohibition At Its Worst*, pp. 156-64, and *The Noble Experiment*, pp. 136-38.

thereof, and in a longer average working life. On the other hand, since alcohol promotes the relaxation of the higher brain centers, and its moderate use after working hours may in this way contribute to efficiency, these results might not be fully realized.

Moreover, prohibition may have had a favorable effect upon industrial efficiency without the complete cessation of drinking, or even without reduction in the national consumption of alcohol. The abolition of the open saloon has probably reduced drinking by workingmen on the way to work, at lunch and during working hours, with a consequent lessened concentration of alcohol in the blood during working hours, even though there is more drinking at home and with friends in the evening. Also, prohibition may have reduced the consumption of alcohol by the working class, if not that of the nation as a whole, and evidence will be given later to indicate that this has been the case.[2] It is therefore possible that prohibition has raised the efficiency of labor, even though there has been no reduction in the consumption of strong drinks.

In considering the effect of prohibition upon industrial efficiency, it must be borne in mind that since 1919 changes in industrial technique and in personnel management have been rapid, and that it is not possible to isolate with precision the various factors contributing to increased efficiency.[3]

Statistical Evidence Regarding the Effect of Prohibition Upon Productivity. The best available measure of industrial efficiency over a period including a number of years

[2] *Cf. infra*, pp. 233-37.

[3] For discussions of recent changes in technology and management, see L. P. Alford, "Technical Changes in Manufacturing Industries," ch. 2, part 2, in *Recent Economic Changes in the United States*, (New York, 1929), and Henry S. Dennison, "Management," ch. 8 in the same report.

both before and since the adoption of prohibition is Mr. Wolman's index of the output per person engaged in manufactures. This index, and also indexes of the consumption of pure alcohol and of beer, are given in Table 94.

There is no significant relationship in the pre-prohibition period between the annual changes in the output per person in manufactures and the annual changes in the consumption of alcohol or of beer, the coefficients of correlation being —.073 and —.135, respectively. The minus signs by themselves would indicate that efficiency increases as less alcoholic beverages are used; but since there are about four chances out of five that the computed correlation between output per person and alcohol consumption is due solely to chance, and two out of three that the correlation between output and beer consumption is due to chance, it would be improper to interpret the signs in this way.

Since the adoption of prohibition the greatest increase in output per person occurred in 1922, the year showing the greatest increase in the consumption of alcohol; and the next greatest increase in output per person occurred in 1925, the year showing the greatest increase in the consumption of beer.

There is thus no indication in the year to year changes in output per person in manufacturing, either before or since the adoption of prohibition, that reductions in the consumption of alcoholic beverages have had any appreciable effect upon industrial efficiency.

On the other hand, the average annual change in output per person during the eight years from 1920 to 1927 was 5.1 per cent of the average output in 1911-14, while the average annual change during the nineteen years from 1900 to 1918 was only .02 per cent. During two of the

TABLE 94

INDEXES OF PRODUCTIVITY AND OF ALCOHOL CONSUMPTION

(1911-14=100)

Year	Output per person in manufactures	Per capita consumption of alcohol	Per capita consumption of beer	Annual changes Output	Annual changes Alcohol consumption	Annual changes Beer consumption
1899	90.3	75.7	74.0			
1900	86.9	81.7	78.2	— 3.4	6.0	4.2
1901	92.0	81.7	77.7	5.1	0.0	— 0.5
1902	93.4	88.2	83.5	1.4	6.5	5.8
1903	91.0	90.5	85.9	— 2.4	2.3	2.4
1904	93.9	91.7	87.1	2.9	1.2	1.2
1905	102.3	90.5	87.6	8.4	— 1.2	0.5
1906	103.0	97.0	95.0	0.7	6.5	7.4
1907	98.0	103.6	100.0	— 5.0	6.6	5.0
1908	91.7	97.0	98.5	— 6.3	— 6.6	— 1.5
1909	99.0	92.3	92.7	7.3	— 4.7	— 5.8
1910	98.2	97.0	96.3	— 0.8	4.7	3.6
1911	93.4	100.6	100.8	— 4.8	3.6	4.5
1912	103.5	98.2	97.5	10.1	— 2.4	— 3.3
1913	105.0	101.2	100.9	1.5	3.0	3.4
1914	98.0	98.8	100.8	— 7.0	— 2.4	— 0.1
1915	106.1	86.4	89.6	8.1	—12.4	—11.2
1916	107.7	89.3	86.6	1.6	2.9	— 3.0
1917	99.2	97.0	88.5	— 8.5	7.7	1.9
1918	94.6	66.9	72.4	— 4.6	—30.1	—16.1
1919	94.4	47.3	39.0	— 0.2	—19.6	—33.4
1920	97.5			3.1		
1921	96.9	32.0	6.1	— 0.6		
1922	116.1	53.8	8.3	19.2	21.8	2.2
1923	119.7	63.3	10.9	3.6	9.5	2.6
1924	120.1	62.1	13.8	.4	— 1.2	2.9
1925	131.3	65.1	16.9	11.2	3.0	3.1
1926	134.3	69.8	20.5	3.0	4.7	3.6
1927	135.0	66.3	24.5	0.7	— 3.5	4.0

SOURCES OF DATA:

Index of output per person in manufactures: Leo Wolman, "Labor," ch. 6, p. 454, in *Recent Economic Changes in the United States.* Figures shifted from 1899 to 1911-14 base.

Indexes of per capita consumption of alcohol and of beer: 1910 to 1919, computed from consumption estimates in Table 1, *supra*, p. 24; 1899 to

1909, computed from the same sources in the same manner; 1921 to 1927, computed from estimates of consumption given in Tables 29 and 45, *supra*, pp. 71 and 104. Figures refer to fiscal years ending June 30 from 1910 to 1919, and to calendar years from 1921 to 1927.

years since the adoption of prohibition, 1922 and 1925, the increase in output per person in manufactures has been greater than in any of the eighteen pre-prohibition years covered by the data; while in only one year since the adoption of prohibition has the output per person declined, and then only slightly, as it did during nine out of the nineteen years between 1900 and 1918.

Output per person has been on a definitely higher level since 1922 than during the two decades preceding that year. Whether this higher level of efficiency in recent years should be attributed in part to prohibition, or wholly to improvements in technology and management, may be debated. If it is due in part to prohibition, it is difficult to understand why output per person did not increase during 1920 and 1921, immediately after the prohibition laws became effective and when drinking was at the minimum, or during 1918 and 1919, when the consumption of liquors was drastically curtailed by war-time restrictions.

The Effect of Prohibition upon Industrial Accidents. The data on industrial accidents prior to the World War are very meagre, and this makes it difficult to analyze the relation of prohibition to accidents. In Table 95 there is given an index of the accident frequency rate in the United States since 1913, based on the limited data available, which may be compared with the indexes of consumption of alcohol and of beer given in the preceding section.

Judged by the coefficients of correlation, there was in pre-prohibition times a high degree of relationship between

TABLE 95

INDEXES OF ACCIDENT FREQUENCY RATES AND OF ALCOHOL CONSUMPTION

Year	Accident frequency rate 1913-14 = 100	Per capita consumption of alcohol 1911-14 = 100	Per capita consumption of beer 1911-14 = 100	Annual changes Accident frequency rate	Annual changes Alcohol consumption	Annual changes Beer consumption
1913	101.5	101.2	100.9			
1914	98.3	98.8	100.8	— 3.2	— 2.4	— 0.1
1915	93.1	86.4	89.6	— 5.2	—12.4	—11.2
1916	102.7	89.3	86.6	9.6	2.9	— 3.0
1917	103.4	97.0	88.5	0.7	7.7	1.9
1918	91.8	66.9	72.4	—11.6	—30.1	—16.1
1919	86.3	47.3	39.0	— 5.5	—19.6	—33.4
1920	89.7			3.4		
1921	80.2	32.0	6.1	— 9.5		
1922	84.8	53.8	8.3	4.6	21.8	2.2
1923	86.9	63.3	10.9	2.1	9.5	2.6
1924	81.3	62.1	13.8	— 5.6	— 1.2	2.9
1925	79.2	65.1	16.9	— 2.1	3.0	3.1
1926	73.7	69.8	20.5	— 5.5	4.7	3.6
1927	63.8	66.3	24.5	— 9.9	— 3.5	4.0
1928	57.7	69.8	29.5	— 6.1	3.5	5.0
1929	55.8	71.0	34.6	— 1.9	1.2	5.1
1930	41.6	62.7	33.6	—14.2	— 8.3	— 1.0

SOURCES OF DATA:

Index of accident frequency rate: 1913 to 1927, computed from the accident frequency rates in the following industries: iron and steel, metal mining, quarrying, ore dressing, smelting, metallurgical auxiliary works, coke ovens, and railroads, weighted according to the number of full-time workers in each industry. Data for railroads refer only to trainmen, and for the years 1913 to 1915 refer only to the first five industries named. (*Statistics of industrial accidents in the United States to the end of 1927,* Bulletin of the United States Bureau of Labor Statistics, No. 490). For the years 1928 to 1930 this index has been computed from the annual percentage changes in the frequency rate in industrial establishments reporting to the National Safety Council (*Monthly Labor Review,* June, 1931, p. 73, and October, 1931, p. 92).

Indexes of per capita consumption of alcohol and of beer: same as Table 94, *supra*, p. 198.

the frequency of accidents and the consumption of alcohol and of beer. The coefficient of correlation between the annual changes in the accident frequency rate and the annual changes in the consumption of alcohol, for the period from 1913 to 1919, is +.841, and that between the annual changes in the accident frequency rate and annual changes in the consumption of beer +.622. It is possible, but not probable, that these are spurious correlations, for with only six cases, there is one chance in twenty-five that a coefficient of correlation as high as the former, and one chance in five that a coefficient as high as the latter, would occur without any true relationship. There is the possibility also that the observed correlation is a correlation of trends, due to unrelated causes: yet this does not appear probable, when both the accident frequency rate and the consumption of alcohol decline the first two, advance the next two, and decline the last two of the six years. On the other hand, it is possible that the coefficients of correlation would have been still higher, had consumption figures for calendar years been available, as there is no reason to suppose a six-months lag in the accident frequency rate.

During most of the years since the adoption of prohibition the accident frequency rate continued to decline, while the consumption of alcohol has increased. Yet the two years in which the increase in alcohol consumption was the greatest, 1922 and 1923, were the only two years in which accidents became more frequent; while the two years in which the consumption of alcohol declined, 1927 and 1930, showed the largest declines in the frequency of accidents.

It is reasonable to conclude from these figures, fragmentary as they are, that variations in the consumption of alcohol, both prior to and since the adoption of prohibition, have had some influence upon the frequency of industrial accidents; and that the reduced consumption of alcohol by industrial workers under war-time restrictions and under prohibition, as compared with pre-war conditions, is partially responsible for the reduced frequency of accidents. It is possible also that changes in drinking habits, apart from changes in the quantity of alcohol consumed, have been a contributory factor in the lower accident rates of recent years. This conclusion is by no means certain, however, for it is possible that the observed correlation between the annual variations in the accident frequency rate and the consumption of alcohol is due to the fact that both tend to rise during periods of industrial expansion and to drop during periods of business depression, rather than to the direct effect of the use of alcohol upon the frequency of accidents.

Upon the frequency of fatal industrial accidents, however, variations in the consumption of alcohol appear to have no measurable effect. In Table 96 there are given the death rates per 100,000 from industrial accidents among industrial policy-holders of the Metropolitan Life Insurance Company and the per capita consumption of alcohol. The coefficient of correlation between the two series for the years from 1912 to 1919 is only +.19, which does not indicate any relationship, as there are two chances out of three that a coefficient of this size, with as few cases, might occur solely by chance. There is considerable year-to-year variation in the death rate from industrial accidents among industrial policyholders of the Metropolitan Life Insurance Company, but the rate during the first five years after prohibition did not differ appreciably from the rate prior to prohibition.

TABLE 96

INDUSTRIAL ACCIDENT DEATH RATES AND THE CONSUMPTION OF ALCOHOL

Year	Fatal industrial accidents, deaths per 100,000 insured	Consumption of alcohol, gallons per capita
1912	39.6	1.66
1913	45.7	1.71
1914	35.2	1.67
1915	27.5	1.46
1916	33.5	1.51
1917	32.5	1.64
1918	40.9	1.13
1919	32.1	.80
1920	34.9	
1921	28.8	.54
1922	34.7	.91
1923	39.7	1.07
1924	34.4	1.05

SOURCES OF DATA:

Fatal industrial accidents: *Statistical Bulletin,* Metropolitan Life Insurance Company, December, 1925, p. 1. Rates for years since 1924 have not been compiled.

Consumption of alcohol: Table 1, *supra,* p. 24 and Table 45, *supra,* p. 104. Figures are given as rates in this table and as index numbers in the preceding two tables in order to be similar in form to the series with which they are correlated.

The Effect of Prohibition upon Absenteeism. Many industrial executives, speaking from personal observation, have reported that the efficiency of their plants has been improved since the adoption of prohibition because workmen are not so frequently absent on Monday while sobering up from week-end drinking bouts.[4] It is doubtful, however, whether the improvement in absenteeism noted by executives is due primarily to less drinking among working-men, though evidence will be presented in a later chapter that there has been such a reduction. With

[4] Feldman, *Prohibition: Its Economic and Industrial Aspects,* pp. 200-210.

long hours and inadequate facilities for healthful recreation, drinking was formerly often the only method available for obtaining escape from the sense of continuous fatigue, the oppression of unhealthful working conditions, and the drabness of home life in the slums.[5] Absenteeism following a day of drinking was probably due primarily to the desire to get away from unpleasant work, a desire more readily gratified with inhibitions removed by alcohol. It is, therefore, to be expected that the shorter work-days and longer week-ends, the lightening of work with the introduction of mechanical devices, and the greater facilities for recreation which have been introduced in recent years would have resulted in a reduction in absenteeism, regardless of the coming of prohibition. The influence of reduced hours of work appears to have been especially great at the time prohibition came into operation, for during the three years from 1917 to 1920 the average hours of work per week in manufacturing industries were reduced as much as they had been during the previous fifteen years.[6]

The only statistical evidence available regarding industrial absenteeism before and since the adoption of prohibition is the experience of a powder company in Delaware, for the years 1907, 1913. 1924 and 1929, cited by the Bureau of Prohibition as an example of the effect of prohibition upon the disappearance of "Blue Monday."[7] These figures are given in Table 97.

[5] The borough of Bermondsey, London, where these conditions still prevail, exemplifies this situation. *Cf. supra*, pp. 125-27.

[6] Douglas, *Real Wages in the United States*, 1890-1926, p. 116.

[7] Bureau of Prohibition, *The Value of Law Observance*, p. 11. These figures, except for 1929, were originally furnished to Mr. Feldman, in reply to his questionairre regarding the effect of prohibition upon industrial absenteeism (Feldman, *Prohibition: Its Economic and Industrial Aspects*, p. 210).

TABLE 97

ABSENTEEISM IN A DELAWARE POWDER PLANT

Day	Per cent. absent 1907	1913	1924	1929
Monday	7.41	6.17	3.66	2.35
Tuesday	6.89	5.22	2.86	2.10
Wednesday	5.77	5.49	2.90	2.15
Thursday	5.68	5.06	2.37	2.01
Friday	5.38	5.05	2.10	1.89
Saturday	6.94	6.59	3.93	2.95
Average for week	6.35	5.59	2.96	2.24

SOURCE OF DATA: see footnote 7, p. 204.

When these figures are reduced to the basis of the average annual percentage decline in absenteeism, as they must be in order to make a fair comparison between the years before and since the adoption of prohibition, and allowance is made for the shortening of the working week, it is clear that they provide no valid evidence for the conclusion that prohibition has tended to eliminate Monday absenteeism. The figures in this form are given in Table 98.

TABLE 98

AVERAGE ANNUAL PERCENTAGE DECLINE IN ABSENTEEISM IN A DELAWARE POWDER PLANT

Day	1907-13	1913-24	1924-29
Monday	.21	.23	.26
Tuesday	.28	.21	.15
Wednesday	.05	.24	.15
Thursday	.10	.24	.07
Friday	.06	.27	.04
Saturday	.06	.24	.20
Percentage decline in hours of work per week in manufacturing industries	3.14	9.19	None

SOURCES OF DATA:

Percentage decline in absenteeism: computed from Table 97.
Percentage decline in hours of work per week: 1907 to 1913 and 1913

to 1924, Douglas, *Real Wages in the United States, 1890-1926*, p. 116; 1924 to 1929, *Survey of Current Business, Annual Supplement, 1931*, pp. 184-85.

It may be noted that the annual percentage reduction in Monday absenteeism between 1913 to 1924, covering the period when the prohibition laws went into effect, did not differ appreciably from the reduction in Monday absenteeism during the pre-prohibition period from 1907 to 1913, or during the period from 1924 to 1929. Nor was the reduction in absenteeism during the period from 1913 to 1924 appreciably greater on Monday than on other days in the week. It may also be noted that the reduction in hours of work per week in manufacturing industries during the period from 1913 to 1924 was 9 per cent, compared with only 3 per cent during the period from 1907 to 1913 and no reduction from 1924 to 1929. In the absence of information to the contrary, it may be assumed that hours in this powder plant were reduced in a similar manner, and that this was a factor in the reduction of absenteeism between 1913 and 1924.[8]

The Efficient Use of Productive Resources. It is sometimes claimed that prohibition has also improved efficiency by promoting the more advantageous uses of productive resources. Especially is this said to be true of resources

[8] An attempt was made by the author to obtain figures regarding absenteeism in this plant for the years immediately before and after the introduction of prohibition, and figures regarding the hours of work. Though no figures on these points could be obtained, the official responsible for collecting the data in Table 97 made the following statement: "The general improvement in absenteeism is undoubtedly due to efforts made over a long period of time to get men to work more regularly and cannot be credited to prohibition, especially as there is very little difficulty in getting a drink in New Jersey under prohibition." He cited a superintendent as authority for the statement that there were ten times as many places where one could get a drink as existed prior to prohibition.

formerly devoted to the production and sale of alcoholic beverages. On the other hand, it has been pointed out that because of the specialized character of buildings and equipment much property formerly used in the production of liquor is now idle or being used inefficiently in other ways.[9]

There appears to be no doubt that some former brewing and distilling centers, especially Louisville, have benefitted by the substitution of other industries for the production of alcoholic beverages, or that many former saloon sites have since the adoption of prohibition been yielding as high or higher rentals for other purposes.[10] But without an inventory, or well distributed sample, both of the properties formerly devoted to the production and sale of alcoholic beverages, and of those now devoted to this purpose, the net effect of prohibition upon the use of productive resources cannot be gauged by citing specific cases.

The first decade after the adoption of prohibition was a period of numerous changes in the locations of industrial plants, office buildings, retail stores and other business establishments. The substitution of motor vehicles for other forms of transportation facilities and of electricity for other forms of power, and also the growing proportion of urban population, profoundly altered the relative advantages of various locations, raising real estate values and rentals in some areas and depressing them in others.

[9] *Cf.* Feldman, *Prohibition: Its Economic and Industrial Aspects*, chs. 17 and 18.

[10] Robert E. Corradini, "The Bowery, New York City" and "Saloon Survey of New York City," U. S. Congress, Senate, Subcommittee of the Committee on the Judiciary, *The National Prohibition Law*, pp. 1535-81; and Henry M. Johnson, U. S. Congress, House, Committee on the Judiciary, *The Prohibition Amendment*, pp. 603-08. *Cf.* also Feldman, *op. cit.*, ch. 17.

The elimination of saloons and the substitution of speak-easies and bootleggers, and the substitution of illegal for legal establishments producing alcoholic beverages have doubtless had a similar, though probably much less important, effect.

Whether such changes in the relative desirability of locations mean more or less efficient use of resources depends upon the technical changes in methods of production which accompany (perhaps as cause, perhaps as effect) changes in the location of industrial and business enterprises. There is no reason to suppose that prohibition has had any significant effect upon industrial or business technique, except possibly upon the hotel business, in which it seems to have forced managers to focus attention upon restaurants and room services instead of upon bars.[11]

More important, however, than changes in the relative desirability of locations is the change in the relative quantity of resources devoted to the production of alcoholic beverages. In both the brewing and distilling industries there has been a great de-centralization, reversing the pre-prohibition trend. There is no doubt that this de-centralization means inefficiency: that is, the use of a larger quantity of resources than formerly, relative to production. Whether or not this inefficiency is enough to make the resources devoted to the production of beer as great as in pre-prohibition days cannot be determined. But the resources devoted to the production of spirits under prohibition must be far greater than the resources devoted to their production prior to prohibition.

Moreover, under prohibition there is a considerable destruction of resources each year in the apparatus and materials seized by prohibition agents. The appraised

[11] Feldman, *Prohibition: Its Economic and Industrial Aspects*, ch. 17.

value of property seized by Federal prohibition agents during the fiscal years from 1921 to 1930 was nearly twice as great as the value of the capital invested in the distilling of liquor in 1914, and about one-sixth as great as the capital invested in the production of all alcoholic beverages. Not all of this property seized is an economic waste, for some of it is sold and diverted to other purposes.

In Table 99 there are given the number and value of establishments devoted to the production of alcoholic beverages for a number of pre-prohibition years; and in Table 100 the number of distilleries, stills and fermenters and the appraised value of property seized by Federal agents in recent years. Statistics of seizures by state and local authorities are not obtainable, but were estimated in 1929 at about the same number as those seized by Federal agents.[12]

TABLE 99

RESOURCES DEVOTED TO THE PRODUCTION OF ALCOHOLIC BEVERAGES 1899 TO 1914

Year	Number of distilleries operated	Distilling establishments: Number	Distilling establishments: Value (millions of dollars)	Number of breweries operated	Malt liquor establishments: Number	Malt liquor establishments: Value (millions of dollars)	Vinous liquor establishments: Number	Vinous liquor establishments: Value (millions of dollars)
1899	3,745	965	32.5	1,771	1,507	413.8	359	9.8
1904	2,172	805	50.1	1,741	1,530	515.6	435	17.8
1909	1,292	613	72.5	1,622	1,414	671.2	290	27.9
1914	743	434	91.3	1,392	1,250	792.9	318	31.5

SOURCES OF DATA:

Number of distilleries and number of breweries operated: *Statistics Concerning Intoxicating Liquors*, December, 1930, pp. 72 and 60. Figures in the 1899 row are for 1901, the earliest year available.

Distilling, malt liquor and vinous liquor establishments: *Census of Manufactures*, 1921, pp. 684-86.

[12] National Commission on Law Observance and Enforcement, *Report on the Enforcement of the Prohibition Laws of the United States*, p. 29.

TABLE 100

RESOURCES SEIZED BY FEDERAL PROHIBITION AGENTS, 1921 TO 1930

Year ending June 30	Number of distilleries	Number of stills	Number of still worms	Number of fermenters	Appraised value of property (millions of dollars)
1921	9,746	10,991	5,182	70,014	8.2
1922	8,313	10,994	10,203	81,640	5.9
1923	12,219	14,000	7,512	124,401	11.5
1924	10,392	15,853	8,211	124,720	10.8
1925	12,023	17,854	7,850	134,810	11.2
1926	12,227	12,248	6,974	130,530	13.8
1927	14,512	11,881	8,024	173,656	24.5
1928	16,220	18,980	9,133	217,278	23.2
1929	15,792	11,544	7,982	211,924	25.7
1930	16,180	8,138	8,805	248,999	29.2
Ten-year totals	127,624	132,583	79,876	1,517,972	164.0

SOURCE OF DATA:

Statistics Concerning Intoxicating Liquors, December, 1930, p. 73.

An indication, though not an accurate measure, of the de-centralization of the alcoholic beverage industry can be obtained by comparing the figures in Tables 99 and 100. It will be noted that the number of distilleries seized in 1930 is more than twenty times, and the total number of distilleries, stills and still worms seized forty-five times the number of distilleries in operation in 1914. The number of fermenters seized is one hundred eighty times the number of breweries in operation in 1914. It is hardly conceivable that seizures represent more than ten per cent of the number in operation, so that for each distillery and brewery formerly operated there are now probably hundreds of illicit stills and thousands of illicit fermenters in operation.

The marketing of liquor has also been de-centralized. Business formerly done by saloons is now scattered over a much larger number of speakeasies and bootleggers.[13] Distribution costs are inordinately high, due to the necessity of using uneconomic methods of shipment, of maintaining private guards and of paying for "protection." There has, to be sure, been a considerable centralization of control over the liquor traffic, especially in the largest cities, by gangs and "syndicates;" perhaps a greater centralization than existed prior to prohibition. This centralization of control, however, does not reduce the necessity of maintaining many more producing establishments and retail outlets when alcoholic beverages are contraband than when they are sold legally.

This de-centralization of the alcoholic beverage industry and the frequent seizure of its equipment are economic losses: the industry must utilize more labor and materials than would be required were its products not forbidden.

[13] The number of speakeasies in New York City was estimated in 1930 by the police commissioner at 32,000, in comparison with less than 12,000 licensed saloons and liquor stores in pre-war years. There were, however, several thousand speakeasies in New York prior to prohibition, for the number of permits to sell liquor issued by the Federal internal revenue collectors in the state of New York was fifty per cent greater than the number of state licenses granted. Mr. Walter W. Liggett estimates that there are 700 speakeasies in the city of Washington and 4,000 bootleggers in the District of Columbia compared with 300 legally licensed saloons prior to prohibition; and that there are 4,000 speakeasies and 15,000 bootleggers in Boston compared with 1,000 saloons in the state of Massachusetts prior to prohibition. (*New York Times*, Sept. 15, 1929, X, p. 3; U. S. Congress, Senate, Subcommittee of the Committee on the Judiciary, *The National Prohibition Law*, pp. 1164 and 1544; and U. S. Congress, House, Committee on the Judiciary, *The Prohibition Amendment*, pp. 13-14.)

CHAPTER X

Prohibition and Public Health and Safety

The degree of health and safety enjoyed by citizens and other residents of the nation is one of the most vital aspects of their welfare. The effect of prohibition upon public health and safety is more important, from the point of view of national welfare, that its effect upon expenditures for liquor or upon the efficiency of the alcoholic beverage industry. But despite its importance, and despite the fact that public health and safety have genuine, though inseparable and non-measurable, inter-relations with economic welfare, only a cursory examination can be made in this study of prohibition of its effects upon public health and safety.

The Effect of Prohibition upon Deaths Directly Associated with the Use of Alcohol. In chapter three it was shown that variations in the death rate from alcoholism and that from cirrhosis of the liver are very closely related to variations in the consumption of alcohol: so closely, in fact, that variations in the death rate from these two diseases may be used to estimate the quantity of alcohol consumed in the United States since the advent of prohibition. Another disease, nephritis, or Bright's disease, is also apparently due to alcohol or associated with its use to such a degree that variations in the incidence of this disease are directly associated with variations in the consumption of alcoholic beverages.

In Table 101 the death rates since 1900 for these three

TABLE 101

DEATH RATES FROM DISEASES ASSOCIATED WITH THE USE OF ALCOHOL
1900 TO 1930

(rate per 100,000 inhabitants or insured)

(1) Registration area of the United States.
(2) Registration states of 1900.
(3) Industrial department, Metropolitan Life Insurance Company.

Year	Alcoholism			Cirrhosis of the liver			Nephritis			Wood and denatured alcohol
	(1)	(2)	(3)	(1)	(2)	(3)	(1)	(2)	(3)	(1)
1900	6.4	5.3		12.9	12.6		89.0	88.7		
1901	6.0	5.0		13.6	13.0		89.3	89.6		
1902	6.1	5.2		13.9	12.9		90.9	90.3		
1903	6.6	6.1		14.5	13.5		97.3	96.0		
1904	5.8	5.3		15.1	13.9		103.1	102.4		
1905	6.2	6.0		14.7	14.0		103.4	101.6		
1906	6.4	6.4		14.5	14.6		97.5	103.0		
1907	7.3	7.5		15.4	15.6		102.4	107.3		
1908	5.0	5.1		14.3	14.1		93.7	99.2		
1909	5.1	5.5		13.8	14.2		95.2	103.2		
1910	5.4	5.6		13.9	14.4		99.1	107.3		
1911	4.9	5.3	4.0	14.0	14.4	16.3	97.7	109.8	95.0	
1912	5.3	5.9	5.3	13.5	13.8	16.7	103.2	113.9		
1913	5.9	6.6	5.2	13.4	13.7	16.0	103.0	113.1		
1914	4.9	5.4	4.7	13.0	13.8	13.9	102.6	114.5	95.4	
1915	4.4	4.8	4.1	12.6	13.5	14.0	105.1	113.1	95.7	
1916	5.8	7.4	5.1	12.3	13.8	13.6	105.6	117.7	99.0	
1917	5.2	6.4	4.9	11.4	12.4	12.4	107.9	118.8	95.7	
1918	2.7	3.0	1.8	9.6	10.2	9.7	97.6	107.1	86.8	
1919	1.6	1.8	1.4	7.9	8.3	7.4	88.1	96.3	73.5	
1920	1.0	1.2	0.6	7.1	7.7	6.3	89.2	97.4	70.8	0.4
1921	1.8	1.9	0.9	7.4	8.0	6.5	85.0	89.5	68.0	0.2
1922	2.6	3.3	2.1	7.4	8.1	5.8	87.9	94.3	70.3	0.2
1923	3.2	4.3	3.0	7.2	7.6	5.8	89.3	94.9	69.6	0.1
1924	3.2	4.5	2.9	7.3	7.9	5.8	88.8	91.8	66.5	0.2
1925	3.6	5.1	3.0	7.3	8.2	6.9	96.5	100.7	71.2	0.2
1926	3.9	5.3	3.7	7.2	8.0	6.7	98.5	102.7	74.9	0.2
1927	4.0	5.4	3.5	7.5	8.0	6.7	92.6	94.6	70.8	0.3
1928	4.0	4.3	3.3	7.6	8.4	6.7	95.2	94.6	71.9	0.3
1929	3.7	5.2	3.5	7.2	8.1	6.6	91.2	90.8	70.6	0.2
1930			3.2			6.8			68.9	

SOURCES OF DATA:

Registration area and registration states of 1900: Bureau of the Census.

Industrial department, Metropolitan Life Insurance Company: *Statistical Bulletin,* Metropolitan Life Insurance Company, January, 1920, and January, 1931, and letters from the statistician of the company.

diseases are given for the entire registration area of the United States, for the registration states of 1900, and for the industrial population insured by the Metropolitan Life Insurance Company. Death rates from wood and denatured alcohol are also given since 1920 for the registration area.

The effect of prohibition upon death rates from these diseases is shown more clearly in Table 102, in which average rates are given for five periods: (1) the first four years of the century; (2) the last four pre-war years; (3) the period of war-time restrictions, 1918 and 1919 (including six months of the War Prohibition Act); (4) the early prohibition period, 1920 to 1922; and (5) the late prohibition period, 1927 to 1929.

TABLE 102

AVERAGE ANNUAL DEATH RATES FROM DISEASES ASSOCIATED WITH THE USE OF ALCOHOL BEFORE AND SINCE THE ADOPTION OF PROHIBITION

(average annual rate per 100,000 persons)

Period	Alcoholism			Cirrhosis of the liver			Nephritis		
	(1)	(2)	(3)	(1)	(2)	(3)	(1)	(2)	(3)
1900-03	6.3	5.4		13.7	13.0		91.6	91.2	
1911-14	5.3	5.8	4.8	13.5	13.9	15.7	101.6	112.6	
1918-19	2.2	2.4	1.6	8.8	9.3	8.6	92.9	101.7	80.2
1910-22	1.8	2.1	1.2	7.3	7.9	6.2	87.4	93.7	69.7
1927-29	3.9	5.0	3.4	7.4	8.2	6.7	93.0	93.3	71.1

SOURCE OF DATA:

Table 101, *supra*, p. 213.

In Table 103 there are given data from hospital records

TABLE 103

HOSPITALIZATION OF ALCOHOLIC CASES

(rate per 10,000 population)

Year	New York City Discharged for acute alcoholism from public hospitals	Boston Alcoholic admissions at three hospitals	New York New cases of alcoholic mental disease at 56 civil hospitals	Massachusetts Alcoholic first admissions to hospitals for the insane	Connecticut Commitments for alcoholic insanity
1912		33.0	.61	.85	1.05
1913		35.9	.61	1.02	1.24
1914	18.23	36.5	.49	.82	1.26
1915	16.13	36.8	.36	.81	1.30
1916	20.34	43.6	.41	.76	1.28
1917	16.00	44.0	.60	1.33	1.04
1918	6.82	24.6	.35	.77	.74
1919	6.35	22.1	.26	.77	.33
1920	5.89	14.1	.12	.26	.32
1921	6.79	26.4	.18	.38	.42
1922	11.85	41.7	.21	.54	.28
1923	16.15	46.5	.26	.56	.26
1924	17.83	42.8	.34	.59	.31
1925	17.63	36.8	.38	.42	.40
1926	18.40	41.8	.37	.44	.52
1927	18.54	35.7	.48	.49	.53
1928	18.89	35.4	.43	.48	.66
1929	18.30	35.7	.44	.53	
1930	19.04	35.3	.44		

SOURCES OF DATA:

New York City: Director of the Department of Public Hospitals for New York City. Figures relate to the Bellevue and Allied and Department of Public Welfare Hospitals.

Boston: Stoddard and Woods, *Fifteen Years of the Drink Question in Massachusetts,* (Boston, 1929), p. 107, and Supplement 1, p. 4. Figures relate to the Washingtonian Home, the Foxboro-Norfolk Institution and the Boston City Hospital. Rate per 10,000 population computed by the author on the basis of interpolations of census reports. In 1916 and again in 1921 changes in the handling of alcoholic cases were made at the Boston City Hospital so that the figures prior to, and after, these dates are not strictly comparable.

New York: Frederick W. Brown, Director, Department of Information and Statistics, The National Committee for Mental Hygiene.

Massachusetts: Stoddard and Woods, *Fifteen Years of the Drink Question in Massachusetts,* p. 108, and Supplement 1, p. 4.

Connecticut: Ralph H. White, "Prohibition in Connecticut," U. S. Congress, House, Committee on the Judiciary, *The Prohibition Amendment*, p. 860.

regarding alcoholism in two large cities, and regarding alcoholic insanity in three states.[1]

Again, the effect of prohibition can be seen more clearly if we average the figures for various periods: (1) the pre-war period, 1912 to 1915; (2) the period of war-time restrictions, 1918 and 1919; (3) the early prohibition period, 1920 to 1922; and (4) the late prohibition period, 1927 to 1930. Averages for these periods are given in Table 104.

TABLE 104

AVERAGE ANNUAL RATES OF HOSPITALIZATION OF ALCOHOLIC CASES BEFORE AND SINCE THE ADOPTION OF PROHIBITION

Period	New York City Discharges from acute alcoholism from public hospitals	Boston Alcoholic admissions at three hospitals	New York New cases of alcoholic mental disease at 56 civil hospitals	Massachusetts Alcoholic first admissions to hospitals for the insane	Connecticut Commitments for alcoholic insanity
1912-15	17.18	35.6	.52	.88	1.21
1918-19	6.59	23.4	.31	.77	.54
1920-22	8.18	27.4	.17	.39	.34
1927-30	18.69	35.5	.45	.50	

SOURCE OF DATA:

Table 103, *supra*, p. 215. Figure for New York City in the 1912-15 row is an average of the years 1914 and 1915 only; and that for Massachusetts in the 1927-30 row is for 1927-29.

It may be concluded from these statistics of death rates and of hospitalization that both during the period of war-time restrictions and during the early years of prohibition the frequency of cases of alcoholism, cirrhosis of the

[1] The author has made no especial attempt to collect data regarding hospitalization of alcoholic cases. The data given in Table 103 are taken from published sources, though in part verified and brought up-to-date by correspondence.

liver, nephritis, and alcoholic insanity decreased to a marked degree. In recent years these diseases have occurred more frequently than during the early years of prohibition, but for the most part are still somewhat below the pre-war rates.

The Effect of Prohibition Upon the General Death Rate and the Death Rate from Tuberculosis. That prohibition has had a favorable effect upon the general health of the American people has been argued not only by active protagonists of the Eighteenth Amendment, but also by eminent scholars.[2] It has been recognized by those presenting this argument that the basic cause of improvement in public health during the post-war years has been the improvement in economic conditions and standards of living, but prohibition has been considered the chief factor in bringing about better conditions of life. That is, the argument that prohibition has benefited public health has rested on the assumptions that prohibition made important changes in the national patterns of consumption and expenditure, and raised the productive efficiency of the nation. In preceding chapters these assumptions have been found to have little validity. Their fallacy, however, does not prove that prohibition has not been a factor in the improvement of public health, for it is possible that changed habits of drinking and the reduced consumption of beer have been of direct benefit to the health of the nation.

The general death rate and the death rate from tuberculosis are probably two of the best indicators available

[2] Louis I. Dublin, "Has Prohibition Improved the Public Health?" *The American Journal of Public Health,* January, 1928; reprinted in *Health and Wealth,* (New York, 1928), ch. 14. Haven Emerson, "Prohibition and Public Health," *The Survey,* December 1, 1928, pp. 289-336.

TABLE 105

DEATH RATES FROM ALL CAUSES, AND FROM TUBERCULOSIS, 1900 TO 1930

(1) Registration area of the United States.
(2) Registration states of 1900.
(3) Industrial department, Metropolitan Life Insurance Company.

Year	Death rate from all causes per 1,000 population			Death rate from tuberculosis per 10,000 population		
	(1)	(2)	(3)	(1)	(2)	(3)
1900	17.6	17.2		20.2	19.5	
1901	16.5	16.1		19.7	19.0	
1902	15.9	15.2		18.5	17.4	
1903	16.0	15.3		18.9	17.7	
1904	16.5	16.0		20.1	18.9	
1905	16.0	15.6		19.2	18.1	
1906	15.7	15.7		18.0	17.8	
1907	16.0	14.5		17.9	17.6	
1908	14.8	14.9		16.8	16.9	
1909	14.4	14.8		16.1	16.3	
1910	15.0	15.6		16.0	16.5	
1911	14.2	15.0	12.5	15.9	15.9	22.5
1912	13.9	14.6	12.0	15.0	15.0	
1913	14.1	14.7	12.0	14.9	14.9	
1914	13.6	14.4	11.5	14.7	14.9	20.5
1915	13.6	14.3	11.3	14.6	14.7	19.8
1916	14.0	15.0	11.7	14.2	14.4	19.0
1917	14.3	15.0	11.6	14.7	14.7	18.9
1918	18.1	18.9	15.6	15.0	15.1	18.9
1919	12.9	13.5	10.6	12.6	12.5	15.7
1920	13.0	13.8	9.9	11.4	11.2	13.8
1921	11.6	12.1	8.7	9.7	9.4	11.7
1922	11.7	12.5	8.8	9.6	9.1	11.4
1923	12.2	12.8	9.0	9.3	9.0	11.1
1924	11.7	12.2	8.5	9.0	8.6	10.4
1925	11.8	12.3	8.5	8.7	8.2	9.8
1926	12.3	12.8	8.9	8.7	8.2	10.0
1927	11.4	11.7	8.4	8.1	7.5	9.4
1928	12.1	12.3	8.7	7.9	7.5	9.1
1929	11.9	12.3	8.9	7.6	7.2	8.7
1930	11.3		8.3			8.1

SOURCES OF DATA:

Registration area of the United States, and registration states of 1900: Bureau of the Census.

Industrial department, Metropolitan Life Insurance Company: *Statistical Bulletin*, Metropolitan Life Insurance Company, January, 1924, and January, 1931.

of the state of the public health. Both of these rates have been substantially lower during the post-war period than prior to the war. These rates are given in Table 105 for the registration area of the United States, the registration states of 1900, and the industrial policyholders of the Metropolitan Life Insurance Company.

For many years the trend of the death rate from all causes and that from tuberculosis have both been downward. The rate of decline was accelerated at about the time prohibition went into effect, but there has been no reversal of the downward trend in recent years, as in the case of diseases directly associated with the use of alcohol. It is known that death rates from all causes, and especially that from tuberculosis, are affected by industrial exposure and occupation. Thus, the highest rate of deaths from tuberculosis among females occurs in the age group from 20 to 24, while that among males occurs in the age group from 35 to 64, which are the ages when the largest proportions of females and males, respectively, are engaged in gainful occupations. The death rate from tuberculosis among industrial policyholders of the Metropolitan Life Insurance Company is considerably above the rate for the general population, while the rate among ordinary policyholders in that company is below the rate for the general population.[3]

These considerations suggest that the accelerated rate of decline from 1919 to 1921 in the death rate from all causes and the death rate from tuberculosis is probably

[3] A. J. Lanza and R. J. Vane, "The Prevalence of Tuberculosis in Industry," *Statistical Bulletin*, Metropolitan Life Insurance Company, July, 1930, pp. 6-10.

due to some factor more directly connected than prohibition with industrial exposure and the standard of living. Probably the best measure of industrial exposure available is the weekly hours of work, and in Table 106 the average hours of work, and the estimated consumption of alcohol are given for several periods, together with the death rate from all causes and from tuberculosis. These periods are: (1) the first four years of the century; (2) the last four pre-war years, 1911 to 1914; (3) the years of war-time restrictions on alcoholic beverages, 1918 and 1919; (4) the early prohibition period, 1920 to 1922; and (5) the late prohibition period, 1927 to 1929.

TABLE 106

DEATH RATES, HOURS OF LABOR, AND THE CONSUMPTION OF ALCOHOL

Period	Death rate per 1,000 from all causes (1)	(2)	Death rate per 10,000 from tuberculosis (1)	(2)	Average weekly hours in industry	Consumption of alcohol, gallons per capita
1900-03	16.0		18.4		56.6	1.45
1911-14	14.7	12.0	15.2		54.0	1.69
1918-19	16.2	13.1	13.8	17.3	51.8	.97
1920-22	12.8	9.1	9.9	12.3	50.4	.73
1927-29	12.1	8.7	7.4	9.1	49.6	1.14

SOURCES OF DATA:

Death rates: Table 105, *supra*, p. 218. Rates in columns (1) are for the registration states of 1900, and those in columns (2) for the industrial department, Metropolitan Life Insurance Company. The death rate from all causes for the 1918-19 period is abnormally high on account of the influenza epidemic of 1918.

Average weekly hours in industry: all periods except 1927-29, Douglas, *Real Wages in the United States, 1890 to 1926*, p. 208; 1927-29, *Survey of Current Business*, Annual Supplement, 1931, p. 185. For the years 1925 and 1926 there was no substantial difference between the hours of work in all industry, as estimated by Douglas, and the hours in factories, as reported in the *Survey of Current Business*, and it is assumed that this was true also from 1927 to 1929.

Consumption of alcohol: Table 1, *supra*, p. 24, and Table 45, *supra*, p. 104. Figures given in the 1920-22 row relate to 1921 and 1922 only.

It is apparent that the death rates from all causes and from tuberculosis are more closely related to hours of labor than to the consumption of alcohol. There is thus no statistical evidence, at least so far as these death rates are concerned, that prohibition has had a measurable influence upon the general public health, either directly or indirectly through the standard of living.[4]

The Effect of Prohibition Upon Automobile Accidents. In view of the effect of alcohol upon the nervous system, it is reasonable to suppose that there is considerable relation between the frequency of automobile accidents and the consumption of alcohol. In Table 107 there is given an index of fatalities caused by motor vehicles since 1913, together with an index of the consumption of alcohol.

[4] This conclusion, it should be noted, though at variance with those drawn by Dr. Emerson and Mr. Dublin, is in accord with their actual findings. Mr. Dublin summarizes his analysis of the death rate as follows:

"The improvement in mortality during the period between 1921 and 1926 . . . was entirely limited to the group of white females. We may summarize our findings as follows: that the prohibition period is characterized by sharply declining mortality rates among children and adolescents of both sexes; and that this decline is characteristic of a number of additional age periods among women. The improvement is retarded among young male adults and disappears altogether during the middle years of life in that sex. In fact, the mortality has definitely risen among men, after age 35.

"At the children's ages, the greatest improvement in the death rate has taken place from accidents, from diarrheal diseases and from pneumonia. Infectious diseases have likewise declined considerably.

"It would appear, therefore, that the improvement is a response, in some measure, to the direct attack made by health and social service agencies, both public and private, which has been going on for years against the communicable diseases and against the diarrheal diseases of childhood. But, in addition, it may be considered a reaction to a rising standard of living, and this is especially evidenced by the lower tuberculosis and the lower pneumonia rates." (Dublin, "Has Prohibition Improved the Public Health?" *The American Journal of Public Health*, January, 1928).

The index of motor vehicle fatalities has been constructed by adding together the death rate per million population and the death rate per hundred thousand registered motor vehicles. This is a simple, though not entirely satisfactory, method of making allowance both for population growth and for the increased use of automobiles.

TABLE 107

INDEXES OF MOTOR VEHICLE FATALITIES AND OF ALCOHOL CONSUMPTION

Year	Index of motor vehicle fatalities 1913-14=100	Index of alcohol consumption 1911-14=100	Annual changes Motor vehicle fatalities	Annual changes Alcohol consumption
1913	107.7	101.2		
1914	92.3	98.8	—15.4	— 2.4
1915	96.0	86.4	3.7	—12.4
1916	95.8	89.3	— 0.2	2.9
1917	95.5	97.0	— 0.3	7.7
1918	91.1	66.9	— 4.4	—30.1
1919	82.7	47.3	— 8.4	—19.6
1920	82.0		— 0.7	
1921	84.3	32.0	2.3	
1922	86.5	53.8	2.2	21.8
1923	93.4	63.3	6.9	9.5
1924	93.0	62.1	— 0.4	— 1.2
1925	98.1	65.1	5.1	3.0
1926	100.3	69.8	2.2	4.7
1927	108.2	66.3	7.9	— 3.5
1928	113.8	69.8	5.6	3.5
1929	124.8	71.0	11.0	1.2

SOURCES OF DATA:

Index of motor vehicle fatalities: *Statistical Abstract of the United States,* 1931, p. 407. Index constructed by adding for each year the deaths per 1,000,000 population and the deaths per 100,000 cars registered, and converting to relative numbers.

Index of alcohol consumption: Table 94, *supra*, p. 198.

The coefficient of correlation between the annual changes in the consumption of alcohol and in motor vehicle fatalities, during the pre-prohibition period from 1913 to 1929, is only +.397, which is no proof of relationship, since with the small number of cases there is nearly one chance out of two of obtaining a coefficient as large as this by chance.

On the other hand, the index of motor vehicle fatalities is lower during the years from 1919 to 1922 than in other years, and these are also the years of lowest consumption of alcohol. This may be due to a genuine relationship between the two series, or the lower rates of the index of motor vehicle fatalities during the middle years of the period covered may be due to the method of combining the rates for the human and the automobile populations.

Furthermore, it is possible, as in the case of industrial accidents, that there is little relationship between fatalities from motor vehicle accidents and the consumption of alcohol, but considerable relation between the frequency of accidents, or the number of persons injured, and the consumption of alcohol. In other words, the cursory analysis made here is entirely inconclusive as to the relation of the consumption of alcohol to motor vehicle accidents, or as to the effect of prohibition upon motor vehicle accidents.[5]

The Effect of Prohibition upon Crime. To make a statistical examination of the relation of prohibition to crime is still more difficult than to analyze its relation to motor vehicle accidents. There are no statistics avail-

[5] Application of the method of multiple correlation to the problem of automobile accidents, taking into account various factors, such as improvements in braking power and car control, highway construction and traffic regulation, as well as the increased use of automobiles and the consumption of alcohol, would probably throw considerable light on the relative importance of various causes of motor vehicle accidents. Special methods would have to be devised for obtaining numerical measurements or estimates of some of these factors; and the amount of work required has precluded the making of this kind of analysis in connection with the present study of prohibition.

TABLE 108

ALCOHOL CONSUMPTION AND CRIMINAL ACTIVITY

Year	Homicides in large cities per 100,000 population	Prosecutions begun in lower courts in Massachusetts per 100,000 population	Convictions in New York State per 100,000 population: Courts of record	Convictions in New York State per 100,000 population: Courts of special sessions	Consumption of alcohol per capita in United States (gallons)
1900	3.4	1340	57	428	1.38
1901	3.6	1305	62	450	1.38
1902	3.8	1285	62	474	1.49
1903	4.2	1280	49	465	1.53
1904	4.6	1343	58	508	1.55
1905	6.1	1317	61	550	1.53
1906	7.2	1420	64	570	1.64
1907	8.5	1352	68	602	1.75
1908	8.0	1597	81	634	1.64
1909	6.9	1541	75	684	1.56
1910	8.0	1488	66	616	1.64
1911	7.9	1551	73	577	1.70
1912	7.7	1555	81	570	1.66
1913	8.6	1680	80	625	1.71
1914	8.5	1757	94	739	1.67
1915	8.2	1823	105	749	1.46
1916	8.5	1625	75	716	1.51
1917	9.5	1749	82	702	1.64
1918	8.5	1507	70	482	1.13
1919	8.9	1580	77	456	.80
1920	8.4	1386	66	323	
1921	9.2	1612	86	448	.54
1922	9.2	1460	104	421	.91
1923	10.0	1339	74	548	1.07
1924	10.8	1512	76	595	1.05
1925	11.1	1499	80	612	1.10
1926	10.5	1381	84	597	1.18
1927	10.5	1399	71	634	1.12
1928	10.2	1375			1.18
1929	9.8	1390			1.20

SOURCES OF DATA:

Homicides: *Statistical Abstract of the United States*, 1931, p. 91.

Prosecutions in lower courts, Massachusetts: Emma A. Winslow, "Relationships between Employment and Crime Fluctuations as Shown by Massachusetts Statistics," *Report on the Causes of Crime*, National Commission on Law Observance and Enforcement, Report No. 13, vol. 1, pp. 364-77. Prosecutions for drunkenness and for violations of liquor and traffic laws not included.

Convictions in New York State: Mary Van Kleeck, "Notes on Fluctuations in Employment and Crime in New York State," *Report on the Causes of Crime*, National Commission on Law Observance and Enforcement, Report no. 13, vol. 1, pp. 388-89. Convictions in courts of record include crimes against persons and against property; and those in courts of special session include assault of the third degree, intoxication, misdemeanor, petit larceny, vagrancy and tramping, and violation of the liquor laws. These rates may be somewhat distorted for some years by the method of computation, as it is doubtful whether interpolations have been made for population in inter-censal years.

Consumption of alcohol: Table 1, *supra*, p. 24, and Table 45, *supra*, p. 104.

able in the United States either for the entire nation, or a fair sample thereof, regarding the frequency of crimes, with the exception of homicides. Statistics of crimes known to the police are not collected in the United States. Neither statistics of arrests, prosecutions nor convictions for causes other than drunkenness and violations of traffic ordinances are collected in a sufficiently uniform manner or over a large enough area to make them representative of conditions throughout the nation.[6] In only two states, in fact, are reliable criminal statistics available for a number of years before, as well as since, the adoption of prohibition.

In Table 108, therefore, the consumption of alcohol is compared only with the rate of homicides in large cities, with prosecutions begun in the lower courts in Massachusetts for causes other than drunkenness and violations of liquor and traffic laws, and with convictions in New York State in courts of record and courts of special sessions.

In Table 109 these statistics of homicides in large cities, prosecutions in Massachusetts and convictions in New

[6] See the *Report on Criminal Statistics*, National Commission of Law Observance and Enforcement, Report No. 3, April 1, 1931.

York State are summarized for several periods: (1) the first four years of the century; (2) the last four pre-war years, 1911 to 1914; (3) the years of war-time restrictions on alcoholic beverages, 1918 and 1919; (4) the early prohibition period, 1920 to 1922; and (5) a later prohibition period, 1925 to 1927.

TABLE 109

ALCOHOL CONSUMPTION AND CRIMINAL ACTIVITY: ANNUAL AVERAGE RATES FOR VARIOUS PERIODS

Period	Homicides in large cities per 100,000 population	Proceedings begun in lower courts in Massachusetts per 100,000 population	Convictions in New York State per 100,000 population: Courts of record	Convictions in New York State per 100,000 population: Courts of special sessions	Consumption of alcohol in the United States, gallons per capita
1900-03	3.8	1303	58	454	1.45
1911-14	8.2	1636	82	628	1.69
1918-19	8.7	1544	74	469	.97
1920-22	9.0	1486	85	397	.73
1925-27	10.7	1426	78	614	1.13

SOURCE OF DATA:

Table 108, *supra*, p. 224.

It will be noted that the trend of the homicide rate has been upward since the beginning of the century. This trend conceals the relationship between homicides and the consumption of alcohol, for when it is removed for the pre-prohibition period from 1900 to 1918, there is a coefficient of correlation of +.75 between the two series. This indicates that about 56 per cent of the deviations in the homicide rate from the trend are associated with variations in the consumption of alcohol. During the entire prohibition period, and also in 1918 and 1919, the homicide rate has been below the trend projected from the pre-prohibition period.

It will also be noted that the rate of prosecutions begun in the lower courts of Massachusetts showed an upward trend in pre-war years, and that this rate has been lower during the prohibition years than during the previous decade. In New York State the rate of convictions in the courts of special sessions was considerably reduced in 1918 and 1919, dropped still further during the early years of prohibition and has since increased nearly to the pre-prohibition level. When the rates for specific offences are examined, it appears that convictions for assault in the third degree, for intoxication and for misdemeanors were all reduced during the period of war-time restrictions and during the early prohibition period, and that all have since increased. Convictions for petit larceny and for vagrancy and tramping appear to have been little affected, while convictions for violation of liquor laws have practically ceased since 1919. The rate of convictions for crimes against persons and property in courts of record appear also to have been affected but little, if at all, by prohibition.

These statistics are fragmentary and so many other factors than the consumption of alcohol are associated with the frequency of crimes that conclusions with respect to the effect of prohibition must be stated with caution. The statistics available, however, point to the conclusion that there is some association between criminal activity and the consumption of alcohol, and that the frequency of some types of crime has been reduced to some extent by prohibition. But this reduction is slight in recent years.

CHAPTER XI

Prohibition and Economic Groups

Any far-reaching change in the conditions of production and sale of a commodity, such as have resulted from the Eighteenth Amendment and the Volstead Act, cannot fail to have significant effects on particular economic groups. When the nation as a whole is considered, these effects may more or less offset each other; but that does not lessen the effects of the change upon the persons within those groups.

The Farming Class. It has been claimed, on the one hand, that prohibition has brought disaster to the farmers; and on the other, that it has been a boon to them.[1] Both these contentions are in part true, for some farmers have lost markets and others have gained new ones as a result of prohibition. Thus farms formerly producing grains especially for the use of large breweries and distilleries found these markets suddenly curtailed, but many other farmers now sell to corn sugar manufacturers or themselves produce alcoholic beverages to be sold in nearby cities.

The most important material used in producing beverage spirits prior to prohibition was corn. A comparison of the quantity used at that time with the quantity used in recent years indicates that the total market has been

[1] See, for example, Loring M. Black, "What the 'Noble Experiment' Costs the Growers of Grain," *Plain Talk*, October, 1928; "Dry Law Proves Economic Boon to Agriculture," *The Christian Science Monitor*, June 12, 1930; and Louis J. Tabor, U. S. Congress, House, Committee on the Judiciary, *The Prohibition Amendment*, pp. 674-82.

affected but little. From 1901 to 1914 the annual quantity of corn used in the production of alcoholic beverages varied from 17 to 24 million bushels, while that used in recent years in the production of corn sugar and corn meal later converted into beverage spirits is apparently about 21 million bushels.[2] This does not take into account the corn converted into beverage spirits by the farmers themselves.

In regard to rye, of which about 5 million bushels per year were used in pre-prohibition times in the production of alcoholic spirits, no direct comparison is possible, since it is not possible to estimate the quantity now used in producing illicit beverage alcohol. The acreage devoted to the production of rye has not declined, averaging in recent years about 3.5 million acres as compared with 2.3 million acres from 1909 to 1914; and the price received by the farmers has been slightly higher in recent years than during that period. This is on account of larger exports than in pre-war years, the total quantity of rye sold in the domestic market being in recent years about 10 per cent less than that sold prior to 1914.[3] It is

[2] Corn used from 1901 to 1914 from *Statistics Concerning Intoxicating Liquors*, December, 1930, p. 63. In 1929 the corn products industry produced 3 billion pounds of cornstarch, dextrin, corn syrup and corn sugar from 87 million bushels of corn, or an average of 35 pounds of these products per bushel of corn (*The Story of a Grain of Corn*, Associated Corn Products Manufacturers, p. 23). Since 70 and 80 corn sugar contain, probably, more water than cornstarch but less than corn syrup, it may be assumed that the above rate is approximately the rate of conversion of corn into corn sugar. The average annual quantity of corn sugar used in the production of beverage alcohol is apparently about 600 million pounds, which means the use of about 17 million bushels of corn. To this must be added about 4 million bushels of corn used for beverage alcohol in the form of corn meal. (See Table 16, *supra*, p. 52, and Table 18, *supra*, p. 56).

[3] *Yearbook of Agriculture*, 1930, p. 617.

not possible to determine from these figures whether the export market has taken rye that, without prohibition, would have been made into whisky, or whether the export market would have developed to its present size without prohibition.

The only other materials used to a large extent in the production of beverage spirits were molasses and barley, the latter used also in making beer. In the case of molasses the quantity used in recent years appears to be fully as great, and is probably greater, than in pre-war days. Molasses is the principal material used in making alcohol which is to be denatured, and when allowance is made for the ethyl alcohol withdrawn for denaturation in pre-prohibition years, the quantity used for the production of beverage spirits does not differ greatly from the quantity estimated to be so used under prohibition.[4] Besides, the major part of the molasses used in the United States is imported, and changes in the quantity used have no appreciable effect upon farmers in this country.

Farmers producing materials used in the making of beer have undoubtedly suffered a loss of markets, since the production of beer is estimated to be only about a third as much as formerly, and during the early years of prohibition was much less than a third. The chief materials used in producing beer are barley, hops, rice, corn and corn products, and sugar and sugar products. In Table 110 an estimate is made of the direct losses to farmers on account of these corps.

During the early years of prohibition the loss to the farmers was greater than the estimate in the above table, since during those years the consumption of beer was

[4] See Table 23, *supra*, p. 64, and *Statistics Concerning Intoxicating Liquors*, December, 1930, pp. 27 and 63.

TABLE 110

ESTIMATED ANNUAL LOSSES OF FARMERS ON ACCOUNT OF REDUCED PRODUCTION OF BEER

Barley: 38 million bushels at 57 cents per bushel..........	$21,660,000
Hops: 29 million pounds at 18 cents per pound.............	5,220,000
Rice: 140 million pounds at 2.1 cents per pound...........	2,940,000
Corn and corn products: 9 million bushels at 75 cents per bushel	6,750,000
Sugar and sugar products: more than offset by increased use for beverage spirits..................................	....
Total	$36,570.000

SOURCES OF DATA:

Reduction in use of barley, rice and corn: estimated by increasing the quantities used in producing beer in the fiscal year ending June 30, 1915, by one-fourth on account of the increase in population, and then taking two-thirds of this quantity (*Statistics Concerning Intoxicating Liquors,* December, 1930, p. 64). In the case of barley, the full amount used in producing spirits, increased by one-fourth, has been added, on the assumption that this material is not used appreciably in the production of spirits under prohibition.

Reduction in use of hops: quantity used in the fiscal year ending June 30, 1915, increased by one-fourth on account of population increase, less the average quantity estimated to be used from 1928 to 1930 in the production of beer (Table 4, *supra,* p. 31, and *Statistics Concerning Intoxicating Liquors,* December, 1930, p. 64).

Prices: averages of prices received by producers for the years 1927 to 1929 (*Yearbook of Agriculture,* 1930, pp. 626, 649, 667 and 812). Prices in 1930 are not included so as to avoid in these estimates the effect of the business depression.

curtailed more than two-thirds. It is possible that in addition to this direct loss the price received for these materials has been reduced on account of the loss of a part of the total market. However, the United States exports all of these products, and except in the case of corn, the price is set in the world market; and the reduced market for use in making beer in the United States does not appear to be a sufficiently great percentage of the world production to affect the price greatly. Moreover, there should be offset against these losses the gains derived from substitute crops or activities. It is an ample allowance, therefore, if we estimate the total loss to the farmers at a maximum of 50 million dollars per year.

Grape producers appear to have gained on account of prohibition. On account of the provision in the Volstead Act permitting the home manufacture of non-intoxicating fruit juices the market for wine grapes was stimulated during the early years of prohibition. The price paid the producers for wine grapes rose from an average of $10 per ton from 1909 to 1916 to $80 in 1921, a more than five-fold increase after allowance is made for the rise in the general price level. By 1929, however, the price had dropped to little more than half that in 1921, still far above the pre-prohibition price.[5] The average increase in price as a result of prohibition, allowing for the higher price level, is apparently about $40 per ton, which, at an average production of about 400,000 tons, would provide $16,000,000 added income per year to California producers.

The production of wine grapes does not appear to have been greatly increased on account of prohibition, despite the higher prices. The production of both raisin and table grapes has increased very rapidly in recent years, but the present production is little more than a continuation of the trend for many years prior to the adoption of prohibition. Producers of these varieties undoubtedly received larger incomes on account of prohibition during its early years, but it is not certain that they have done so in recent years.

In chapter eight it was estimated that the annual per

[5] Shear, *Economic Status of the Grape Industry*, pp. 94 and 120, and the *Yearbook of Agriculture*, 1930, p. 733. *Cf.* also Shear, *op. cit.*, p. 30, for the estimated California production of wine grapes.

capita use of milk is now about nine gallons higher than would have resulted from continuation of the pre-prohibition trend of use. If this is considered a direct substitute for beer, and there is little doubt that it is so in part, an added income to dairy farmers of about $240,000,000 may be attributed to prohibition.[6] If only a fourth of this unusual increase in the use of milk is to be attributed to prohibition, the gain to the dairy farmers more than balances the loss to the grain and hop growers.

The producers of sugar have probably also benefited to a slight extent, as a result of the use of approximately 400,000 tons per year in the production of illicit spirits.[7]

It is difficult to estimate the effect of prohibition upon farmers as consumers of alcoholic beverages. It is quite likely that they spend less upon liquor than formerly, since a considerable part of the alcoholic beverages used in rural regions is produced on the farms at low cost. In a former chapter it was roughly estimated that the expenditure of the farming class for liquor in 1910 was about $200,000,000, and a considerable part of this may have been made available for other uses.[8]

The Working Class. The best evidence available regarding the consumption of alcohol among the working class as compared with that of the general population is the death rate from alcoholism and cirrhosis of the liver among that class. In Table 111 there are given the percentage declines in the death rates from these diseases, both among the general population and among the industrial policyholders of the Metropolitan Life Insurance Company, under war-time

[6] Nine gallons of milk per capita amounts to 77.4 pounds, and the average price to the producers from 1927 to 1929 was $2.55 per 100 pounds (*Yearbook of Agriculture*, 1930, pp. 594 and 908).

[7] Table 21, *supra*, p. 62.

[8] Table 64, *supra*, p. 138.

restrictions and during the early and late prohibition periods.

TABLE 111

CHANGES IN DEATH RATES FROM DISEASES ASSOCIATED WITH THE USE OF ALCOHOL

	Percentage change compared with the four years ending June 30, 1914		
	War-time restrictions 1918-19	Early prohibition period 1920-22	Late prohibition period 1927-29
Alcoholism			
Registration area	—58	—66	—26
Registration states of 1910	—52	—63	—13
Registration states of 1900	—59	—64	—14
Industrial department, Metropolitan Life Insurance Company.	—67	—75	—29
Cirrhosis of the liver:			
Registration area	—35	—46	—45
Registration states of 1910	—28	—40	—35
Registration states of 1900	—33	—43	—41
Industrial department, Metropolitan Life Insurance Company.	—45	—61	—57
Both causes:			
Registration area	—41	—52	—40
Registration states of 1910	—35	—47	—28
Registration states of 1900	—41	—49	—33
Industrial department, Metropolitan Life Insurance Company.	—50	—64	—51

SOURCES OF DATA: Bureau of the Census and Table 101, *supra*, p. 213.

It should be borne in mind in considering the figures in this table that the rates for the registration area of 1900 or that of 1910 are more significant that the rates for the entire registration area. The latter are affected by the enlargement of the registration area, which in recent years includes a larger part of the sections of the nation with a lower consumption of alcohol than other sections.

Reference to Table 101 shows that prior to the World

War the death rate from alcoholism among the industrial population was less than that among the general population, but that the death rate from cirrhosis of the liver was higher among the industrial than the general population. This is in accord with the lower consumption of spirits and higher consumption of beer by members of the working class than by members of other classes. In recent years, however, both the death rate from cirrhosis and that from alcoholism among the industrial population have been below the rates for the general population. It is reasonable to assume, therefore, that the working class now consumes not only less spirits, but also less beer, than the population as a whole.

It may be observed that the combined death rate from alcoholism and cirrhosis of the liver among the industrial population is only 49 per cent as high from 1927 to 1929 as from 1911 to 1914. This indicates, on the basis of the relationship between the death rate from these diseases and the consumption of alcohol disclosed in chapter three, that the consumption of alcohol per capita by the industrial population has declined about sixty per cent.[9]

In a former chapter it was estimated that in 1910 the urban and village wage-earning class was responsible for about two-fifths of the total liquor bill, the amount spent by this class in that year being estimated at six hundred million dollars.[10] Since 1910 the general population has

[9] This is computed in the following way. In the registration states of 1910 the average annual death rate from alcoholism and cirrhosis of the liver during the period from 1911 to 1914 was 191 per million population, of which 49 per cent would be 94 per million. Applying the equation of relationship utilized in Table 36 (see footnote to that table, *supra*, p. 86), the corresponding consumption of pure alcohol by the general population would be .65 gallons, which is 38 per cent of the average annual consumption in 1911-14.

[10] *Cf.* Table 64, *supra*, p. 138.

increased by about one-third, but the wage-earning population has probably increased about forty per cent.[11] The annual liquor bill of the wage-earning class in recent years, under the conditions of 1911-14, would thus be nearly a billion dollars; which would be raised to nearly two billions if allowance is made for the probable effect upon prices of higher taxation and higher commercial costs of production.[12] This should be considered a maximum estimate, as no allowance is made for reduced consumption on account of the higher prices.

Under prohibition the working class probably pays less for its alcoholic beverages than other classes, since there is probably more home production among its members than among other classes, except the farmers. The cheaper grades of beverage spirits can also be obtained at as low a price as the average pre-war retail price.[13] It is thus possible that the wage-earning class is paying no higher prices, on the average, for its liquor than it paid prior to the World War. If so, the total liquor bill of the wage-earning class under prohibition may be estimated at about half a billion dollars, computed on the

[11] From 1910 to 1927 the number of wage-workers, outside of agriculture, increased by more than 38 per cent (King, *The National Income and Its Purchasing Power*, p. 56). This increase in the wage-earning population is an accompaniment of a relative decrease in the number of farmers and of proprietors of small business establishments.

[12] See Table 68, *supra*, p. 149, where the probable post-war price of beer, had prohibition not been adopted, is estimated at 1.8 times the pre-war price, and the probable post-war price of spirits at 2.7 times the pre-war price. Since the working class formerly purchased more beer than spirits, it is reasonable to assume that the average cost of liquors purchased by that class would approximately have doubled.

This estimate may also be obtained by assuming that without prohibition the wage-earning class, as in 1910, would be responsible for about two-fifths of the maximum estimate in Table 82, *supra*, p. 168.

[13] *Cf.* Tables 49 and 76, *supra*, pp. 113 and 158.

basis of 40 per cent as much consumption per capita and an increase of 40 per cent in numbers. But if, along with the rest of the urban population, the working class is paying higher prices for alcoholic beverages than prior to the World War, its total liquor bill may be nearly as great as it would have been without prohibition. The author believes that the most reasonable estimate, in view of both these considerations, is that the working class is now spending between half a billion and a billion dollars a year for alcoholic beverages, and has transferred about a billion dollars a year to other purposes, mostly other beverages. A billion dollars per year is about $35 per wage-earner, or $55 per family in the wage-earning class, and is about three per cent of the total income of the wage-earning class.[14]

The Business, Professional and Salaried Class. In 1927 the total number of persons normally attached to industry was about 45,400,000, of which 55 per cent were wage-earners outside of agriculture, 19 per cent were engaged in farming, and 26 per cent were entrepreneurs and salaried employees outside of agriculture.[15] While there may be some difference among these three major economic classes of the population as to the ratio between the number of persons gainfully employed and the number of persons dependent upon them, it is reasonable to sup-

[14] The number of wage-workers in 1927, outside of agriculture, is estimated by King at 25 millions, and the total income of wage-earners, including pensions and compensations, at 33 billion dollars in 1928 (King, *The National Income and Its Purchasing Power*, pp. 56 and 74). At the rate of increase in preceding years, the number of wage-workers in 1930 may be estimated at about 27½ million. In 1930 the total number of gainfully employed was 49 million and the total number of families 30 million, or about 1.6 persons per family gainfully employed. ("Gainful Workers in the United States by Industry Groups," and "Number of Families in the United States," Bureau of the Census, releases of September 9, 1931, and November 30, 1931.)

[15] King, *op. cit.*, pp. 50, 56, 60 and 62.

pose that the above percentages are approximately accurate as to the division of the entire population among these three classes.

If the death rate from alcoholism and cirrhosis of the liver among the wage-earning class, or 55 per cent of the population, has declined by 51 per cent, as is indicated by the experience of the Metropolitan Life Insurance Company, and that among the entire population by only 28 per cent, as is indicated by the experience of the registration states of 1910, the death rate among the 45 per cent of the population which do not belong to the industrial wage-earning class must be at the same level as in the period from 1911 to 1914. It is therefore reasonable to suppose that the consumption of alcoholic beverages by the farming class, and the business, professional and salaried class taken together, has been changed but slightly, if at all, by the Eighteenth Amendment and the Volstead Act.

The best evidence available regarding the consumption of alcoholic beverages by these classes separately is the difference in death rates from alcoholism and cirrhosis of the liver in rural and urban regions, allowance being made for the wage-earning part of the urban population. In Table 112 there are given the average annual death rates from these diseases, for 1911-14 and for 1926-28, in the rural and in the urban parts of the registration States and among the industrial population.

It will be noted from this table that the death rate from alcoholism in the urban parts of the registration States in 1926-28 was only 15 per cent below that in 1911-14, as compared with 35 per cent in the rural parts of the registration States and 27 per cent among industrial wage-earners. In view of the fact that the business, professional and salaried class constitute less than half the urban population, it appears probable that the death rate from alcoholism among members

TABLE 112

URBAN AND RURAL DEATH RATES FROM ALCOHOLISM AND CIRRHOSIS OF THE LIVER, 1911-14 AND 1926-28

	Average annual death rate per 100,000 population 1911-14	1926-28	Percentage change, 1911-14 to 1926-28
Alcoholism			
Rural part of registration States	4.0	2.6	—35
Cities in registration States	6.5	5.5	—15
Industrial department, Metropolitan Life Insurance Company	4.8	3.5	—27
Cirrhosis of the liver			
Rural part of registration States	10.0	5.9	—41
Cities in registration States	16.1	9.1	—43
Industrial department, Metropolitan Life Insurance Company	15.7	6.7	—57

SOURCES OF DATA:

Registration States: 1911-14, Table 56, *supra*, p. 122; 1926-28, computed from population statistics and from the number of deaths reported by the Bureau of the Census, *Mortality Statistics*, 1928, pp. 13-14.

Industrial department, Metropolitan Life Insurance Company: Table 101, *supra*, p. 213.

of that class is fully as high in recent years as it was prior to prohibition. The death rate from cirrhosis of the liver in the urban parts of the registration States was in 1926-28 43 per cent below that in 1911-14, as compared with 41 per cent in the rural part of the registration States and 57 per cent among industrial wage-earners. This indicates that there has probably been some reduction in the consumption of beer by the business, professional and salaried class, but a much smaller reduction than by the wage-earning class. Allowance must also be made for the expansion of the registration area between the two periods under consideration, and for the fact that this expansion has been for the most part in those sections of the country which are relatively "dry." This tends to make the computed reductions in the death rates from alcoholism and cirrhosis of the liver larger than the true reductions, both in the rural and the urban parts of the registration States.

When all of these facts are taken into consideration, it is reasonable to conclude that the per capita consumption of alcoholic beverages by the business, professional and salaried class is fully as great in recent years as it was prior to prohibition. It appears probable that this class consumes the major portion of the alcohol sold illegally under prohibition, and that most of this is in the form of distilled spirits, since about 70 per cent of the alcohol used in recent years is in the form of spirits.[16]

The business, professional and working class has increased in numbers about 50 per cent since 1910.[17] This class probably purchases most of its alcoholic beverages from speakeasies and bootleggers at average prices from three to four times as high as those prevailing prior to the War.[18] If the eight hundred fifty million dollars estimated to have been spent for liquor by the business, professional and salaried class in 1910,[19] is increased by 50 per cent to allow for the increase in numbers in the class, and multiplied by three to allow for higher cost, the total liquor bill of this class in 1929 may be estimated at about four billion dollars. In 1930, with reduced consumption and lower prices for liquor, the expenditure of this class for liquor may be put at about three billion dollars.

16 Table 30, *supra*, p. 72.

17 King estimates the number of entrepreneurs and salaried employees outside of agriculture at 8,190,000 in 1910 and 11,919,000 in 1927, an increase of 46 per cent (*The National Income and Its Purchasing Power*, pp. 60 and 62). Extending these figures would make the increase nearly to 50 per cent in 1929 and slightly over 50 per cent in 1930.

18 Tables 49 and 79, *supra*, pp. 113 and 164, respectively.

19 Table 64, *supra*, p. 138.

The total income of the business, professional and salaried class may be estimated at slightly over 50 billion dollars in 1929.[20] This class, then, is apparently spending about 8 per cent of its total income for alcoholic beverages, as compared with about 2 per cent by the wage-earning class.

It is reasonable to suppose that without prohibition the average price of alcoholic beverages used by the business, professional and salaried class would have been two or two and a half times the price prevailing prior to the World War.[21] If the use of liquor by this class were not reduced by higher prices, as it might have been without prohibition even though it has not been with prohibition, the liquor bill of the class, without prohibition, would probably now be two and a half or three billion dollars.[22] It may thus be concluded that the business, professional and salaried class is spending about a billion dollars per year for alcoholic beverages which without prohibition would have been available for other purposes.

The business, professional and salaried class includes most of the families in the nation with incomes of more

[20] King estimates the income of entrepreneurs, other property owners and salaried persons outside of agriculture at $50,253,000,000 in 1928 (*The National Income and Its Purchasing Power*, pp. 74, 108 and 138). The net income reported by individuals filing Federal income tax returns increased in 1929 by only .62 per cent over 1928 (*Statistics of Income for 1929*, preliminary report, p. 2). While some of the income from property is received by wage-earners and some farmers and wage-earners file income tax reports, these figures refer almost entirely to the business, professional and salaried class.

[21] Table 68, *supra*, p. 125.

[22] An estimate of two and a half billion dollars as the liquor bill of the business, professional and salaried class, without prohibition, may also be obtained by assuming that this class, as in 1910, would have been responsible for about half the maximum estimate of the total liquor bill as given in Table 82, *supra*, p. 149.

than three thousand dollars; and practically the entire sales of medium and high priced automobiles, high-class radios, electric refrigerators, and all the "quality" goods profusely advertised in weekly and monthly magazines are made to members of this class. In fact, this class constitutes by far the major portion of the market in the United States for all kinds of consumer goods except the absolute necessities of life. It is not reasonable to argue that the expenditure of money for liquor by the working class diverts it from other uses and thus detracts from prosperity, while that spent by the business and professional class does not so detract.[23] The conclusion reached in chapter eight that prohibition has not, since its early years, appreciably affected the total amount of purchases of other goods is not invalidated by the discussion in this chapter: for the release in purchasing power among wage-earners on account of a reduction in their consumption of beer has been offset by an absorption of purchasing power from the business, professional and salaried class in higher prices paid for liquor.

The Producers of Alcoholic Beverages. The effect of prohibition upon the producers of alcoholic beverages is of less economic importance than its effect upon large classes of the population, such as farmers and wage-earners. Yet the producers of alcoholic beverages are the persons who have been most vitally affected by the adoption of prohibition.

The personnel of the former legitimate industry, consisting of about 300,000 persons, was almost entirely dispersed during the period of restriction and the first year of prohibition.[24] While some of these persons may have

[23] Samuel Crowther, *Prohibition and Prosperity*, pp. 19-21.

[24] In 1910 there were 101,000 persons who gave their occupation as bar tenders and 68,000 as saloon keepers, and in 1914 there were 70,567

remained unemployed for a long time, it is probable that most of them obtained other jobs during the "boom" of 1919-20. Many of them, especially the skilled workers, doubtless had to accept lower wages in their new jobs.[25]

The conditions of production and sale in the illicit industry under prohibition differ greatly from those in the former legitimate industry. Both producing plants and retail outlets are located in less conspicuous places, materials are used in different forms, and methods of production and transportation have changed. Because of these changes, it is not probable that the personnel of the illicit industry, built up principally between 1922 and 1926, includes many of the same persons as the former legitimate industry. But since an industry that was centralized in the hands of about 2,000 producing establishments and 150,000 saloons has been driven into the hands of a multitude of small producers, bootleggers and speakeasies, and forced to provide private guards and armies of gangsters, it is highly probable, despite a reduction of two-thirds in the consumption of beer, that the number of persons engaged in the industry is larger than before prohibition.[26]

With the de-centralization of production there has doubtless come, despite the toll taken by gangsters and syndicates, a tendency toward a wider distribution of the receipts of the industry. Instead of taxes paid to the public treasury, "protection" money flows to police and

wage earners and 25,586 salaried persons employed by breweries, wineries and distilleries (*United States Census*, 1910, and *Census of Manufactures*, 1914).

[25] *Cf.* Feldman, *Prohibition: Its Economic and Industrial Aspects*, pp. 322-23.

[26] *Census of Manufactures*, 1921, pp. 682-86; and Feldman, *Prohibition: Its Economic and Industrial Aspects*, p. 146.

government officials. Many of the new small producers are farmers whose incomes have been reduced by the relatively low prices of agricultural products prevailing since the World War; others are workingmen without jobs as a result of industrial depression and changing industrial technique.[27] Prohibition may thus be a factor ameliorating for some people the hardships resulting from economic adjustments in farming, mining and manufacturing.

On the other hand, the illicit character of the industry has brought to the producers a high degree of uncertainty and danger. Not only do they face the possibility of raids, arrests and prison sentences, but also of gang warfare and reprisals and the uncertain results of frequent changes in the location of their producing and selling establishments.

[27] Walter W. Liggett, "Georgia, Godly but Guzzling," *Plain Talk*, May, 1930; Martha B. Bruere, *Does Prohibition Work?*, pp. 293-95.

CHAPTER XII

Prohibition and Public Finance

With the collapse in late 1929 and early 1930 of the "new economic era" most of the arguments dealt with in the preceding pages, especially those relating to the effect of prohibition upon prosperity, have rapidly become obsolete. The protagonists of prohibition who from 1925 to 1929 claimed that our national prosperity was due to the elimination of the drink bill have not yet credited the Eighteenth Amendment and the Volstead Act with responsibility for the ensuing depression.

On the contrary, it is now being argued that the abandonment of prohibition, at least in respect to beer, would lead to business revival, and that the taxation of alcoholic beverages would provide the best means of balancing the Federal government budget.[1] The former of these arguments is of little importance; but the latter deserves more serious consideration.

The Cost of Enforcing Prohibition. In view of the estimates in the preceding chapter that both the national per capita consumption of alcoholic spirits and the consumption of pure alcohol by the business, professional and salaried class are as great as in pre-war times, it is hardly appropriate to speak of the cost of enforcing pro-

[1] "Mr. Mellon's Oversight," editorial in the *Atlanta Constitution*, May 31, 1931; Leonidas C. Dyer, statement to President Hoover, *New York Times*, June 11, 1931, p. 1; John I. Haas, letter to the *New York Times*, May 2, 1931, p. 18. Other references could be cited to these arguments.

hibition: it would be more nearly in accord with the actual situation to speak of the cost of reducing the consumption of beer by the wage-earning class. It is, then, the expenditures upon attempted enforcement of the prohibition law rather than the cost of complete enforcement that are given in Table 113.[2]

TABLE 113

FEDERAL EXPENDITURES UPON THE ENFORCEMENT OF PROHIBITION
(thousands of dollars)

Year ending June 30	Direct cost: Bureau of Prohibition	Direct cost: Coast Guard	Indirect cost	Less fines and penalties	Total net expenditures
1920	2,200	.....	1,390	1,149	2,441
1921	6,350	.....	5,658	4,571	7,437
1922	6,750	.....	7,153	4,356	9,547
1923	8,500	.....	10,298	5,095	13,703
1924	8,250	.....	10,381	6,538	12,093
1925	10,012	13,407	11,075	5,873	28,621
1926	9,671	12,479	10,441	5,647	26,944
1927	11,993	13,959	11,482	5,162	32,272
1928	11,991	13,667	16,930	6,184	36,404
1929	12,402	14,123	16,839	5,474	37,890
1930	13,374	13,558	17,100	5,357	38,675

SOURCES OF DATA:

Bureau of Prohibition: *Statistics Concerning Intoxicating Liquors*, December, 1930, p. 2. Appropriations for narcotic work of the Bureau have been deducted.

Coast Guard, 1930: National Commission on Law Observance and

[2] The estimates given here for expenditures upon enforcement, though obtained in part by different methods, differ but little from those presented by Mr. J. M. Doran, former Commissioner of Prohibition (*New York Times*, June 16, 1929) and by the Association Against the Prohibition Amendment (*Cost of Prohibition and Your Income Tax*). Mr. Doran, however, deducted not only fines and penalties collected from violators of the law, but also taxes collected on distilled spirits and fermented liquors. These taxes are collected from legitimate sales of alcoholic beverages for medicinal, sacramental and scientific purposes, and to deduct them from the cost of enforcement is both illogical and misleading.

Enforcement, *Report on the Cost of Crime,* No. 12, p. 96. This is based on an estimate by the Commandant of the Coast Guard that half the total expenditure of the coast guard is incurred in connection with the enforcement of prohibition (see pages 97 and 98 of this report). Other years, 1925 to 1929, estimated in the same way from the total expenditures of the coast guard reported in the *Statistical Abstract of the United States,* various issues. These estimates appear reasonable, for the balance of expenditures by the Coast Guard is similar in amount to its annual expenditures prior to 1925.

Indirect cost, 1930: total cost as estimated by the National Commission on Law Observance and Enforcement (*Report on the Cost of Crime,* No. 12, pp. 98 and 149), less amounts spent by the Bureau of Prohibition and the Coast Guard. Other years estimated from the ratios between the number of criminal prosecutions under the National Prohibition Act in Federal courts each year and the number in the year 1930 (*Statistics Concerning Intoxicating Liquors,* December, 1930, p. 78).

Fines and penalties collected: *Statistics Concerning Intoxicating Liquors,* December, 1930, p. 2.

Figures for 1920 relate only to the latter half of the fiscal year.

To the expenditures of the Federal government should be added those of states and local governments. The states have been spending about seven hundred thousand dollars a year in the direct enforcement of prohibition, but their indirect expenditures, as well as the expenditures of local governments, cannot be estimated.[3] There is no evidence, however, that they have spent any larger sums for the enforcement of national prohibition than they formerly spent for the enforcement of state and local regulatory or prohibitory laws.

We may then consider the net annual expenditures upon the enforcement of prohibition to be approximately forty million dollars, which is slightly over one per cent of the total ordinary expenditures of the Federal government, and is not a sufficiently great burden to be an important factor in considering the merits of prohibition.

[3] Bureau of the Census, *Financial Statistics of States,* annual issues.

TABLE 114

INTERNAL REVENUE TAX RATES ON ALCOHOLIC BEVERAGES

Spirits: Period	Spirits: Rate per gallon	Beer: Period	Beer: Rate per barrel	Wine: Period	Wine: Rate per gallon, Alcohol content, Up to 14%	Wine: 14% to 21%	Wine: 21% to 24%
1862-1864	$.20	1862-1863	$1.00				
1864-1868	$2.00	1863-1864	.60				
1868-1872	.50	1864-1898	1.00				
1872-1875	.70	1898-1901	2.00				
1875-1894	.90	1901-1902	1.60	1862-1916	None		
1894-1917	1.10	1902-1917	1.50	1916-1917	$.04	$.10	$.25
1917-1919	3.20	1917-1919	3.00	1917-1919	.08	.20	.50
1919-	6.40	1919-	6.00	1919-	.16	.40	1.00

SOURCES OF DATA:

1862-1894: Frederic C. Howe, *Taxation and Taxes in the United States* (New York, 1896), p. 154.

1894-1919: Bender, *Federal Revenue Act of 1916*, and Feldman, *Prohibition: Its Economic and Industrial Aspects*, p. 26.

The rates given in this table are subject to a few exceptions. From March to June, 1864, the rate on spirits was $.60 per gallon. Spirits made from grapes, apples and peaches were taxed at lower rates than other spirits during part of the period prior to 1868. Since 1916 wines of more than 24 per cent alcoholic content have been classed as spirits for tax purposes.

The tax on spirits is on gallons of proof strength, that is, 50 per cent alcohol by volume.

The Loss of Government Revenues. The loss of government revenue is not, in the strict sense, a part of the cost of prohibiting the manufacture and sale of alcoholic beverages: or rather, it would not be so if prohibition were actually effective. The cost of government must be borne by the taxpayers in one form or another; and while the replacement of one tax by another may raise serious questions regarding the justice of tax incidence, the elimination of taxes upon alcoholic beverages is not of itself an economic loss.

When prohibition is ineffective, however, the situation

TABLE 115

GOVERNMENT REVENUE FROM ALCOHOLIC BEVERAGES
(thousands of dollars)

	Federal Government					
	Internal revenue					
Year	Distilled spirits	Fermented liquors	Customs	Total	States	Cities
1890	81,687	26,009	8,518	116,214	24,786	
1900	109,869	73,551	8,427	191,847		
1902	101,138	71,989	10,149	203,276	55,241	
1903	131,953	47,548	11,207	190,708	9,750	27,672
1905	135,959	50,361	12,093	198,415		29,616
1910	148,029	60,572	17,605	226,207		39,075
1911	155,280	64,368	16,663	219,648		40,387
1912	156,391	63,269	16,765	219,660		41,143
1913	163,879	66,267	18,833	230,147	20,993	51,947
1914	159,098	67,082	19,205	226,180		
1915	144,620	79,329	13,105	223,949	20,799	39,607
1916	158,682	88,771	15,286	247,453	19,263	38,025
1917	192,111	91,897	13,390	284,009	22,440	36,975
1918	317,554	126,286	6,969	443,840	20,849	35,576
1919	365,211	117,840	2,543	483,051	14,228	32,319

SOURCES OF DATA:

Federal Government: *Statistical Abstract of the United States,* various issues.

States and Cities: United States Bureau of the Census, *Wealth, Debt and Taxation,* 1890, 1902 and 1913; *Financial Statistics of States* and *Financial Statistics of Cities,* various issues.

Figures for states and cities for 1890 and 1902 include all local governments. The figure for cities in 1903 is for 148 cities and that for 1913 for all cities with over 2,500 population. Figures for cities for other years are for cities with over 30,000 population.

is somewhat different. Alcoholic beverages pay no tax, but the cost of evading the law and the inefficiencies of small scale, hidden and interrupted production keep the price of such beverages high. These costs of "protection" and of inefficiency are economic wastes, which constitute a burden upon the consumers of alcoholic beverages. The elimination of these costs would constitute an economic gain, a part of which might be absorbed by taxation and provide, as in pre-prohibition times, a considerable part of the revenue of the Federal government.

For nearly sixty years prior to the adoption of prohibition taxes on alcoholic beverages were an important source of Federal government revenue. The various rates of tax in force during this period are given in Table 114; and the amount of revenue obtained, for a number of pre-prohibition years, in Table 115.

It is apparent that various estimates may be made of the revenue which the Federal government might now be collecting, were alcoholic beverages subject to taxation instead of prohibition. In Table 116 five such estimates are given, based on the tax rates in force prior to the World War, those levied in 1917 and the still higher rates imposed in 1919, and on the average per capita consumption from 1911 to 1914 and during the fiscal years of 1918 and 1919.

TABLE 116

ESTIMATES OF LOSS OF FEDERAL GOVERNMENT REVENUE AS A RESULT OF PROHIBITION

(millions of dollars)

Year ending June 30	Based on average per capita consumption from 1911 to 1914, and tax rates in force from 1902 to 1917	from 1917 to 1919	since 1919	Based on average per capita consumption in the fiscal years 1918 and 1919, and tax rates in force from 1917 to 1919	since 1919
1920	278	725	1,451	405	809
1921	282	737	1,473	411	822
1922	287	748	1,496	417	835
1923	291	759	1,519	424	847
1924	295	771	1,541	430	860
1925	300	782	1,564	436	872
1926	304	793	1,586	443	885
1927	308	804	1,609	449	898
1928	313	816	1,631	455	910
1929	317	827	1,654	461	923
1930	321	838	1,677	468	935
1931	326	850	1,700	474	948

SOURCES OF DATA:

Per capita consumption, 1911-14 and 1918-19: Table 1, *supra*, p. 24.

Tax rates: Table 114, *supra*, p. 248.

Estimates of loss of revenue: computed from consumption and tax rates and population estimates. This method does not give the precise amount of revenue obtained in pre-prohibition years, because import duties differed from internal tax rates, but the error is not large. The difference between the first of these five estimates and that given in Table 65, *supra*, p. 141, is due principally to the inclusion of state and city revenues in the latter, but in part to a difference in the method of computation. The method used in Table 65 could not be used for all of the estimates of this table, and so a method has been used which could be made uniform.

In view of the large obligations of the Federal government after the close of the World War and the growing demand for restrictions on the sale of alcoholic beverages, it is not likely, had the Eighteenth Amendment not become effective, that tax rates would have been reduced to the pre-war level. The first estimate in the above table is therefore unreasonably low. On the other hand, the third estimate is unreasonable large, because the high rates imposed in 1919 could hardly have failed both to check consumption and to foster the sale of bootleg liquor.

It is impossible, however, to estimate with reasonable accuracy the extent to which taxation at the 1919 rate would have reduced consumption. There was a marked reduction in consumption after the change in tax rates in 1917; but since there were also other restrictions on the production and sale of liquor and the area under state and local prohibition was being rapidly extended, this reduction cannot be attributed solely, or even principally, to the increase in taxation. It has been estimated in a preceding chapter that prohibition, in spite of prices considerably higher than would have been necessary under the 1919 rates of tax, has not reduced the consumption of spirits. In view of this fact, and of the general prosperity from 1922 to 1929, it seems reasonable to suppose that consumption would have tended, under the 1917 rates but without prohibition, to return toward the 1911-14 level, and this might also have been true with the 1919 rates in force.

The tax collected from alcoholic beverages would, however, have tended to drop below the third estimate in Table 116 because of the relatively heavier increase in tax upon spirits than upon beer and wine, which would have tended to encourage the use of beer and wine in the place of spirits.

Furthermore, it is usual for excessively high taxation on any article of common use to result in the development of a contraband traffic. State taxes on gasoline, for example, have created a large bootleg traffic.[4] Even the low rates of taxation imposed on liquor prior to the World War were not readily collected in some parts of the country; and the rates in force from late 1917 to early 1919 tended to increase the illicit production of liquor, for in the fiscal year 1918-19 the seizures of stills and liquor increased about 70 per cent over the level of the preceding four years.[5]

In view of these tendencies, it is reasonable to assume that the tax rate on spirits in force from 1917 to 1919 was nearly as high as could readily be collected without a marked reduction in legitimate production. A tax of four dollars per gallon, which is six cents for a drink containing one ounce of pure alcohol, is probably the highest rate that it would be practicable to levy except in time of war.

The tax rate on beer has always been relatively lighter

[4] *The Business Week*, July 2, 1930, p. 12, and November 11, 1931, p. 10.

[5] *Statistics Concerning Intoxicating Liquors*, December, 1930, p. 72.

than that on spirits, being about half as much in proportion to alcoholic content prior to 1917, and a third as much since then. As beer is bulkier than spirits, it is less likely to be produced illicitly to avoid taxation, and should be able to bear without evasion as heavy a tax relative to alcoholic content as spirits. Ten dollars a barrel on beer is the equivalent of four dollars a gallon on spirits, assuming the beer to have an alcoholic content of 4½ per cent. This is two cents per half-pint drink, or three cents per seidel. But this tax would tend to check consumption more than the corresponding rate of tax on spirits, on account of the greater consumption of beer by the working class.

Rates of four dollars per gallon on spirits and ten dollars per barrel on beer, with corresponding rates on wine, would yield in 1932, at the 1911-14 rate of consumption, a total tax of $1,650,000,000; and at the rate of consumption during the last two fiscal years prior to prohibition, $930,000,000.[6] It is reasonable to suppose that the repeal of the Eighteenth Amendment and the levy of these rates would result in a lower consumption than in 1911-14, but greater than under war-time restrictions, and thus yield about one and one-fourth billion dollars. A rate of four dollars per gallon on spirits and five dollars per barrel on beer would probably yield about one billion dollars. If beer and light wines alone were legalized, with the tax on beer ten dollars per barrel, there would tend to be some substitution of these drinks for illicit spirits, and the total tax would probably be about three-fourths of a billion dollars. These are estimates of the probable maximum revenues. It is possible that with the knowl-

[6] This revenue would be reduced by the costs of collection. These costs, however, would be offset by the elimination of expenditures upon the enforcement of prohibition.

edge of processes of manufacture and distribution acquired under prohibition, bootleggers would continue to operate extensively under these rates of tax so that these amounts could not be raised for some years after legalization.

The amount of Federal government revenue which it would be possible to obtain from the taxation of alcoholic beverages is thus comparable in magnitude to each of the three principal sources of Federal revenue: the personal income tax, the corporation income tax, and the customs and excise taxes.[7]

The Incidence of Liquor Taxation. The respective merits of various kinds of taxes depend to a large extent upon the incidence of those taxes. Income taxes, which are generally considered the most just type of tax, are graduated so as to fall more heavily upon the well-to-do and the rich than upon the less well-to-do; and in the United States practically the entire farming and wage-earning classes are exempt.

Taxes on alcoholic beverages, like other taxes on articles of common consumption, fall on the users thereof. If the Eighteenth Amendment were repealed and the rates of 1917 or the rates discussed in the preceding paragraph levied upon liquor, the larger part of the tax would be paid by the business, professional and salaried class, since this class uses more liquor than either the farming or wage-earning class, or at least spends more upon it. This would be especially true if, as in pre-prohibition times,

[7] Each of these three sources brought to the Federal Treasury a little over one billion dollars in 1929 and in 1930, but the first two yielded only about half as much in 1931 (calendar year) (U. S. Treasury Dept., *Statistics of Income for 1930*, preliminary report, pp. 12 and 17; *Monthly Summary of Foreign Commerce of the United States*, December, 1931).

tax rates on spirits were relatively higher than on beer. The added tax burden on this class would not, however, be a serious one, for it would be more than offset by the reduction in liquor prices. Not all of the tax would fall upon this class, for the wage-earning class would doubtless resume its use of beer, and thus bear a considerable part of the liquor tax. If the Volstead Act were modified and beer and light wines alone taxed, the burden would be divided between the wage-earning class and the business, professional and salaried class; but in what proportions is difficult to estimate, because of the impossibility of determining to what extent the business, professional and salaried class would substitute legal beer and light wine for contraband spirits.[8]

It is the wealthy persons among the business, professional and salaried class who would gain the most by the taxation of alcoholic beverages, because they would be the greatest gainers from reductions in other types of Federal taxation. The amount of customs receipts is determined by tariff rather than by fiscal policies, and there is little likelihood that taxes on tobacco, which constitute the bulk of the internal revenue aside from income taxes, would be eliminated or reduced to offset taxes on alcoholic beverages. It is therefore highly probable that the imposition of high tax rates on alcoholic beverages would be accompanied by a substantial reduction in the personal income or corporation income tax or both.[9]

[8] The incidence of taxation discussed here is the permanent incidence. During the period of adjustment to new conditions, a great part of the tax burden on alcoholic beverages would fall upon those who now live directly and indirectly upon protection money and the profits from the illicit alcoholic beverage industry.

[9] If taxes on alcoholic beverages were introduced during a period of business depression and treasury deficits, like that of 1931 or 1932, they

In 1929, persons with incomes of over $100,000 per year, constituting only four-tenths of one per cent of all the persons filing income tax returns, paid 65 per cent of the total income tax; and persons with incomes of over $25,000, constituting but two and a half per cent of all the persons filing returns, paid 93 per cent of the individual income tax. These same persons received the major part of the dividends paid by domestic corporations, and therefore also paid the major part of the corporation income tax.[10] This wealthy class, consisting of only a hundred thousand persons and their dependents, would undoubtedly receive most of the benefit from tax changes.

The imposition of liquor taxes would thus be a means of shifting part of the burden of Federal income taxation from wealthy persons to the rest of the business, professional and salaried class and to the wage-earning class. That this is recognized by some members of the wealthy class and by advocates of the repeal of the Eighteenth Amendment is shown by evidence gathered by the lobby investigation committee of the United States Senate in 1930.[11]

would take the place of a general sales tax, or other new taxation, rather than resulting in reduced income taxes. The permanent effect, however, would probably be a reduction in income taxes.

[10] Bureau of Internal Revenue, *Statistics of Income for 1929*, pp. 9, 32 and 34.

[11] The argument that repeal of the Eighteenth Amendment would reduce income taxes has been used by the Association Against the Prohibition Amendment in soliciting subscriptions from wealthy persons; and Mr. Irenee du Pont is quoted as saying that one of his companies would save $10,000,000 a year in corporation tax if the United States were to adopt the British rate of tax on beer (U. S. Congress, Senate, Committee on the Judiciary, *Lobby Investigation*, pp. 3953, 3992-93 and 4165-67).

PART FOUR

SUMMARY AND CONCLUSIONS

CHAPTER XIII

The Economic Results of Prohibition

The alcoholic beverage industry is an outlaw industry in the United States. Because it is illegal, the statistical facts collected in regard to it are meagre. In the foregoing pages an attempt has been made to bring together such statistics as are available regarding this outlaw industry, to make the most reasonable estimates by indirect means where statistics are lacking, and thus to appraise the economic effects of outlawing the industry. The conclusions resulting from this statistical and economic analysis may now be summarized.

These conclusions must be read in the light of the bases upon which they rest, and are subject to margins of error which in some cases may be quite large. In the preceding analysis more than one basis of estimation has been used whenever possible, and care has been taken to ensure consistency among the assumptions upon which the estimates rest. Nevertheless, on account of the character of the data and of the assumptions which must be made in interpreting them, the range within which reasonable estimates may be made is considerable. Especially is this true in regard to expenditures upon alcoholic beverages, which may have been as much as a fourth, or even a third, greater or less than the estimates given here.

In these circumstances no study of the results of prohibition can claim high precision and unquestionable proof. The conclusions stated here can claim, however, to be reasonable inferences, after intensive study and analysis, from such data as are available.

The Effect of Prohibition upon the Consumption of Alcoholic Beverages. In the light of the available evidence, it may reasonably be concluded:

(1) That prohibition has reduced the per capita consumption of alcoholic beverages in terms of pure alcohol nearly one-third, when the years 1927-1930 are compared with the pre-war years 1911-1914; that is, from 1.69 to 1.14 gallons per year.

(2) That the per capita consumption of beer has been reduced about 70 per cent, from 20.53 gallons per year in 1911-1914 to 6.27 gallons in 1927-1930; the per capita consumption of wine has increased about 65 per cent, from .59 gallons per year in 1911-1914 to .98 gallons in 1927-1930; and that the per capita consumption of spirits has increased about 10 per cent, from 1.47 gallons per year in 1911-1914 to 1.62 gallons in 1927-1930.

(3) That during the first three years of prohibition, the consumption of alcoholic beverages was curtailed to a much greater extent than since that early period.

(4) That the per capita consumption of wine and of spirits has been fairly constant since 1923, subject to annual variations as a result of business fluctuations and other disturbing factors; and that the per capita consumption of beer increased steadily up to 1929, but dropped in 1930.

(5) That except for the first three years, the per capita consumption of alcohol has been greater under prohibition than during the war period, with high taxation and restricted production and sale.

The Effect of Prohibition upon National Expenditures. From the evidence available, it is reasonable to conclude:

1. That the total expenditure upon alcoholic beverages in the prosperous year of 1929 was nearly five billion dollars, and in the depression year of 1930 nearly four

billions; that this is about what the liquor bill would have been if alcoholic beverages had been sold under the conditions of 1911-1914 and taxed at the rates imposed in 1917; and that the expenditure upon beer is less, but that upon spirits more, than it would have been without prohibition.

2. That during the first three years of prohibition the liquor bill was reduced about two billion dollars per year.

3. That prohibition was not a significant factor in the increased purchases of automobiles, radios, electrical appliances, household equipment or other consumers' goods during the period of business prosperity from 1923 to 1929; and that prohibition, aside from the first year or two, has had no appreciable effect upon savings deposits, life insurance carried, deposits in building and loan associations, or other forms of saving and investment.

4. That the consumption of milk, coffee and carbonated beverages has increased considerably since the adoption of prohibition, and that each of these, as well as distilled spirits, may be a partial substitute for beer; but that it is not possible to determine the relative degree of substitution.

The Effect of Prohibition upon Industrial Efficiency. In regard to the efficiency of industry, it may reasonably be concluded:

1. That prohibition has not been a factor of measurable significance in the increased industrial productivity of recent years; and that statistical evidence is lacking as to the effect of prohibition upon industrial absenteeism.

2. That reduced consumption of alcohol under wartime restrictions and under prohibition may have been partially responsible for the decrease in the frequency of industrial accidents; but that the data available do not show a

measurable relation between prohibition and the frequency of fatal industrial accidents.

3. That there has been a great economic waste involved in the decentralization of the alcoholic beverage industry, both in the use of productive resources and of labor.

The Effect of Prohibition upon Economic Groups. The effect of prohibition upon the principal economic classes of the nation may be summarized as follows:

1. That some farmers have lost markets on account of prohibition, but that the farming class as a whole has gained more than it has lost.

2. That under prohibition the working class is consuming not more than half as much alcohol per capita as formerly; and that the expenditure of this class upon alcoholic beverages is probably a billion dollars less than it would be without national prohibition.

3. That the per capita consumption of alcohol by the business, professional and salaried class has been affected but little by prohibition; and that due to higher prices this class is spending at least a billion dollars a year more for alcoholic beverages than it would be spending without national prohibition.

4. That the wealthy class, with annual incomes per income-receiver of more than $25,000, has had to make up in higher income taxes most of the loss of Federal revenue due to prohibition, amounting approximately to three-fourths of a billion dollars a year.

The Effect of Prohibition upon Public Health and Safety and upon Public Finance. It may reasonably be concluded:

1. That prohibition has reduced to some extent the death rate from diseases directly associated with the excessive use of alcoholic beverages, especially among the

working class; but that prohibition has not had a measurable effect upon the general health of the nation.

2. That as indicated by fragmentary statistics, there is some association between criminal activity and the use of alcohol and that the frequency of some types of crime has been reduced slightly by prohibition.

3. That the great increase in the use of automobiles during the past decade has masked the effect of prohibition upon automobile accidents, so that the relationship is not determinable by elementary statistical analysis.

4. That the Federal government might collect a maximum of about a billion and a quarter dollars from the taxation of all alcoholic beverages, or a maximum of three-fourths of a billion from beer alone; and that this would make possible lower income taxes than would otherwise be necessary.

BIBLIOGRAPHY

The literature on the alcohol problem and on prohibition is so enormous that a separate volume would be required to present a reasonably complete bibliography. Only those publications are listed here to which reference has been made in the preceding pages.

Books

Leon P. Alford, editor. *Management's Handbook.* New York: Ronald Press Co. 1924.

Bender's Federal Revenue Law, 1916. New York. 1917.

F. H. Cherrington, editor-in-chief. *Standard Encyclopedia of the Alcohol Problem.* 5 vols. Westerville, Ohio: American Issue Publishing Co. 1925.

R. C. Chapin. *Standard of Living among Workingmen's Families in New York City.* New York: Charities Publication Committee. 1909.

Committee on Prohibition, National Federation of Settlements; Martha Bruere, editor. *Does Prohibition Work?* New York: Harper and Brothers. 1927.

Samuel Crowther. *Prohibition and Prosperity.* New York: The John Day Company. 1930.

Rheta Childe Dorr. *Drink: Coercion or Control?* New York: Frederick A. Stokes Co. 1929.

Paul Douglas. *Real Wages in the United States.* Boston: Houghton Mifflin Co. 1930.

Louis I. Dublin. *Health and Wealth.* New York: Harper and Bros. 1928.

Ralph C. Epstein. *The Automobile Industry.* New York and Chicago: A. W. Shaw Co. 1928.

Mordecai Ezekiel. *Methods of Correlation Analysis.* New York: John Wiley and Sons, Inc. 1930.

Fannie Farmer. *The Boston Cooking School Cook Book.* Boston: Little, Green and Co. 1923.

Herman Feldman. *Prohibition: Its Economic and Industrial Aspects.* New York: D. Appleton and Co. 1927.

Irving Fisher. *Prohibition at Its Worst.* New York: Alcohol Information Committee. 1927.

Irving Fisher. *Prohibition Still At Its Worst.* New York: Alcohol Information Committee. 1928.

Irving Fisher, assisted by H. Bruce Brougham. *The Noble Experiment*. New York: Alcohol Information Committee. 1930.

R. A. Fisher. *Statistical Methods for Research Workers*. London: Oliver and Boyd. 1928.

Fabian Franklin. *The A B C of Prohibition*. New York: Harcourt, Brace and Co. 1927.

Ernest Gordon. *When the Brewer Had the Stranglehold*. New York: Alcohol Information Committee. 1930.

House of Representatives, State of Massachusetts. *Report of the Commission on the Cost of Living*. Boston: Wright and Potter Printing Co. 1910.

Reginald E. Hose. *Prohibition or Control?* New York: Longmans, Green and Co. 1928.

Albert A. Hopkins, editor. *Scientific American Cyclopedia of Formulas*, New York: Munn and Co. 1911.

Frederic C. Howe. *Taxation and Taxes in the United States*. New York: Thomas Y. Crowell Co. 1896.

Willford I. King. *The Wealth and Income of the People of United States*. New York: The Macmillan Co. 1915.

Willford I. King. *The National Income and Its Purchasing Power*. New York: National Bureau of Economic Research. 1930.

Charles Merz. *The Dry Decade*. Garden City, N. Y.; Doubleday, Doran and Co. 1930.

Ministère du Travail et de la Prèvoyance Sociale (France). *Salaires et Coût de l'Existence à diverses époques, jusqu'en 1910*. Paris: Statistique Generale de la France. 1911.

National Bureau of Economic Research. *Income in the United States*, vol. 1. New York: Harcourt, Brace and Co. 1921.

National Bureau of Economic Research. *Recent Economic Changes in the United States*. New York: McGraw-Hill Co. 1929.

Paul H. Nystrom. *Economic Principles of Consumption*. New York: The Ronald Press Company. 1929.

Francis Peabody. *The Liquor Problem*. Boston: Houghton Mifflin Co. 1925.

Stuart A. Rice, editor for the American Statistical Association. *Statistics in Social Studies*. Philadelphia: University of Pennsylvania Press. 1930.

Sir Humphrey Rolleston and John Wm. McNee. *Diseases of the Liver, Gall-gladder and Bileducts*, third edition. New York: The Macmillan Co. 1929.

Gunter Schmolders. *Prohibition im Norden*. Berlin: Gebr. Unger. 1926.

G. Findlay Shirras. *Report on an Inquiry into Working Class Budgets in Bombay*. Bombay: Government Central Press. 1923.

Ernest H. Starling. *The Action of Alcohol on Man.* London: Longnans, Green and Co. 1923.

Cora Francis Stoddard and Amy Woods. *Fifteen Years of the Drink Question in Massachusetts,* and Supplement 1. Boston: Scientific Temperance Federation. 1929.

Francis J. Tietsork, editor. *Temperance—or Prohibition?* New York: The Hearst Temperance Contest Committee. 1929.

Millard E. Tydings. *Before and After Prohibition.* New York: The Macmillan Company. 1930.

PAMPHLETS AND BULLETINS

American Automobile Chamber of Commerce. *Facts and Figures of the Automobile Industry,* 1930.

Associated Corn Products Manufacturers. *The Story of a Grain of Corn.* Chicago: 1930.

Association Against the Prohibition Amendment. *Cost of Prohibition and Your Income Tax.* Washington, D. C. 1929.

Association Against the Prohibition Amendment. *Does Prohibition Pay?* Washington, D. C. 1930.

Association Against the Prohibition Amendment. *Government Liquor Control in Canada.* Washington, D. C. 1929.

Association Against the Prohibition Amendment. *Scandals of Prohibition Enforcement.* Washington, D. C. 1929.

Board of Temperance, Prohibition and Public Morals of the Methodist Episcopal Church. *The Facts About Prohibition—Illustrated—Trust Your Eye.* Washington, D. C. 1927.

Board of Temperance, Prohibition and Public Morals of the Methodist Episcopal Church. *Prohibition Prosperity.*

Board of Temperance, Prohibition and Public Morals of the Methodist Episcopal Church. *What Has Prohibition Done?* Washington, D. C.

Board of Temperance, Prohibition and Public Morals of the Methodist Episcopal Church. *Why I Am For Prohibition.*

Department of Research and Education, Federal Council of the Churches of Christ in America. Research Bulletin No. 5, *The Prohibition Situation.* New York. 1925.

Harvard University Graduate School of Business Administration, *Bulletins of the Bureau of Business Research,* 1922 to 1929.

International Association of Ice Cream Manufacturers, *Dairy Products and Kinds of Sugar Used in the Manufacture of Ice Cream.* Harrisburg, Pa. 1928.

S. W. Shear in cooperation with H. F. Gould. *Economic Status of the Grape Industry.* Berkeley, Calif.: University of California, College of Agriculture, Agricultural Experiment Station. 1927.

Wm. A. Schoenfeld, John Marshall, Jr., and Paul C. Newman. *A Compendium of Hop Statistics.* Portland, Oregon. 1930.

George B. Wilson, editor. *The Alliance Year Book and Temperance Reformers' Handbook*, 1929, 1930 and 1931. London: United Kingdom Alliance.

UNITED STATES GOVERNMENT PUBLICATIONS

Bureau of the Census. *Thirteenth Census of the United States*, 1910.

Bureau of the Census. *Fourteenth Census of the United States*, 1920.

Bureau of the Census. *Fifteenth Census of the United States*, 1930.

Bureau of the Census. *Financial Statistics of Cities.*

Bureau of the Census. *Financial Statistics of States.*

Bureau of the Census. *Wealth, Debt and Taxation.*

Bureau of the Census. *Statistical Abstract of the United States.*

Bureau of the Census. *Census of Distribution*, 1930.

Bureau of Prohibition, Department of Justice. *Possible Production of Illegal Liquor in the United States for the fiscal year ending June 30, 1930.*

Bureau of Prohibition. *The Value of Law Observance.* 1930.

Department of Agriculture. *Yearbook of Agriculture.*

Department of Labor. *Cost of Living in the United States*, Bulletin of the Bureau of Labor Statistics, No. 357.

Department of Labor. *Statistics of Industrial Accidents in the United States to the end of 1927*, Bulletin of the Bureau of Labor Statistics, No. 490.

Department of Labor. *Wholesale Prices, 1890 to 1926*, Bulletin of the Bureau of Labor Statistics, No. 440.

Department of Labor. *Wholesale Prices, 1913 to 1928*, Bulletin of the Bureau of Labor Statistics, No. 493.

Department of Labor. *Sixth, Seventh and Eighteenth Annual Reports of the United States Commissioner of Labor.*

National Commission on Law Observance and Enforcement. *Report on the Observance of the Prohibition Laws in the United States.* Printed as 71st Congress, 3d Session, House Document No. 722. January 7, 1931.

National Commission on Law Observance and Enforcement. *Report on Criminal Statistics.* 1931.

National Commission on Law Observance and Enforcement. *Report on the Causes of Crime.* 1931.

National Commission on Law Observance and Enforcement. *Report on the Cost of Crime.* 1931.

Treasury Department. *Annual Reports of the Commissioner of Internal Revenue*, 1911 to 1928.

Treasury Department, Bureau of Industrial Alcohol. *Statistics Concerning Intoxicating Liquors*, December, 1930 and December, 1931.

69th Congress, 1st Session, Senate, Subcommittee of the Committee on the Judiciary. *The National Prohibition Law.* Hearings on S. 33, S. 34, S. 591, S. 592, S. 3118, S. J. Res. 34, S. J. Res. 85, S. 3823, S. 3411, and S. 3891, April 5 to 24, 1926.

71st Congress, 2nd Session, House of Representatives, Committee on the Judiciary. *The Prohibition Amendment,* Hearings on H. J. Res. 11, 38, 99, 114, 219 and 246, February 12 to April 24, 1930.

71st Congress, 2nd Session, Senate, Subcommittee of the Committee on the Judiciary, *Lobby Investigation,* Hearings pursuant to S. Res. 20, 1930 and 1931.

PERIODICALS

Louis I. Dublin, "Has Prohibition Improved the Public Health?" *The American Journal of Public Health,* January, 1928.

Haven Emerson. "Prohibition and Public Health," *The Survey,* December 1, 1928, pp. 289-336.

Hugh H. Fox. "The Present Consumption of Alcohol in the United States," *The Periscope,* April, 1927.

A. J. Lanza and R. J. Vane. "The Prevalence of Tuberculosis in Industry," *Statistical Bulletin,* Metropolitan Life Insurance Company, July, 1930, pp. 6-10.

Bert Park. "The Bootlegger and His Forerunners," *The American Mercury,* July, 1926.

George B. Waldron. "Economics of the Drink Traffic," *The Chautauquan,* v. 51, pp. 96-107.

George B. Wilson. "A Statistical Review of the Variations during the Last Twenty Years in the Consumption of Intoxicating Drinks in the United Kingdom, and in Convictions for Offenses Connected with Intoxication, with a Discussion of the Causes to which these Variations may be Ascribed," *Journal of the Royal Statistical Society,* January, 1912, pp. 183-247.

Holbrook Working. "The Decline in Per Capita Consumption of Flour in the United States," *Wheat Studies of the Food Research Institute,* vol. ii, pp. 278-279, and vol. iv, p. 86.

INDEX

Absenteeism, industrial, effect of prohibition, 203-06

Accidents
- automobile, effect of prohibition, 221-23, 262
- industrial, effect of prohibition, 191-203, 261

Alcohol, industrial and denatured, diversion to beverage use, 40-49

Alcoholic insanity, hospitalization prior to and since prohibition, 214-17

Alcoholism
- deaths related to consumption of alcohol, 73-98
- hospitalization prior to and since prohibition, 214-17

Alford, L. P., recent changes in technology and management, 196

Arrests for drunkenness, relation to consumption of alcohol, 99-103

Association Against the Prohibition Amendment
- assertion that repeal of the Eighteenth Amendment would reduce income taxes, 256
- estimate of government expenditures upon enforcement of prohibition, 246
- references to publications, 19-20

Barley, loss to farmers from prohibition, 231

Beer
- estimate of consumption, prior to and since prohibition, 107
- estimate of expenditure, 169-170
- substitutes for, 142, 184-92, 261

Bermondsey (London), expenditures for liquor, 126-27

Beverages, non-alcoholic, consumption, 185-90

Black, Loring M., effect of prohibition upon grain producers, 228

Board of Temperance, Prohibition and Public Morals of the Methodist Episcopal Church, 18, 173

Brown, Frederick W., statistics of alcoholic insanity, 215

Bruere, Martha B., effect of prohibition, 244

Buckner, Emory R., estimate of diversion of industrial alcohol, 41

Building and loan associations, effect of prohibition, 182-84

Bureau of Prohibition
- estimate of possible production of illegal liquor, 31, 33, 37-38, 45, 52, 53, 68
- reports regarding materials seized by prohibition agents, 66, 67, 70
- statement regarding industrial absenteeism, 204

Buying habits, influence of prohibition, 172-79, 260

Carbonated beverages
- consumption prior to and since prohibition, 186-89
- use of sugar in, 60-61

Carver, Thomas Nixon, effect of prohibition, 18

Chapin, R. C., family budgets, 128-29, 135, 136

Cherrington, Ernest H., effect of prohibition, 18, 172

Christian Science Monitor, articles on prohibition, 18, 172, 228

Cirrhosis of the liver, deaths related to consumption of alcohol, 73-98
Coca-Cola, consumption prior to and since prohibition, 186-89
Coefficients of relationship
 consumption of alcohol and arrests for drunkenness, 100
 consumption of alcohol and automobile accidents, 222-23
 consumption of alcohol and deaths from alcoholism and cirrhosis of the liver
  Denmark, 81, 83
  United Kingdom, 75-76, 79-81
  United States, 84-87, 91-96
 consumption of alcohol and homicides, 226
 consumption of alcohol and industrial accidents, 201-02
 consumption of alcohol and industrial production, 197
 consumption of sugar and related factors, 57
Coffee, as substitute for beer, 185-88
Confectionery, as substitute for beer, 59-60, 190-92
Consumption of alcoholic beverages
 foreign countries, 26
 methods of estimating under prohibition
  beer, 27-33
  spirits, 34-40
  wine, 40-70
 United States, prior to prohibition, 23-26
 United States, since prohibition
  beer, 33, 71, 259
  spirits, 70, 71, 259-60
  wine, 40, 71, 259-60
Consumption of pure alcohol in beverages
 prior to prohibition, 23-26
 since prohibition, 72, 259
Corn (maize)
 effect of prohibition upon market, 228-31
 use in making alcoholic beverages, 56-57
Corn meal, use in making alcoholic beverages, 55-56
Corn starch, use in making alcoholic beverages, 54-55
Corn sugar
 estimate of amount used in making beverage spirits, 52
  production and use, 49-54
Corn syrup, use of, 54-55
Corradini, Robert E.,
 effect of prohibition on real estate values, 207
 report on arrests for drunkenness, 101
 use of corn sugar, 50
Cost of producing alcoholic beverages
 at home, 161-63
 commercial, 145-46
Crowther, Samuel, relation of prohibition to prosperity, 18, 130, 172, 242

Death rates, alcoholism and corrhosis of the liver
 industrial insurance policyholders, 133-34
 related to consumption of alcohol
  Denmark, 81-84
  United Kingdom, 74-81
  United States, 84-98, 212-14, 233-35, 238-40
 urban and rural, 121-22, 133, 238-39
Death rate, general, effect of prohibition, 217-21
Decentralization of alcoholic beverage industry, 210-11
Denatured alcohol, diversion to beverage use, 40-49
Dennison, Henry F., technological change, 196
Diseases associated with the use of alcohol
 see alcoholism, alcoholic insanity, cirrhosis of the liver, nephritis
Doran, J. M.
 diversion of industrial alcohol, 41-47

estimate of expenditures upon enforcement, 246
Dorr, Rheta Childe, effects of prohibition, 19
Douglas, Paul, hours of work in industry, 204, 206, 220
Drinking habits
convival drinking, 88-89, 143
effect upon efficiency, 195-96
industrial and misery, 88
Drunkenness, arrests for, related to consumption of alcohol, 99-103
Dublin, Louis I., relation of prohibition to health, 217, 221
du Pont, Irenee, relation of liquor taxes to corporation taxes, 256
Dyer, Leonidas C., effect of taxing beer, 245

Economic classes in the United States
distribution of population among, 130-32
effect of prohibition
business, professional and salaried class, 237-42, 262
farmers, 228-33, 261
producers of alcoholic beverages, 242-44
wage-earners, 233-37, 261
wealthy class, 255-56, 262
Efficiency, effect of prohibition, 195-99
Emerson, Haven, relation of prohibition to public health, 217, 221
Enforcement of prohibition, cost of, 245-47
Expenditures for alcoholic beverages
by principal economic classes
business, professional and salaried class, 135-38
farmers, 134, 138
wage-earners, 134-35, 138
effect of prohibition, 168-71
national liquor bill prior to prohibition, 113-15
related to business fluctuations, 115-18
related to national income, 115
related to price changes, 118-19
national liquor bill since prohibition, 168-71, 260
per capita and per family, 119-30
probable liquor bill, 1921-1930, without prohibition, 135-38
related to family income, 127-30
Ezekiel, Mordecai, statistical methods, 61, 77, 80, 87, 91, 94

Federal Council of Churches in Christ in America, research report on prohibition, 19
Feldman, Herman, effect of prohibition, 18, 203-4, 207, 208, 243
Fisher, Irving
arguments for prohibition, 18, 195
use of hops, 30
uses of corn sugar, 50
yield of wine from grapes, 37
Fisher, R. A., statistical method, 87
Food Control Act, 25
Fox, Hugh F., use of hops and malt syrup, 30, 65
Franklin, Fabian, arguments against prohibition, 19
Fruit drinks, use of, 188-90

Gebhart, John C.
police severity regarding drunkenness, 103
statistics of arrests for drunkenness, 101
Gin, price of, 160-61
Government revenue, loss on account of prohibition, 250-53
see also taxation
Grapes
effect of prohibition upon production, 232
use of, 34-38

Haas, John I., taxation of beer, 245
Hearst Temperance Contest Committee, 19, 88

Home-brew, 30
Hops, use in making illegal beer, 27-31
Hose, Reginald E., effects of prohibition, 19

Ice cream, as substitute for beer, 190-92
Industrial alcohol, diversion to beverage use, 40-49
Insurance, life, effect of prohibition, 181-84
Johnson, Henry M., effect of prohibition in Louisville, 207

King, Willford I.
  estimates of number of entrepreneurs, salaried workers and wage-earners, 132, 236, 237, 240
  estimates of national and class income, 137, 141, 237, 241

Lanza, A. J., deaths from tuberculosis, 219
Law enforcement
  cost of enforcing prohibition, 245-47
  seizures by prohibition agents, 208-10
Life insurance, effect of prohibition, 181-84

Malt extract and malt syrup, 30, 65
Malt liquor
  see beer
Materials used in making alcoholic beverages
  barley, 231
  corn (maize), 56-57, 228, 231
  corn meal, 55-56
  corn starch, 54-55
  corn sugar, 49-54
  corn syrup, 54-55
  fruits, 65
  grapes, 34-38
  hops, 27-31
  industrial alcohol, 40-49
  malt syrup, 65
  molasses, 63-65
  prices of, 144-45, 161-62
  relative importance, 67
  rye, 56-57
  sugar, beet and cane, 57-63, 231, 233
  vegetables, 65
McNee, John Wm.
  see Ralleston, Sir Humphrey
Medicinal alcohol, 68-69
Metropolitan Life Insurance Company, industrial policyholders, 133, 233-35, 238
Merz, Charles, reference to, 25
Milk, as substitute for beer, 186-90, 233
Molasses, use in making alcoholic beverages, 63-65

National Commission on Law Observance and Enforcement, 18, 224-25, 246-47
Near-beer, as substitute for beer, 186-88
Nephritis, death rate related to consumption of alcohol, 212-14
Nystrom, Paul H., effect of prohibition, 18

Park, Bert, quality of liquor prior to prohibition, 88
Peabody, Francis, strength of alcoholic liquors, 164
Pickett, Deets, effect of prohibition upon buying habits, 173
Prices of alcoholic beverages
  estimated probable post-war, without prohibition, 147-49
  prior to prohibition, 111-13
  under prohibition, 152-65
Prices of materials used in producing alcoholic beverages, 144-45, 161-62
Production of alcoholic beverages under prohibition
  beer, 27-31
  cost of, 145-46, 161-63
  materials used
    see materials
  spirits, 40-57
  wine, 34-39
Proof gallons, meaning of, 23

Randolph, Robert Isham, commercial beer production in Chicago, 163-64

Real estate, effect of prohibition, 207-8
Rolleston, Sir Humphrey, relation of cirrhosis of the liver to the consumption of alcohol, 73
Rye
effect of prohibition upon production, 229-31
use in making alcoholic beverages, 56-57

Saloon, substitutes for, 142
Savings deposits, effect of prohibition, 179-83
Schmolders, Gunter, convivial drinking, 89
Schoenfeld, Wm. A., data regarding hops, 144
Seizures by prohibition agents, 32, 39, 70, 208-210
Shear, S. W., grape industry, 34, 35, 37, 144, 232
Shirras, G. Findlay, workingmen's budgets, 129
Smuggled liquors, 31-33, 39, 67-68
Speak-easies, number of, 211
Starling, Ernest H., effects of alcohol, 19
State prohibitory laws, effect on consumption, 25

Tabor, Louis J., effect of prohibition upon farmers, 228
Taxation of alcoholic beverages
effect of anticipated increase in taxes upon withdrawals, 25
incidence of, 254-56
government revenue, prior to prohibition, 114, 249
loss of government revenue as result of prohibition, 248-54
maximum tax rates, 252-63
rates of tax prior to prohibition, 248
Tea, as substitute for beer, 185-88
Tobacco, as substitute for beer, 190-92
Tuberculosis, death rate related to consumption of alcohol, 217-21
Tydings, Millard E., effect of prohibition, 19

Vane, R. J.
see Lanza, A. J.
Van Kleeck, Mary, data regarding criminal convictions in New York, 224-25

Waldron, George B., estimates of liquor bill prior to prohibition, 113
Webb Kenyon Act, 139
Wilson, George B.
liquor consumption in Bermondsey, 127
liquor consumption in Great Britain, 75, 79
Winslow, Emma M., data regarding criminal prosecutions in Massachusetts, 224
Working, Holbrook, flour consumption, 174
Wolman, Leo, index of productivity, 197-98
Wort, 30

Bei Fragen zur Produktsicherheit wenden Sie sich bitte an:
If you have any questions regarding product safety,
please contact:

Walter de Gruyter GmbH
Genthiner Straße 13
10785 Berlin
productsafety@degruyterbrill.com